੧ੳ ਸਤਿਗੁਰਪ੍ਰਸਾਦਿ॥

Restoration & Renovation of Abandoned Historical Places

Gurdwara Choha Sahib Ji, Rohtas, Jhelum

Dr. Satpreet Singh

Sikh Reference Library USA

1463 Moffat Blvd, Suite 9

Manteca, CA 95336 USA

www.sikhreferencelibraryusa.com

Restoration & Renovation of Historical Abandoned Places
Copyright © 2022 by Satpreet Singh

Library of Congress Control Number: 2021947214

ISBN 978-1-7375532-8-1 (Punjabi)
ISBN 978-1-7375532-5-0 (English)
ISBN 978-1-7375532-7-4 (Punjabi E-book)
ISBN 978-1-7375532-1-2 (English E-Book)

Publisher:
Sikh Reference Library USA
1463 Moffat Blvd, Suite 9
Manteca, CA 95336 USA
www.sikhreferencelibraryusa.com

Dedication

This book is dedicated to "The mother of the Khalsa Panth" Mata Sahib Kaur (Deva) Ji. Mata Sahib Kaur Ji is the mother of the Khalsa Panth, and this title is given to her by Dhan Dhan Guru Gobind Singh Ji

Table of Contents

Foreword 9

Preface 11

Restoration and Renovation 13

   Restoration..15

      Type 16

         Importance 20

         Survival 21

   Renovation..27

      Type 28

      Importance...29

      Survival 29

Sikha Theory of Restoration 31

   Nanak Shahi Bricks 34

   Kanker (Pebbles) 35

   Jute..36

   Dal (Lentils, Peas, Beans) 37

   Saffron..38

   Milk 39

   Seashells 40

   Acacia Gum...41

   Turmeric 42

   Indigo (Neel) 43

   Yogurt...44

   Buffalo Milk Butter 45

   Jaggery..46

Gurdwara Janam Asthan Mata Sahib Kaur Ji 47

    History 49

    Proposals of design..51

    Land Purchase 53

    Contracts...56

Gurdwara Choha Sahib Ji 71

    History 73

    Inspections..83

    Geotechnical Condition...95

    Master Plan..133

    Material 143

    Sarovar..159

    Electric Plan 167

    Restoration Contract...185

    Historical Artifacts 247

    Contributory Religious Organizations..................................279

    Individual Contributors 285

Foreword

The author writes this book from his practical experience by restoring very significant historical buildings, Gurdwara Choha Sahib Ji and Gurdwara Janam Asthan Mata Sahib Kaur Ji in west Punjab. Both buildings were abandoned during the partition of Punjab in August 1947. The Khalsa Panth lost significant historical buildings and trillion-dollar properties and moved to east Punjab.

The author of this traveled to west Punjab in December 2019 to see the Khalsa Panth historical places in west Punjab from the United States of America. His travel experience was very sorrowful by visiting the abandoned historical Gurdwaras. Many encroachments were made, and the condition of the approximately 476 historical Gurdwaras was very critical. He came back to the United States of America after his eight-day visit. But his life was changed by seeing the actual ground realities of the abandoned historical places.

The author is highly educated and has many professional designations as an entrepreneur in the United States of America. He used his expertise and formed a California-based USA non-profit organization named "Ranjit Nagara." After getting all approvals and forming the non-profit organization "Ranjit Nagara," he did arduous work from January 2020 to August 2020 to get approvals from the foreign country outside the United States of America where these historical buildings were located.

The author worked day and night with the architects, restorers, governmental officials, and departments daily to resolve the hurdles during the restoration process. Finally, the restoration was completed. He wrote this book to remove the barriers of the future generation in restoring historical buildings in east and west Punjab.

Rupinder Kaur
Bibliognost
Sikh Reference Library USA

Preface

This book is written from practical experience and for the future generation's reference. The heritage and historical buildings are significant to evident the actual history. The two primary reasons were kept in mind during the writing of this book. First, the historical significance. Second, many self-made scholars put detriment to the Khalsa Panth history and deterring the name of the Historical places with their thoughts without any research. The history given in this book is referenced from the Khalsa Panth authenticated resources like Mahan Kosh of Bhai Kahan Singh Nabha, Suraj Parkash Granth, Prachin Panth Prakash, and the scholars of Damdami Taksal.

This book aims to guide how to restore the centuries-old building with the same material in their original structure. It also explains that the ingredients used in the material are powerful and helpful in the environment for better health. The heritage and historical buildings do not need to destroy by saying that there is no way to save them. This book provides the ways to keep the historically significant building to preserve them for the coming generations. These buildings provide pieces of evidence for the glory of the religions, states, and nations.

The development of the Sikha Theory of Restoration, Renovation, and Reconstruction was based on the guidance from the material used during the Khalsa empires. It explains how that material is beneficial for human and environmental health, how nature made the materials for constructing the buildings, and how we can use them for a better living experience.

Dr. Satpreet Singh

11

Restoration

and

Renovation

Restoration and Renovation

Restoration, Renovation, and Reconstruction are the three different terms used in three different circumstances and situations to rebuild the feeling, attachment, adaptability of the past, and guidance for the future. Every Nation, State, Country, Culture, Society, Community, diversity, group has its own history of thoughts, ideas, buildings, objects, subjects, etc. Restoration, renovation, and reconstruction are essential tools to save and preserve those thoughts, ideas, buildings, structures, objects, subjects, focus. This tool serves to keep and protect history in the present, provide guidance and become the root for the future generation.

Restoration

Restoration means an initial or prior peak beautiful, perfect, acceptable situation or circumstances of history, mind, building, object, asset, structure, subject, etc. In the present world. Restoration is an extensive, complicated, and complex issue in world history. Restoration has the power to save history for generations to use for future references. Restoration can be Historical, thoughts, environmental, climate, physical, tangible, intangible, building, object, asset, etc. Each field has its own significance and importance. Without history, the present is blind, and the future is murky. History works as a driver of the present to place it in the hands of the future. Restoration is a tool for history. Restoration plays a vital role in understanding the value of the heritage,

Gurdwara Choha Sahib in August 2019

inheritance, legacy of any religion, society, community, group, diversity.

Types of Restoration

Restoration is a vast and complex field. It has many branches and is applied to all areas including but not limited to:

History: The first and foremost significant area of restoration is history. The history

impacted by many traditions, cultures, rulers, anti-rulers, and time play a vital role in benevolence, goodwill, decency, indulging, assisting, serving, harm, damage, injury, hurt, and prejudice. When the thoughts of cohorts of tradition, cultures, rulers came into power, then the history of that religion, society, community, group shines. On the other hand, anti-cohorts have always tried to hurt others to detriment history. There is also another side called neutrals, and when they come in powers, history stays at what it is on at the start time of naturalization power. The neutralization period does not shine or provide detriment. The cohorts of every religion, society, group, and community are always concerned about preserving and restoring their true history.

Environment: Ecology word is used to be the concern of the environment. Environmental restoration is the central issue of the globe in the modern world. Initially, humans did pay attention to the environmental issue and became more materialistic in money, fame, or prestige. The recent era of humans forgets about nature. It ignores the damage of the natural environment only to facilitate for the sole personal interest of the human to facilitate himself, family, society, group, community, state, and nation. Environmental restoration is most important to

restore for the actual facilitation of the world's present and future generations. Nature fills its gap by itself. Understanding the natural environment and stopping damaging the natural resources provided by the environment and world creator will help preserve and restore the environment.

Building: History defines through literature, books, scholars, practitioners, characters, buildings, etc. Each religion, society, group, community, state, and nation has its own construction history. The type of construction and buildings represent them in their own way. All governments, most NGOs, private and public heritage businesses are serious about saving their heritage by preserving the old historical buildings. Each state and nation have its own separate building restoration department to keep the history of their State and Nation. It is imperative to save historical buildings because history is mythology without evidence and

reference. History becomes real when it has evidence in the past to serve the present, and the present makes history glorify the past with its own contribution. Historic buildings are the references, evidence, and proof of history to make them real.

Anatomy: Anatomy is another most critical issue of restoration. The human body structure needs repair to make it workable and perfect. Sleep is a natural resource of mind restoration. Physiology is used to examine the body, and psychology explores the mind. Both technologies and methods play a vital role in restoring body and mind. Many surgeries, procedures, abscission, enucleation, incision, resections, aciurgy are used to repair and restore the anatomy. Body tissues, cells, nerves, injuries, and sickness are restorable and get restored by nature and some with medical treatments. Anatomical and functional restoration theories are very successful and used to repair various body parts.

Law, Rules, Regulations: Restoration is also used in courts, laws, rules, and regulations. There are many restoration laws in all the countries, like restoration in kind, restoration of rights, period of restoration, restoration justice, habitat restoration, restoration remedies, etc. Restoration is used for societies, communities, groups, offenders, defenders, victims and to heal them to the prior situation or circumstances as a whole. It is used to implement law and order in towns, cities, states, nations. Political parties used the restoration to better their image in the general public to get occupancies in the assembly and legislation. Many laws, rules, regulations, policies are passed and implemented in every city, state, and nation for some restoration.

Assets or objects: restoration is used to restore the assets and things to preserve them for the future, whether tangible or intangible. The tangible asset includes furniture, money, gold, silver, bronze, or any other things that a person can touch and feel. Intangible assets and an object like air, credibility, prestige, fame, ego, kindness, and anything that a person cannot touch, intangible assets or things can only feel. Restoration of assets and objects provide personal, city, state, and nations satisfaction and honor for their work and prestige.

Throne of Maharaja Ranjit Singh Ji

Economy: Economy restoration becomes forward all towns, cities, states, nations, global at all levels. When the economy collapses, all groups, societies, people, governments, States, and Nations are affected. Poverty increases and prices go high for the daily use of thins, affordability power of the public went down and the lifestyle poorly affected. Economic restoration and theories provide the measure and try to restore the economy to the prior state where prosperity, happiness, and lifestyle glorifies. A restored, stable economy always plays a steady and perfect role in developing the public and government's economic stability. The affordability of all levels gets approached, price hikes get removed or limited, bad competitions get limits, lifestyle gets improved.

Importance

Restoration has vital rules that keep life on track with past ties, a driver for the present, and guidance for the future. Everything, whether it is human-made, nature-made human-nature made is get restored at some point. The future of any religion, society, group, town, city, state, nation, globe and even universe will be blind. There will be no respect, better lifestyle, and growth. The circle of human and natural life will get jammed and deter the values of ethics and morality. Time will never stop, and the clock will run and get restored in the form of day and night, but the matter of time will be limited. The aims, goals, and meaning of life will not be present. The level of mind will get leveled at one place and do not want to grow, and the question will be raised why it grow if there is no meaning. The love in the families will get disturbed with past ties and linage.

The power to fight the involunteer and unexpected circumstances or situations will be limited or none. Cultures, religion, thoughts, love, prosperity will get destroyed and will be meaningless for all. Generations who forget the past, ignore the past, or are forced emotionally to forget the past get destroyed in the future. When the present becomes history, that period becomes the darkest, blackest, obscurest, terrible, awful, horrible era of that generation. That period or era destroyed and molded the culture, tradition, languages to the influence of others or merged to others one day. Good researchers, scholars, cohorts, leaders become heroes in those times and play a significantly vital role in restoring their history at all times. They become history by restoring their history.

Restoration in all fields and areas has significant, meaningful, and vital. It is a must tool to connect with the past, learn from past mistakes and wrongdoing, make corrections, guidance from the righteous doings, and fall into the prosper, glorified future with the contribution. Life aims, goals, meaning, achievements, pride, prestige, fame, kindness all are connected with the past, present, and future. The past motivates and encourages them to contribute to their town, city, state, nation, nature, religion, etc. The present always sets the goals, aims, and achievements from the guidance of the past. The future of the generations and even self become prosper, beautiful, loveable, comfortable, advice with the right deed of the present. Restoration of cultures, societies, groups, communities by developing diversity provides more beauty and glory to the religions, cultures, societies, and communities with the contribution. It makes them able to provide guidance to the future world generation and develop with diversity, peace with others.

Survival

Many methods and techniques are developed for the survival of restoration. All methods and techniques are different, specializing in the particular type of restoration. Researchers, Scholars, Scientists, academics, and NGOs try to develop new ideas, knowledge, management techniques to save the importance and meaning of restoration. Culturally, traditions, communities, and languages are restored with the restoration ideas, methods, and techniques developed by the intelligent, energetic, and active cohorts of researchers, scientists, and scholars.

History: Farsighted and prescient scholars document history in various forms to pass it to the next generation. History explains and defines the future. Good authors and researchers play a significant and vital role as saviors of history. History provides courage, enthusiasm, power, willingness and makes strong ties to the ancestors and successors. Researchers and scholars always develop new ideas and methods to save history for the present and future generations. Presently, history is survived in the form of literature, artifact, books, stories, places. The survival of history becomes the foundation for the present and future generations. Each religion, society, group, community, business, and organization has its own history and provides directions and guidance in the future and present. Dignity, fame, glory, and pride can only be explained to the present and future generations with written documentation and history, whether written, verbal, or place. Some materialistic greedy, and egoist people made fake thoughts and fiction to earn money and fame. Those frugal writers' names are always written

21

as the traitor of history because they are only interested in benefiting themselves, not the world or society.

Sri Harmander Sahib (Darbar Sahib), Amritsar, Punjab

Environment: Many theories have been developed to save the environment like environmental sustainability, green energy, water conservation, air pollution, non-plastic use, etc. All theorists, practitioners, scholars, and nations are concerned about saving and preserving natural resources for the betterment of the public. Human has excellent progress in every field, but still, there are a creator and his creation that the human mind is unable to understand. Humans temporarily find alternatives to facilitate the environment, which are not enough permanent solutions. The perfect example far away from the human mind is life, air, and water. Each individual, organization, society, religion has a responsibility to participate and become the savior of the environment. A clean and clear environment provides peace and a healthy lifestyle for humans and other creatures. Some examples of saving the environment are clean surroundings, planting trees, using natural resources prudently, spreading knowledge, educating communities, etc.

Building: Buildings have a significant role in the world's history. Restoration methods and techniques are used to restore the building to its original shape without changing in the same way it was first built before. Most buildings are constructed and repaired at different times and use other materials. Researchers, Scholars, restorers, and the government develop many different methods, rules, regulations, and techniques to save the building and their history for the future to tell the story of the nation, state, and religion. Development and conservation, heritage conservation, architectural, stylistic

Sri Akal Takhat Sahib Ji, Amritsar, Punjab
Throne of the God

restoration, modern restoration are some theories to restore the building. Buildings are the

23

heritage of religions, nations, and states. The building structure and architectural values represent the glory of their peak era. Building and their architecture are the precious evidence of the realities and tell the real stories by themself. Demolishing a historical building means destroying history. Usually, enemies of the nation destroy the historical and religious buildings to enslave them. They believe that the historical building will remind them about their glorious era. Unfortunately, mental slavery pushes some false leaders or religious leaders to destroy their own buildings, so the anti-nation, anti-religion, and anti-society do not get the blame. It is required to understand the importance of the historical building to pass the historical values and pieces of evidence. Human is very advanced in the

Gurdwara Choha Sahib Ji February 2022 after restoration by Ranjit Nagara, A California based USA non-profit organization

present world, and there are many universities laboratories. It is easy in the current 21st century to find out about the construction of historical buildings, like what material was used, how much was used, the combination of material, different ingredients, the life span of the material, etc.

Two case studies of very significant historical buildings of Khalsa Panth (Sikhs) have been given in this book where resources are significantly less: the first one is about the birthplace of the mother of the Khalsa Panth called Gurdwara Janam (birth) Asthan (place) Mata Sahib Kaur Ji also known as Gurdwara Mata Sahib Deva Ji shown in the picture. The second case study is about Gurdwara Choha Sahib Ji belongs to the founder of Sikhism. Both were abandoned in the partition of Punjab in 1947 AD. There are approximately 476 abandoned Gurdwaras present and waiting for restoration.

Picture one has taken February 2021: Gurdwara Janam Asthan Mata Sahib Kaur (Deva) Ji (The Mother of the Khalsa Panth), Rohtas Jhelum, Punjab, Pakistan

Anatomy: Anatomy is a study, methodology, techniques to examine the body's structure. It looks at the various parts and organs. Each part of the body and organ has its own anatomy. Many anatomy types are human, gross, comparative, embryology, phytotomy, microscopic, zootomy, and radiology. The necessary resources to restore the anatomy system are water, food, air, shelter, etc. Medical surgery and treatment are also used to restore the fractured part or organ of the body. Surgery restores the part of the body with the support of anatomy. Literature review of the body is significant before the surgery of any part of the body. Without understanding the anatomy, the procedures can have the worst results. Doctors, researchers, and scholars in the medical field always generate new strategies and adapt technologies to implement them.

Law, Rules, and Regulations: Restoring the law, rule, and regulation means implementing the law. For traffic control, traffic laws and regulations are applied to control the speed of the vehicles as per law. Protecting democracy laws are used to apply checks and balances on various fields of power. Without restoring the law, rule, and regulations world, Nation, States, and even different religious systems will be disturbed. Following rules and regulations are the only way to achieve dignity and glory. Lawmakers, researchers, scholars always develop new laws and regulations to restore and implement the existing laws, rules, and regulations to make life better as a whole.

Assets or Objects: Assets and objects are a part of history and represent the history of their era. Historical assets like the throne of Maharaja Ranjit Singh (The lion of Punjab in history) are in the museum of the United Kingdom. People from the world went there to see the throne of the Maharaja Ranjit Singh, and it represents the glory of the empire of the Khalsa Panth. Similarly, many historical assets are saved by the various era of the great kingdoms. To keep them as it is and maintain them in their original shapes has a significant impact on the coming generations. These assets remind the history with their presence. Archeology departments are established to find, save and preserve historical assets and objects.

Economy: Expansion, peak, contraction, and trough are the four main stages of the economy is defined by economy scholars. The average spending, lifestyle, prices are the factor that helps to understand the economic cycle. Nation and states have different ways to restore the economy by increasing infrastructure, reducing regulation, implementing new laws, developing rural areas, etc. The general public changes their spending and habits to revive their economy.

Renovation

Renovation is a technique or method in which the existing structure is updated and made functional with news standards. This term is widely used in the restoration of historical buildings. Renovation does not change the existing structure of buildings and bring them back in a better shape. Many factors are considered to renovate the historical buildings like Historical Significance, Current Physical condition, Proposed Use, and Intended Interpretation.

Introduction

Historical significance is the most crucial matter in renovating any historical building. The historical values of the building must be the same or superior after the renovation, especially in the renovation of the religious, historical buildings. This book's two case studies are completed on the most important abandoned historical buildings shown as Gurdwara Choha Sahib Ji and Gurdwara Janam Asthan Mata Sahib Kaur Ji. The renovation is only possible when there is an existing structure present.

The current Physical condition of the building and the material used to make that building decide to what extent the changes are possible with maximum survivor of the existing structure. The material used to build the picture two case study was a superior material in 1834 AD by Maharaja Ranjit Singh (also known as the architect of the emperors). That material has a life of at least 200 years. The material details are discussed in the following chapter of this book.

The proposed use of the historical building also forced to make some changes. For example, there was no electricity in the old eras, and in the present age, electricity is a necessary utility for all kinds of buildings. The ratio and the capacity of the load that the building can handle also impact the renovation strategy of the historic building. After some decades, renovation is always required to upgrade the facilities, whether historic or non-historic. Religious and landmark buildings are constantly renovated to facilitate the religious communities or societies by keeping the historical significance in mind.

Intended interpretation means the code of conduct, rules, regulations, the system, historical values, and religious values must be maintained. Any renovation project aims to keep the maximum level of heritage saved with minor changes. The interpretation of the renovated projects must be the same as it was before the renovation. Renovation only repairs or maintains the portion of the building or project that is required with its historical values.

Types of Renovation

The renovation added historical values and improved the buildings' quality. There are four types of renovations basic, appeal, heritage, and Personal

Basic: The primary type of renovation provides patches and repairs to the existing weak areas to maintain and use in the present and future. The primary method and techniques that concentrate the building are in good condition and useable. Smaller, cheaper improvements are made to make them in a weak state. The improvement with basic methods and techniques does not add value to the project or building.

Appeal: Appeal methods make the project or final look of the project better for the first impression of the visitors. These methods include the surrounding, landscape, fountains, lighting, boundaries, etc.

Heritage: Heritage renovation add value to the existing legacy for the future. The renovation completed with heritage methods and techniques becomes the heritage and adds importance and value. These renovation methods are used to renovate the nations, states, religious history, heritage sites, and places.

Personal: Personal methods and techniques are used for the nation, state, or religious preferences. Renovation of the nation, state, or religious heritage add value and represent them in the future. Therefore, in wars, enemies always destroy the historical and heritage buildings of the other side.

Importance

Renovation is always required to keep the building in usable condition. Renovation is needed to make the glory of the building high, increase space, maximize facilitation, add value, make it eco-friendly, confirmable, etc. Abandoned historical buildings are always required to renovate to preserve and save their historical importance. Another benefit of renovation is that it conserves resources, reduces waste, and preserves heritage instead of destroying them and building a new one. Renovate by using the existing structure save the original footprint of the building with the original material of the construction. The renovation adds the history to connect the future generation with their past as witnesses. Renovating and saving heritage is a social responsibility of the present age to transfer it to the next generation with evidence from the past.

Survival

Survival in renovation has many different ways. Survival methods and techniques define how to survive by respecting the historical heritage and buildings. Researchers, Scholars, and leaders are always curious to find new survival methods. Here we will discuss three strategies: Plus, Unique Quality, and Housing.

Plus: the plus method or technique is used to extend, expand, narrow the existing structure with minimal changes to the heritage. This method facilitates the public and survives the legacy for a more extended period. It also adds value to the heritage and becomes the heritage by itself.

Unique Quality: Unique quality is a process in which the old material and superior quality are made to renovate the existing structure of the building. It keeps the uniqueness of the heritage and value to its previous glory. It is unique then the modern world and provides the feeling of the old eras of ancestors. It gives the sense of their bravery, superiority, and confidence.

Housing: Renovating a building or structure that needs replacing the current use or activity with another place is called the housing method. During the renovation, the historical building can not be used for any other purpose. To keep the standard of work and quality with the emotion and feeling of the public are continually significant. Providing a similar environment during the renovation is called the housing method.

Sikha Theory

Of

Restoration, Renovation & Construction

Sikha (Sikh-Khalsa) Theory
of Restoration, Renovation, & Construction

The Sikha theory of restoration is derived from the word Sikh and Khalsa with various experiments from the material used during the three different eras of the Khalsa empire:

1) Baba Banda Singh Bahadar during 1708-1716 AD,

2) Empire of Sikh Misls during 1732-1789 AD, and

3) Khalsa empire during Maharaja Ranjit Singh Ji from 1790 to 1849.

The material used in the Sikha theory of restoration, renovation, and construction is a material made by nature instead of chemicals. The three Khalsa empire eras have used this material since 1708 in ancient Punjab. This ancient material is potent, economical, and has an age of approximately two hundred years. This material is also beneficial in stopping the bacteria in the air and killing the spreadable bacteria. The material used in the Sikh Theory of restoration and renovation also helps calm the mind and help to concentrate or focus on the right direction. The beautiful light scent remains with the life of the building. These material ingredients are explained briefly in this chapter.

The historically significant building is the heritage for the present and future generations. These buildings are history by themselves. It is the duty of the present to save them for their coming generation to preserve history in facts. True history always requires evidence, and evidence is always based on facts. Those facts are derived from historic places, buildings, documents, and generations.

The Sikh theory of restoration and renovation concentrates on ancient materials used in ancient Punjab that are chemical-free, have a longer life, stop spreading bacteria, and do not provide any damage to the environment. For researching this material, the 1834 AD building material is drilled in minimal quantity without detriment to the old building of Gurdwara Choha Sahib Ji and tested in the University of Peshawar laboratories. Ranjit Nagara USA uses the same material and process to retore the Gurdwara Choha Sahib Ji used during the Khalsa empire.

There are sixteen different ingredients used in the Sikha theory of restoration, renovation, and construction material. However, more can be added or subtracted as per the need of the building, circumstances, and situations.

1. **Nanak Sahi Bricks:** Nanak Shahi brick was first used by Baba Banda Singh Bahadar during the first Sikh empire 1708 to 1716 AD. Baba Banda Singh Bahadar was a saint and soldier blessed by Guru Gobind Singh Ji. He initiated the Nanak Shahi bricks to build the forts and significant places related to the Sikh Gurus, Khalsa Panth, and prominent Sikhs. The Nanak Shahi brick comes in various sizes, but the main used sizes are 7" x 4" x 1.25", 6" x 4" x 1.25", and 4" x 4" x 1.25". Most of the Gurdwara and forts built by Sikhs are built with Nanak Shahi bricks. Nanak Sahi Brick is made with a particular type of soil available in Punjab on a constant intense heat to get a desired natural color. Nanak Sahi bricks are very decorative and robust. These bricks have a very long life compared to the other bricks and stones used in construction. The building made with Nanak Sahib bricks does not need external plaster because of its beauty.

Nanak Shahi Brick used during the restoration of Gurdwara Choha Sahib Ji (February 2022)

Nanak Sahib Brick is instrumental in making arches, walls, and floors. The mortar used with Nanak Shahi Bricks is also made with nature-made materials like pebbles, acacia gum, lentils, milk, Saffron, etc. the mortar also has a long life and is very environment friendly. It is recommended to use the same Nanak Shahi bricks during the restoration, renovation, and construction of significant historical places.

2. **Kanker (Pebble):** The earth has many different materials naturally available to use in building construction. Kankers are usually found in unproductive land or abandoned places. The powder of Kankers is made by fine crushing and then mixed with other material ingredients to prepare a mortar. These Kankers are readily available in many parts of Punjab. Kankers are collected in large quantities from different areas. They are continuously burned and heated for three to four days with intense fire and then crushed gently to make powder. The powder made from the Kankers used in various ratios depending on the current structure, condition, weather, and area.

Kankers are very inexpensive and readily available. The lifetime of the Kanker powder is very long and helps the other material keep dry and non-shrinking. The raw Kankers are always irregular and crinkled in shape. Even in the 21st century, the concrete road and highways use the Kankers as their base for long life and strongness. The Sikh Theory of restoration and renovation uses the Kankers as part of the material used in ancient Punjab during the Khalsa empires.

3. **Jute**: Jute is grown on the fertilizer with mid or high humidity. The land of Punjab is very productive, and Jute can be quickly grown there. It is also available in Asia. The farmer uses their land to produce Jute because its remains help the ground to keep healthy and productive.

Jute is first seeded in the land. The Jute tree is approximately 8-15 feet high. After the cropping of Jute from the ground, it is tied with nit and put under deep water for 10-30 days. The farmers take the shell of the jute plant is called Jute. The Jute is then used for the various purpose to make bags, window shuttering, roof cover, etc. Jute is also beneficial in the construction material. It is used as required in the material to strengthen enormously.

The outer skin of the jute plant is usually called Jute. The rope made from the Jute is widely used in all the countries around the globe. It provides strength, longer life, and the joint between the different ingredients of the material used in construction. The Khalsa empire constructions of the historical buildings have Jute as the mortar ingredient. Another use of the jute plant is the jute leaves which are very rich in minerals and vitamins, including vitamin C and vitamin A. The jute leaves help to reduce inflammation, promote bone health, and make the immune system strong.

4. **Dal (Lentils, Peas, Beans):** Dal is a beneficial material for the restoration, renovation, and construction of significant and prominent buildings. All Dals have wealthy contents of Vitamin B, folate and manganese, thiamine, iron, and phosphorus. Dal is used as a part of the mortar of the Gurdwaras, forts, and historically significant buildings during the Khalsa empire. The Moong Dal and

Moong Dal is very high in protein and helps reduce fat in the body. The use of the Moon dal in the material provides help to kill bacteria and keep the surrounding environment clean. It also helps to clean the air. Many nutrition recommends the use of the Moon dal in the current era. The Moong Dal is used as required in the construction material and helps to keep the air and environment clean.

Mah Dal (black lentils) is also used during the construction of the building as part of the ingredients. Mah Dal is accommodating to prevent heartaches and improve the digestive system. Improve bones, good for skin and health. The Mah Dal is also very helpful in controlling diabetes. The Mah Dal is used as required in the construction material in the Sikha Theory of Restoration, renovations, and construction.

5. **Saffron:** Saffron is commonly derived from the saffron crocus flower. Saffron crocus flower is the first flower bloomed in spring. The Saffron flower is usually found in jaamni (purple) and Kapahi (yellow). The Saffron is also available in some parts of ancient Punjab. Saffron is a potent spice and antioxidant. The molecules present in the Saffron helps to protect the cells against stress. The main antioxidant in saffron are crocin, crocetin, safranal, and kaempferol. Saffron improves memory learning ability, protects brain cells against progressive damage, reduces appetite, and helps in reducing weight. Saffron is also used to remove depression.

The crimson stigma or styles in the saffron crocus flower is called threads. The thread in the saffron flower has two colors, red and yellow. Each color has its benefits. Sikh Theory of Restoration, renovation, and construction use the saffron thread and leaves both. They are very expanse and beneficial. The Saffron as a material ingredient helps keep the environment calm and scent. Saffron is used in the construction material to provide yellow or purple color. The colors derived from the Saffron never get detriment and has long life than other chemical paints. Saffron is only used as required in the material mortar.

6. **Milk:** The Sikha Theory of Restoration, renovation, and construction use buffalo milk to prepare the lime of mortar. Buffalo milk is naturally very high in fat and protein. It is very readily available in Punjab and is a very creamy dairy product. It contains a very high amount of calcium and minerals needed to develop bones. Buffalo milk reduces the risk of osteoporosis disease. The milk is also very rich in iron and helps reduce the problem of anemia and increase the circulation in the blood. The potassium contents of the buffalo milk help to regulate blood pressure.

The use of the milk in the contraction material for the mortar and the white color. It is used as required in the material depending on the building's current structure, condition, and whitening. It also helps in the waterproofing of the outer layers of the building. It helps smooth the surface like marble and is very healthy for the environment. The milk ingredient in the construction material helps mediate and concentrate with a fresh mind and without stress. It also helps make the human body more active state with environmental factors.

7. **Seashells:** Seashells ha a gar protective layer and are instrumental in the construction material. Seashells make the material dry and robust. Seashells are the outer part of the sea animals and are automatically disposed of their skin and washed by water waves and tides. The Sikha Theory of restorations uses the seashells to strengthen the mortar. The seashell also used a tool because of their strongness. Some seashells are big enough as bathtubs. They are also used for

religious purposes in many religions. Seashells are rich in calcium and very useful in horticulture. For horticulture, seashells are broken into small parts and ground into the soil to raise the power of hydrogen and increase the calcium. In construction, the use of the seashell in two ways. First. Seashells are crushed into powder and then mix it with the lime mortar. Second, the seashells are burned on intense heat for three-four days and then routed to powder for use. The seashell is helped the mortar to provide long life. It helps to prevent the shrinkage of the materials over time. It is only used as required in the lime mortar for various purposes. Seashells help in decorating walls, floors, ceilings, etc. Sometimes the engraving with seashell on the historical building provides a fabulous beauty

8. **Acacia Gum:** Acacia Gum is naturally produced from the acacia tree in east and west Punjab.

Acacia tree is a small tree that grows up to the maximum height of 40 feet. It can grow in any soil. The acacia tree is beneficial for health, and various parts of it are helpful for many medical treatments. The leaves of the acacia trees are useful in bleeding. It is water-resistant and naturally antibacterial. Acacia has been used for medicines, woodwork, and baking food for centuries. The acacia tree contains chemicals naturally like alkaloids, glycosides, and flavonoids. These all are very helpful in healing wounds. Acacia tree also has an ingredient naturally called acacia catechu and is very beneficial for the health of the mouth and teeth.

Acacia Gum is a rich source of fiber called water-soluble. Water-soluble is used in food for diet and keeping the cholesterol under control in the human body. It reduces body fat and keeps the weight in the healthy range. It also relieves and helps in treating cough and sore throat. Acacia Gum used in the construction material of Sikha Theory of restoration make the other ingredients of the lime sticky. The use of acacia gum in the lime plaster help to prevent and remove the bacteria from the building environment. It is used in the construction material as per requirements of the building structure, condition, and weather.

9. **Turmeric:** Turmeric is commonly used in east and west Punjab vegetables. It naturally contains a chemical called curcumin. Turmeric has natural antioxidant and anti-inflammatory properties and is very beneficial for the health of the human body. It is helpful in chronic conditions to prevent the effect on tissues. It improves memory, lessens the pain, lowers the risk of heart attacks, lowers depression, helps in preventing cancer. It is readily available and the most used ingredient of daily life in Punjab. It is widely used in all parts of the world.

The color derived from turmeric is solid. Because of its health benefits, the Sikhs Theory of Restoration, renovation, and construction uses it as a construction material of the building. It first dried for days in natural solar heat to use in the material. It is then ground to make the powder in the 18th, and 19th-century Gurdwaras built by Khalsa Panth used the turmeric powder for the yellow color by mixing it with the actual material used on the building. It provides benefits such as color and as well as health. It makes the material shiny and helps in non-shrinking.

10. Indigo (Neel): Indigofera tinctoria is the scientific name of Neel. It has been used for dye for centuries in Punjab. The maximum height of the indigo plant is 7 feet. The indigo plant has light green leaves and pink or violet flowers. The indigo flower is rich in carbohydrates, proteins, alkaloids, tannins, flavonoids, glycosides, terpenoids, quinines, steroids, gallic acid, dehydrodeguelin, tephrosin, sumatrol, antioxidants, antibacterial, anthelmintic, laxative, anticancer, anti-inflammatory, anti-diabetic, cytotoxic properties. Neel is widely used in the medical field to treat various diseases like cardiopathy, epilepsy, ulcers, skin disorder, splenomegaly, cough, delusion, parasitic infestation, poisoning, mental disturbance, nervine disorder, headache, depression.

The Sikha theory of restoration, renovation, and construction use Neel to construct the buildings. The blue color derived from the Neel is solid and provide help in strengthening the other ingredient in the lime material. It is used to give a blue hue to the material. It helps to keep the environment calm and healthy.

43

11. Yogurt: Yogurt is a product made from milk. It contains protein, fat, carbohydrates, calcium. The yogurt-making process starts with milk by adding various live bacteria cultures, and they are put at a specific temperature to encourage bacteria growth. Yogurt word comes from the Turkish word "yogurmak" which means thick, coagulate, or curdle. It has natural growth sugar

called lactose to give yogurt a different flavor. The process of making yogurt is called yogurt culture. Yogurt contains calcium, vitamin B6 and B12, riboflavin, potassium, and magnesium. It enhances the gut microbiota, prevents the digestive problem, helps in reducing weight, boosts the immune system, helps in reducing type 2 diabetes heavy metal exposure.

The Sikha theory of restoration, renovation, and construction uses yogurt in the construction material. It helps to keep the building material healthy and safe. It enables the outer skin of the plaster to be water-resistant and environmental damage resistant to provide longer life to the material. For use in the material, the yogurt must be fresh and mixed in the lime plaster to give the final finish to the building. The outer layer becomes soft, smooth, and looks like a marble finish using yogurt. The ratio of use in the construction material depends on the building's type, condition, environment, and structure. The material made by adding yogurt has had the same health benefits for a long time and keeps the building's environment clean.

12. **Buffalo Milk Butter:** The butter made from the raw milk of buffalo is called buffalo milk butter. The process that makes butter from the milk is called churning. The raw milk of buffalo is churning clockwise and anti-clockwise continuously to produce butter from the milk. Buffalo butter is rich in antioxidants to help boost the immune system. It improves the human body to absorb nutrients and minerals helps against viruses and bacteria. Buffalo milk butter contains vitamins, protein, calcium, and fat. It improves heart health, strengthens bones, regulates blood pressure, increases muscle mass, boosts skin health, reduces burning, boosts immunity.

The Sikha theory of restoration, renovation, and construction use buffalo milk butter in the construction materials of the historically significant buildings. The butter must be fresh for use as an ingredient in the lime for the outer skin of the plaster. It mixes in the lime mater for the dressing to provide a smooth and lubricating finish. It strengthens the material to minimize friction and allow a smooth finish. It helps waterproof the outer layer of the building plaster and reduces environmental damage over time. It keeps the whitening and glossy finish of the outer plaster layer of the building for beautification. It is used as required in the building material depending on building condition, structure, and environment.

13. Jaggery: Raw Cane Jaggery is a natural sweetener readily available in the east and west Punjab. It is made from sugarcane through a very intellectual process. The sugar cane plant is

a maximum of 20 feet tall with stout, jointed, fibrous stalks and very rich in sucrose. Jaggery has many health benefits and is an ideal sweetener. It contains protein, choline, betaine, vitamin B12, vitamin B6, folate, calcium, iron, phosphorus, magnesium, selenium, and manganese. Jaggery has many health benefits like it prevent constipation, purifying the blood, detoxifying the liver, boosting immunity, treating cold and flu, preventing anemia, relieving joint pain, aiding in weight loss, and promoting intestinal health.

The process to make the jaggery is extraction, filtration, boiling, and cooling.

The sugarcane is crushed for juice extraction; then, the liquid is filtered and boiled on a required heat for a specific time, leaving it for cooling for some time and solidifying in the desired shape. The Sikha theory of restoration, renovation, and construction use jaggery in the construction material used in ancient Punjab. Jaggery is reheated again to mix with the construction material as required. It helps the material be strong and supports the building environment to be healthy for the life of the material.

Gurdwara Janam Asthan
Mata Sahib Kaur Ji

Gurdwara Janam Asthan Mata Sahib Kaur Ji

Gurdwara Janam Asthan Mata Sahib Kaur Ji was first built in the early 18th century by the Sikh Misls. Before building the Gurdwara, it was the home of the parents of the Mother of the Khalsa Panth Mata Sahib Kaur Ji, also known as Mata Sahib Deva Ji.

The Mother of the Khalsa Panth was born in the house of Bhai Ramu Bassi and Mata Jas Devi in November 1681 AD. Bhai Ramu Bassi was the son of Bhai Baghtu, a Guru Nanak Dev Ji follower. Bhai Ramu Bassi and his family were great devotees of Guru Tegh Bahadar Sahib Ji and Guru Gobind Singh Ji. When Mata Sahib Kaur Ji was born, they decided to marry her with Guru Gobind Singh Ji. Guru Gobind Singh Ji revealed the Khalsa Panth at Anandpur Sahib, Punjab, on the first Vaisakh of 1699 AD. Today is known as the inauguration day of the Khalsa Panth and Khalsa Samat.

Bhai Ramu Bassi and the Rohtas resident went to Anandpur sahib in 1700 AD to propose the marriage of Mata Sahib Kaur Ji and Guru Gobind Singh Ji. Guru Gobind Singh Ji was already married and told that it is not possible. Bhai Ramu Bassi and his villagers request the Mata Gujri Ji (Mother of Guru Gobind Singh Ji) and describe their devotion and situation. Later Guru Gobind

49

Singh Ji accepted the marriage proposal and told them that it would be an eternal marriage. Guru Gobind Singh Ji gives her the Mother of the Khalsa Panth title.

Mata Sahib Kaur Ji becomes the Mother of the Khalsa, and her birthplace has become the most religious place for the Sikhs and the Khalsa Panth. Various states developed the Gurdwara structure by the Sikh Misls Empire and Khalsa empires. The Gurdwara existed between the Khaskhani gate of Kashmiri Gate of the Rohtas fort. The Gurdwara was built in the shape of a triangle like an arrow. The adjacent road with the Gurdwara Sahib's boundary wall connected Khaskhani gate and Kashmiri gate and then attached it to the Gurdwara Choha Sahib Ji through Kashmiri Gate.

The Khalsa Pant always organized the big celebration every year on the first week of November before the partition of Punjab in August 1947. 1947 Partition led the detriment to the Khalsa Panth, and this Gurdwara Sahib got abandoned. The Gurdwara Sahib get demolished by the residents of Rohtas after august 1947, and many illegal encroachments were made. They made unlawful residential homes and other development. No one was left there to take care of the Gurdwara Sahib.

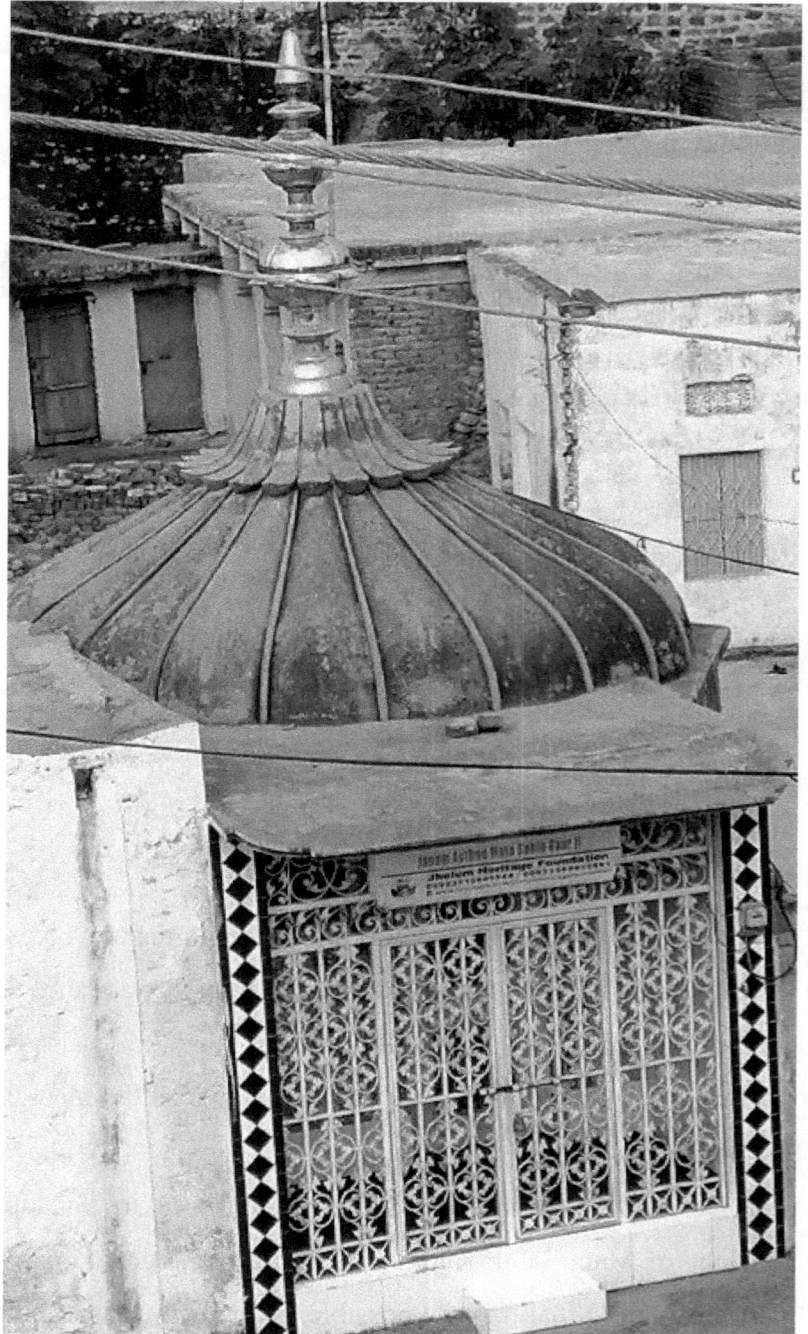

Remaining Dome and 10' x 10' room with lock-in June 2021

50

With the blessing of Mata Sahib Kaur Ji and Khalsa Panth, Ranjit Nagara, the USA, proposed three different plans to restore Gurdwara Janam Asthan Mata Sahib Kaur Ji to purchase five homes, nine homes, or twenty-two homes. The plan was preliminary and entirely depended on the purchase of illegally built homes without trouble from the resident of Rohtas. The local government and the official promised to help acquire the property back to the Gurdwara Sahib from the illegal occupier. The land belongs to the Gurdwara Sahib, but the unlawful occupier refused to give it back to restore the Gurdwara Sahib. Ranjit Nagara offered them that they could take a reasonable price and sell it. Residents of Rohtas still refused and asked for a very high price. Ranjit Nagara paid those unpredictable prices to the illegal occupier and got approximately three and a half Kanals land back in the name of Gurdwara Sahib.

The red covered area was the prosed purchase with twenty-two homes for the restoration purpose of the Gurdwara Janam Asthan Mata Sahib Kaur Ji. All houses were illegally built after the partition of Punjab in 1947 by demolishing the original Gurdwara, and most of those homes are vacant on the land of the Gurdwara Sahib. Still, the illegal land occupiers refused the proposal and did not give them to restore the Gurdwara Sahib. Even they did not give back to Gurdwara by taking the price.

The following proposal was made to purchase the nine homes. But the same situation was faced, and the illegal occupiers refused to give them back to restore the Gurdwara Sahib. Even

they were the illegal occupants of the land and built the illegal house on the Gurdwara Land. It was very disappointing that no one lived in those houses for a long time, and they even refused the purchase offer made by Ranjit Nagara USA because they did not want to see the Gurdwara there.

The last proposal of Ranjit Nagara was made for the five homes adjacent to the Gurdwara Janam Asthan Mata Sahib Kaur Ji. Initially, all the illegal occupiers refused the proposal, then the three homes and the two-shop adjacent to the Gurdwara agreed to sell them at a very high price. Ranjit Nagara paid those high prices because there was no other option left to expand the Gurdwara Sahib on its

own land. The complete details of the purchase are given in the land purchase section of the book.

Gurdwara Janam Asthan Mata Sahib Kaur Ji
Land purchase Contracts

Gurdwara Janam Asthan Mata Sahib Kaur Ji is in Rohtas fort, Rohtas, Jhelum in west Punjab. Before the partition of Punjab in August 1947, the Gurdwara Janam Asthan Mata Sahib Kaur Ji complex was in more than 30 kanals (163,350 square feet) areas from the Khaskhani gate to the Kashmiri gate of the Rohtas fort.

The dark black line represents the old way from Khaskhani gate to Kashmiri Gate of Rohtas fort before the Partition of Punjab in 1947.

The red line in the shape of the arrow represents the actual approximate area and boundary walls of the Gurdwara Janam Asthan Mata Sahib Kaur Ji in Rohtas fort.

Illegally built home on the land of Gurdwara Sahib by demolishing the structure and wall after the partition of Punjab.

Ranjit Nagara USA approaches the ETPB, PSGPC, and the Government authorities to get the land back for the Gurdwara Janam Asthan Mata Sahib Kaur Ji. All government officials and PSGPC were very helpful. But the illegal occupier of the Gurdwara land was refused to give it back to build the Gurdwara Sahib. It is heard from the religious leaders of Sikhism that the original Gurdwara was in the shape of the arrow toward the Khaskhani gate. More research is required at this time.

Gurdwara Choha sahib Ji and Gurdwara Janam Asthan Mata Sahib Kaur Ji are within walking distance of 10-15 minutes through the Kashmiri gate of Rohtas fort

Gurdwara Choha Sahib Ji, Rohtas, Jhelum

Gurdwara Janam Asthan Mata Sahib Kaur Ji remaining 10' x 10' room on August 2020.

As of February 2022, Ranjit Nagara USA purchased three and a half Kanal land on the name of ht gurdwara Mata Sahib Kaur Ji with the blessing of Khalsa Panth and Mata Sahib Kaur

Ji. The Gurdwara has landed by completing the occupied land has been handed over to PSGPC and ETPB on February 28, 2022.

The land is purchased at a very high price because the illegal encroachment and occupiers do not want that Khalsa Panth restores the Gurdwara Sahib. Ranjit Nagara USA is very thankful to Mr. Raza Waqar and Mr. Rao Pervaiz Akhtar, Deputy commissioner of Jhelum, for the help in the purchase of the land.

All sellers sign the contract and receive the selling price in the office of Deputy commissioner Rao Pervaiz Akhtar in his presence. An archeology officer, assistant commissioner, and Jhelum heritage societies witnessed the signature and payment procedure. Ranjit Nagara, CEO Satpreet Singh signed the contract at Ranjit Nagara office located in Manteca, California, USA. All the original documents are present in the Ranjit Nagara USA head office in Manteca, CA. The overpriced land is purchased in the name of the Gurdwara Janam Asthan Mata Sahib Kaur Ji. Ranjit Nagara pays a very high price on behalf of the Khalsa Panth because the Gurdwara Janam Asthan Mata Sahib Kaur Ji has a very high priority in Khalsa Panth. It is apparent in the contract that this land will not belong to any individual, organization (Private or Public), NGO. The

Gurdwara Janam Asthan Mata Sahib Kaur Ji's sole property will only belong to the Khalsa Panth. As clearly seen in the picture (April 2021). the only clue of the Gurdwara Sahib was the Dome only. All the surrounding was illegally made after the partition of Punjab in August 1947.

LAND and HOME PURCHASE CONTRACT in Rohtas Fort, Jhelum, Pakistan
(For JANAM ASHTAN MATA SAHIB KAUR JI)

THIS AGREEMENT, made at <u>Deputy Commissioner (RAO PARVAIZ AKHTAR) Office, Jhelum</u>, each copy of which shall be deemed an original, effective as of the ___29ᵗʰ___ day of ___JULY___, 2021, by and between <u>PARVEEN AKHTAR W/O MALIK MUHAMMAD SHARIF AWAN, MUHAMMAD YASIR S/O MALIK MUHAMMAD SHARIF AWAN, MUHAMMAD HANIF S/O MALIK MUHAMMAD SHARIF AWAN</u>, whose address is <u>NEAR JAMIA MAZHAR, HOUSE NUMBER 225, MACHINE MOHALA NUMBER 3, JHELUM, PUNJAB, PAKISTAN</u>, hereinafter referred to as "Seller", and JANAM ASHTAN MATA SAHIB KAUR JI (PAID BY RANJIT NAGARA, a USA based California Non-Profit Organization), whose address is <u>1463 MOFFAT BLVD, STE 9, MANTECAM CA 95336, UNITED STATES OF AMERICA</u>, hereinafter referred to as "Buyer", upon the following terms and conditions.

A.   Agreement to Sell; Agreement to Purchase. Seller has this day agreed to sell unto Buyer and Buyer has agreed to purchase from Seller premises located at Rohtas Fort, which is more particularly described as follows:

Situated in the City of JHELUM, DINA Tehsil and more particularly described on Exhibit "A" which is attached hereto, estimated to contain thirteen (13) Marla (0.0813 acre(s)) of land or three thousand five hundred thirty nine and twenty six by hundred (3539.26) square feet of land, more or less and including dwelling or structure resides and more particularly described on Exhibit "A" which is attached hereto, specifically incorporated herein, and hereafter referred to as the "Property".

B.   Payment of Purchase Price. Buyer shall pay Seller for the Property the purchase price of ___Two Million Pakistan Rupees___ (___2,000,000___ PKR) That is equal to ___Thirteen thousand three hundred Seventy two dollars & Fifty Six cent___ United States Dollars ($___13,372.56___). The purchase price shall be payable as follows:

1.   Buyer shall pay to Seller the lump-sum (Token Money) of ___One hundred thousand Pakistan Rupees (e-tra)___ (___100,000___ PKR) before the execution of this Land and Home Contract.

2.   The unpaid balance of the purchase price, ___Two Million Pakistan Rupees___ PKR (___2,000,000___ PKR) that is equal to ___Thirteen thousand three hundred Seventy two dollars & Fifty Six cent___ United States Dollars ($___13,372.56___), within ten days after occupy and full control of the property. ___13,372.56___

C.   Delivery of Possession. Buyer shall have exclusive possession of the Property commencing ___31ˢᵗ JULY___, 2021 and continuing.

H.   Encumbering of Property. Seller warrants that, as of the date of this Contract, the Property is free and clear of all liens and encumbrances, mortgages, if any, on the Property.

I.   Assignment. The property can be only used to build for the Gurdwara Janam Asthan Mata Sahib Kaur Ji. The property cannot use for anyone's personal or business use at any time and will

ATTESTED
Mal... ...d Iqbal
Date...   ...lic, Jhelum

Page 1|3

56

be solely used for the Gurdwara Janam Asthan Mata Sahib Kaur Ji as per Sikh Rehat Maryada, Sikh code and Conducts.

K.   Recording of Contract.   The property considered to be recorded upon signature in the Jhelum Deputy Commissioner's office by seller. The property can be only considered recorded on the Name of GURDWARA JANAM ASTHAN MATA SAHIB KAUR JI. No person or entity will not make any type of claim on the property. This property will be owned by the Khalsa Panth and will be only used for the use of Gurdwara Janam Asthan Mata Sahib Kaur Ji.

N.   Successors and Assigns.   This property belongs to Gurdwara Janam Asthan Mata Sahib Kaur Ji and this property will be always on the name of Gurdwara Janam Asthan Mata Sahib Kaur Ji. No individual or entity will ever make claim on this property. This property will be the property of the Khalsa Panth and will be solely used for the purpose of Gurdwara Janam Asthan Mata Sahib Kaur Ji.

O.   Property to be Sold "AS IS".   Buyer hereby acknowledges that they are purchasing the Property in its present "AS IS" condition.

IN WITNESS WHEREOF, the parties have hereunto set their hands on the date set forth above.

SIGNED AND ACKNOWLEDGED IN THE PRESENCE OF JHELUM DEPUTY COMMISSIONER ROA PARVAIZ AKHTAR:

Signatures:

Parveen Akhtar
Seller

Parveen Akhtar Thumbprint

Muhammad Hanif
Seller

Muhammad Hanif Thumbprint

Muhammad Yasir
Seller

Muhammad Yasir Thumbprint

Satpreet Singh
President and Director
Ranjit Nagara
USA Based Non-Profit Organization

Witnesses:

Raja Ahmad Waqar
Jhelum Heritage Society
Jhelum, Punjab
Pakistan

Waqar Husain
Assistant Commissioner
Dina, Jhelum, Punjab
Pakistan

Imran Masood
Archeology Officer
Rohtas Fort, Jhelum
Punjab, Pakistan

Page 2|3

ATTESTED

57

EXHIBIT "A"

Approximately Fourteen (14) Marla home and land adjacent to Janam Asthan Mata Sahib Kaur in between Khaskhani gate and Kashmiri gate near to the Rohtas fort wall.

ATTESTED

The payment made for the first home and land was paid by wire transfer below.

RANJIT NAGARA

RANJIT NAGARA <info@ranjitnagara.org>

Your Same Day wire transfer was successfully sent

3 messages

Online Transfers from Bank of America
<bankofamericatransfers@mail.transfers.bankofamerica.com>
Reply-To: Online Transfers from Bank of America <bankofamericatransfers@mail.transfers.bankofamerica.com>
To: info@ranjitnagara.org

Wed, Jun 16, 2021 at 9:15 AM

We have successfully sent the following transfer:

****

Item #:	343775168
Amount:	$13,372.56 (2,000,000.00 PKR)
To:	WAQAR AHMED RAJA
Fee:	0.00
Rate:	1 USD = 149.56 PKR
Send on Date:	06/16/2021
Service:	International Wire Transfer

****

If there is a problem with executing your request, we will notify you both by email and on the Manage Accounts tab. You can always check your transfer status on the Review Transfer screen at www.bankofamerica.com.

Sincerely,

Member Service

www.bankofamerica.com

This is a service email from Bank of America. Please note that you may receive service emails in accordance with your Bank of America service agreements, whether or not you elect to receive promotional email.

Read our privacy policy: http://www.bankofamerica.com/privacy

Please don't reply directly to this automatically-generated email message.

Bank of America Email, 8th Floor-NC1-002-08-25, 101 South Tryon St., Charlotte, NC 28255-0001

Bank of America, N.A. Member FDIC. Equal Housing Lender:

http://www.bankofamerica.com/help/equalhousing.cfm

(C) 2021 Bank of America Corporation. All rights reserved.

This email was sent to: info@ranjitnagara.org

Online Transfers from Bank of America
<bankofamericatransfers@mail.transfers.bankofamerica.com>
Reply-To: Online Transfers from Bank of America <bankofamericatransfers@mail.transfers.bankofamerica.com>
To: info@ranjitnagara.org

Wed, Jun 16, 2021 at 9:15 AM

We have successfully sent the following transfer:

LAND, SHOP and HOME PURCHASE CONTRACT in Rohtas Fort, Jhelum, Pakistan
(For JANAM ASHTAN MATA SAHIB KAUR JI)

THIS AGREEMENT, made at <u>Deputy Commissioner (RAO PARVAIZ AKHTAR) Office,</u> <u>Jhelum</u> , each copy of which shall be deemed an original, effective as of the ___ **20ᵗʰ** ___ day of ___ **JULY** ___ , 2021, by and between <u>MUHAMMAD DAUD BAIG S/O Mirza</u> <u>ASGHAR BAIG</u>, whose address is <u>NEAR (ADJACENT) JANAM ASTHAN MATA SAHIB</u> <u>KAUR JI, ROHTAS FORT, JHELUM, PUNJAB, PAKISTAN</u>, hereinafter referred to as "Seller", and JANAM ASHTAN MATA SAHIB KAUR JI (PAID BY RANJIT NAGARA, a USA based California Non-Profit Organization), whose address is <u>1463 MOFFAT BLVD, STE 9,</u> <u>MANTECAM CA 95336, UNITED STATES OF AMERICA</u>, hereinafter referred to as "Buyer", upon the following terms and conditions.

A.   Agreement to Sell; Agreement to Purchase. Seller has this day agreed to sell unto Buyer and Buyer has agreed to purchase from Seller premises located at Rohtas Fort, which is more particularly described as follows:

Situated in Rohtas fort in the Tehsil DINA, District JHELUM, , PUNJAB, PAKISTAN and more particularly described on Exhibit "A" which is attached hereto, estimated to contain fifteen (15) Marla or more (0.0938) acre(s) or more) of land or four thousand eighty three and seventy five by hundred (4083.75) square feet of land, or more including dwelling, shop, land or structure resides and more particularly described on Exhibit "A" which is attached hereto, specifically incorporated herein, and hereafter referred to as the "Property".

B.   Payment of Purchase Price. Buyer shall pay Seller for the Property the purchase price of <u>FOUR MILLION FIVE HUNDRED THOUSAND PAKISTAN RUPEES</u> (4,500,000 PKR) That is equal to <u>Twenty nine thousand four hundred four dollars Twenty Seven cent</u> United States Dollars ($ <u>29,404.27</u>). The purchase price shall be payable as follows:

1.   Buyer shall pay to Seller the lump-sum (Token Money) of <u>Fifty THOUSAND Pakistan Rupees</u> (50,000 PKR) before the execution of this Land, Shop and Home Contract.

2.   The unpaid balance of the purchase price, <u>Four Million Five hundred thousand Pakistan Rupees</u> PKR (4,500,000 PKR) that is equal to <u>Twenty nine thousand four hundred dollars</u> United States Dollars ($ <u>29,404.27</u>), within ten days after occupy and full control of the <u>Twenty Seven cent</u> property.

C.   Delivery of Possession. Buyer shall have exclusive possession of the Property commencing **21ˢᵗ** **JULY** , 2021 and continuing.

H.   Encumbering of Property. Seller warrants that, as of the date of this Contract, the Property is free and clear of all liens and encumbrances, mortgages, if any, on the Property.

I.   Assignment. The property can be only used to build for the Gurdwara Janam Asthan Mata Sahib Kaur Ji. The property cannot use for anyone's personal or business use at any time and will be solely used for the Gurdwara Janam Asthan Mata Sahib Kaur Ji as per Sikh Rehat Maryada, Sikh code and Conducts.

Page 1 | 3

A T T E S T E D
Malik Shahid Iqbal
Date_____ Notary Public, Jhelum

MALIK SHAHID IQBAL ADVOCATE
No._____
Date 06/08/2...
NOTARY PUBLIC JHELUM

60

K.   Recording of Contract. The property considered to be recorded upon signature in the Jhelum Deputy Commissioner's office by seller. The property can be only considered recorded on the Name of GURDWARA JANAM ASTHAN MATA SAHIB KAUR JI. No person or entity will not make any type of claim on the property. This property will be owned by the Khalsa Panth and will be only used for the use of Gurdwara Janam Asthan Mata Sahib Kaur Ji.

N.   Successors and Assigns. This property belongs to Gurdwara Janam Asthan Mata Sahib Kaur Ji and this property will be always on the name of Gurdwara Janam Asthan Mata Sahib Kaur Ji. No individual or entity will ever make claim on this property. This property will be the property of the Khalsa Panth and will be solely used for the purpose of Gurdwara Janam Asthan Mata Sahib Kaur Ji.

O.   Property to be Sold "AS IS". Buyer hereby acknowledges that they are purchasing the Property in its present "AS IS" condition.

IN WITNESS WHEREOF, the parties have hereunto set their hands on the date set forth above.

SIGNED AND ACKNOWLEDGED IN THE PRESENCE OF JHELUM DEPUTY COMMISSIONER ROA PARVAIZ AKHTAR:

Signatures:

_____
Muhammad Daud Baig
Seller

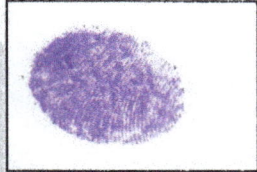

[thumbprint]
Muhammad Daud Baig

Satpreet Singh
Satpreet Singh
President and Director
Ranjit Nagara
USA Based Non-Profit Organization
On Behalf of JANAM ASTHAN MATA SAHIB KAUR JI

Witnesses for:

_____
Raja Ahmad Waqar
Jhelum Heritage Society
Jhelum, Punjab
Pakistan

_____
Waqar Husain
Assistant Commissioner
Dina, Jhelum, Punjab
Pakistan

_____
Sub Imran Masood
Archeology Officer
Rohtas Fort, Jhelum
Punjab, Pakistan

ATTESTED
Malik Shahid Iqbal
Date_____ Notary Public Jhelum

06/08/2021

Page 2 | 3

EXHIBIT "A"

Approximately Fourteen (15) Marla or more home, shop and land adjacent to Janam Asthan Mata Sahib Kaur Ji in between Khaskhani gate and Kashmiri gate near to the Rohtas fort wall.

ATTESTED
Malik Shahid Iqbal
Notary Public, Jhelum

MALIK SHAHID IQBAL ADVOCATE
No.
06/08/2021
NOTARY PUBLIC JHELUM

The payment confirmation that was made to purchase the adjacent home and shop of Gurdwara

RANJIT NAGARA   RANJIT NAGARA <info@ranjitnagara.org>

Your Same Day wire transfer was successfully sent
2 messages

Online Transfers from Bank of America   Tue, Jul 20, 2021 at 6:47
<bankofamericatransfers@mail.transfers.bankofamerica.com>   AM
Reply-To: Online Transfers from Bank of America <bankofamericatransfers@mail.transfers.bankofamerica.com>
To: info@ranjitnagara.org

We have successfully sent the following transfer:

```
*************************************************
Item #:      348052160
Amount:      $29,404.27 (4,500,000.00 PKR)
To:          WAQAR AHMED RAJA
Fee:         0.00
Rate:        1 USD = 153.039 PKR
Send on Date: 07/20/2021
Service:     International Wire Transfer
*************************************************
```

If there is a problem with executing your request, we will notify you both by email and on the Manage Accounts tab. You can always check your transfer status on the Review Transfer screen at www.bankofamerica.com.

Sincerely,

Member Service

www.bankofamerica.com

This is a service email from Bank of America. Please note that you may receive service emails in accordance with your Bank of America service agreements, whether or not you elect to receive promotional email.

Read our privacy policy: http://www.bankofamerica.com/privacy

Please don't reply directly to this automatically-generated email message.

Bank of America Email, 8th Floor-NC1-002-08-25, 101 South Tryon St., Charlotte, NC 28255-0001

Bank of America, N.A. Member FDIC. Equal Housing Lender:

http://www.bankofamerica.com/help/equalhousing.cfm

(C) 2021 Bank of America Corporation. All rights reserved.

This email was sent to: info@ranjitnagara.org

Online Transfers from Bank of America   Tue, Jul 20, 2021 at 7:33
<bankofamericatransfers@mail.transfers.bankofamerica.com>   AM
Reply-To: Online Transfers from Bank of America <bankofamericatransfers@mail.transfers.bankofamerica.com>
To: info@ranjitnagara.org

We have successfully sent the following transfer:

LAND, SHOP and HOME PURCHASE CONTRACT in Rohtas Fort, Jhelum, Pakistan
(For JANAM ASHTAN MATA SAHIB KAUR JI)

THIS AGREEMENT, made at Deputy Commissioner (RAO PARVAIZ AKHTAR) Office, Jhelum , each copy of which shall be deemed an original, effective as of the 12th day of AUGUST , 2021, by and between MOHAMMED SAQIB S/O MOHAMMED SADIE, whose address is NEAR JANAM ASTHAN MATA SAHIB KAUR JI ROHTAS FORT, JHELUM, PUNJAB, PAKISTAN, hereinafter referred to as "Seller", and JANAM ASHTAN MATA SAHIB KAUR JI (PAID BY RANJIT NAGARA, a USA based California Non-Profit Organization), whose address is 1463 MOFFAT BLVD, STE 9, MANTECAM, CA 95336, UNITED STATES OF AMERICA, hereinafter referred to as "Buyer", upon the following terms and conditions.

A.   Agreement to Sell; Agreement to Purchase. Seller has this day agreed to sell unto Buyer and Buyer has agreed to purchase from Seller premises located at Rohtas Fort, which is more particularly described as follows:

Situated in Rohtas fort in the Tehsil DINA, District JHELUM,,, PUNJAB, PAKISTAN and more particularly described on Exhibit "A" which is attached hereto, estimated to contain fifteen (15) Marla or more (0.0938) acre(s) or more) of land or four thousand eighty three and seventy five by hundred (4083.75) square feet of land, or more including dwelling, shop, land or structure resides and more particularly described on Exhibit "A" which is attached hereto, specifically incorporated herein, and hereafter referred to as the "Property".

B.   Payment of Purchase Price. Buyer shall pay Seller for the Property the purchase price of Three Million Pakistan Rupees (3,000,000 PKR) That is equal to Nineteen thousand one hundred Ninety Six dollars & seventysix Cent United States Dollars ($ 19,196.76). The purchase price shall be payable as follows:

1.   Buyer   shall   pay   to   Seller   the   lump-sum   (Token   Money)   of one hundred thousand (pakistan rupee) (100,000 PKR) before the execution of this Land, Shop and Home Contract. (US$639.87)

2.   The unpaid balance of the purchase price. Two Million nine hundred thousand Pakistan Rupees PKR (2,900,000 PKR) that is equal to Eighteen thousand five hundred fifty six dollars +Eighty seven cent United States Dollars ($ 18,556.87), within ten days after occupy and full control of the property.

C.   Delivery of Possession. Buyer shall have exclusive possession of the Property commencing 13th August , 2021 and continuing.

H.   Encumbering of Property. Seller warrants that, as of the date of this Contract, the Property is free and clear of all liens and encumbrances, mortgages, if any, on the Property.

I.   Assignment. The property can be only used to build for the Gurdwara Janam Asthan Mata Sahib Kaur Ji. The property cannot use for anyone's personal or business use at any time and will be solely used for the Gurdwara Janam Asthan Mata Sahib Kaur Ji as per Sikh Rehat Maryada, Sikh code and Conducts.

K.   Recording of Contract. The property considered to be recorded upon signature in the Jhelum Deputy Commissioner's office by seller. The property can be only considered recorded on the Name of GURDWARA JANAM ASTHAN MATA SAHIB KAUR JI. No person or entity will not make any type of claim on the property. This property will be owned by the Khalsa Panth and will be only used for the use of Gurdwara Janam Asthan Mata Sahib Kaur Ji.

N.   Successors and Assigns. This property belongs to Gurdwara Janam Asthan Mata Sahib Kaur Ji and this property will be always on the name of Gurdwara Janam Asthan Mata Sahib Kaur Ji. No individual or entity will ever make claim on this property. This property will be the property of the Khalsa Panth and will be solely used for the purpose of Gurdwara Janam Asthan Mata Sahib Kaur Ji.

O.   Property to be Sold "AS IS". Buyer hereby acknowledges that they are purchasing the Property in its present "AS IS" condition.

IN WITNESS WHEREOF, the parties have hereunto set their hands on the date set forth above.

SIGNED AND ACKNOWLEDGED IN THE PRESENCE OF JHELUM DEPUTY COMMISSIONER ROA PARVAIZ AKHTAR:

Signatures:

Mohammed Saqib
Seller

Mohammed Saqib

Satpreet Singh
President and Director
Ranjit Nagara
USA Based Non-Profit Organization
On behalf of JANAM ASTHAN MATA SAHIB KAUR JI

Witnesses for:

Raja Ahmad Waqar
Jhelum Heritage Society
Jhelum, Punjab
Pakistan

Waqar Husain
Assistant Commissioner
Dina, Jhelum, Punjab
Pakistan

Sub Divisional Officer Archaeology
Government of Punjab

Imran Masood
Archeology Officer
Rohtas Fort, Jhelum
Punjab, Pakistan

EXHIBIT "A"

Approximately Fourteen (15) Marla or more home, shop and land adjacent to Janam Asthan Mata Sahib Kaur Ji in between Khaskhani gate and Kashmiri gate near to the Rohtas fort wall.

The payment for the home and shop is given in two payments because the illegal occupier refused to give possession to Ranjit Nagara of the Home and Shop. Both payments are shown in two separate transactions.

Online Transfers from Bank of America <bankofamericatransfers@r

to me

We have successfully sent the following transfer:

****

Item #:   351527700
Amount: $3,192.46 (500,000.00 PKR)

To: WAQAR AHMED RAJA
Fee: 0.00
Rate: 1 USD = 156.619 PKR
Send on Date: 08/16/2021
Service: International Wire Transfer
****

If there is a problem with executing your request, we will notify you both

Sincerely,

Member Service

www.bankofamerica.com

This is a service email from Bank of America. Please note that you may in accordance with your Bank of America service agreements, whether (promotional email.

Read our privacy policy: http://www.bankofamerica.com/privacy

Please don't reply directly to this automatically-generated email messag

Second Full payment for the third contract of land and shop purchase of Gurdwara Janam Asthan Mata Sahib Kaur Ji.

RANJIT NAGARA

RANJIT NAGARA <info@ranjitnagara.org>

Your Same Day wire transfer was successfully sent
1 message

Online Transfers from Bank of America   Wed, Aug 4, 2021 at 7:52
<bankofamericatransfers@mail.transfers.bankofamerica.com>   AM
Reply-To: Online Transfers from Bank of America <bankofamericatransfers@mail.transfers.bankofamerica.com>
To: info@ranjitnagara.org

We have successfully sent the following transfer:

****

Item #:   350114396
Amount: $16,004.30 (2,500,000.00 PKR)
To: WAQAR AHMED RAJA
Fee: 0.00
Rate: 1 USD = 156.208 PKR
Send on Date: 08/04/2021
Service: International Wire Transfer
****

If there is a problem with executing your request, we will notify you both by email and on the Manage Accounts tab. You can always check your transfer status on the Review Transfer screen at www.bankofamerica.com.

Sincerely,

Member Service

www.bankofamerica.com

This is a service email from Bank of America. Please note that you may receive service emails in accordance with your Bank of America service agreements, whether or not you elect to receive promotional email.

Read our privacy policy: http://www.bankofamerica.com/privacy

Please don't reply directly to this automatically-generated email message.

Bank of America Email, 8th Floor-NC1-002-08-25, 101 South Tryon St., Charlotte, NC 28255-0001

Bank of America, N.A. Member FDIC. Equal Housing Lender:

http://www.bankofamerica.com/help/equalhousing.cfm

(C) 2021 Bank of America Corporation. All rights reserved.

This email was sent to: info@ranjitnagara.org

68

The land of the Gurdwara Janam Asthan Mata Singh Kaur Ji was acquired successfully by Ranjit Nagara USA, and Ranjit Nagara developed the following plan to restore the Gurdwara Sahib.

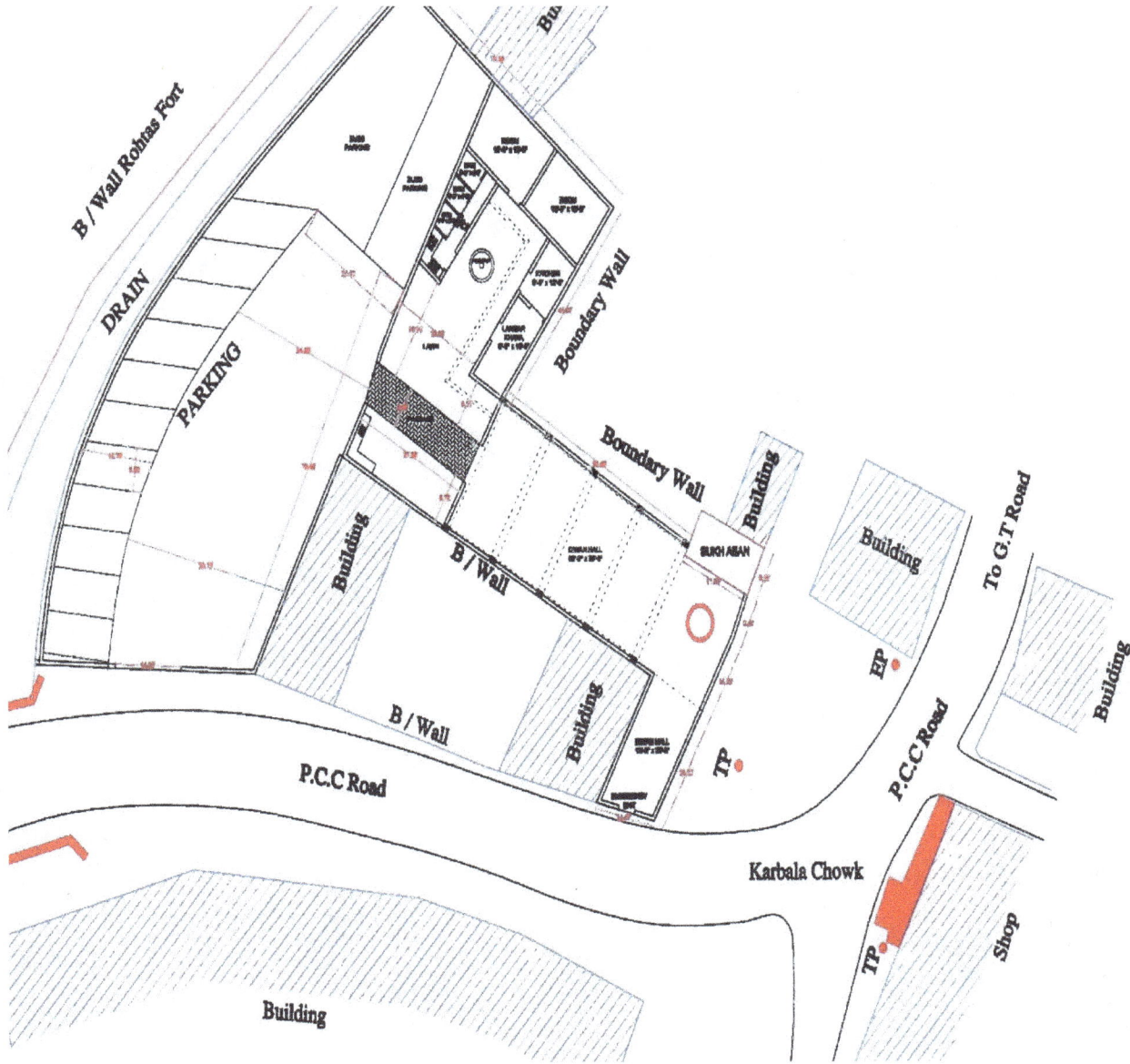

The purchased land was handed over to Evacuee Trust Property Board and Pakistan Sikh Gurdwara Prabandhak Committee on January 31, 2022, by Ranjit Nagara USA. Khalsa Panth is early waiting to visit Gurdwara Janam Asthan and rebuilding like it was before the partition of Punjab.

Gurdwara Choha Sahib Ji, Rohtas

Gurdwara Choha Sahib Ji, Rohtas, Jhelum, Punjab

Gurdwara Choha Sahib Ji is situated in the mountains of the Rohtas village. As per the Mahan Kosh of Bhai Kahan Singh Nabha, Gurdwara Choha Sahib is in Rohtas village in district Jhelum of Punjab. Village Rohtas is approximately three miles to the west of the Dina railway station. Gurdwara Choha Sahib is situated in the mountainous area toward the north of Rohtas. Sri Guru Nanak Dev Ji visited Rohtas around 1521 AD by the invitation of Bhai Bhagtu. Bhai Bhagtu was a great Sikh and grandfather of the Mother of the Khalsa Panth Mata Sahib Kaur Ji.

Gurdwara Choha Sahib Ji during the final stages of restoration by Ranjit Nagara USA on February 13, 2022.

The Gurdwara Choha Sahib Ji is situated in the Pothohar area, which lacked water before the visit of Rohtas by Guru Nanak Dev Ji in the early 16th century. The residents depended on the rainwater. At the request of Bhai Bhagtu and residents of Rohtas Guru, Nanak Dev Ji started the natural drinkable water source from the earth in the early 16th century. This water source started by Guru Nanak dev Ji is still the primary water source for the whole resource area in the 21st century.

Gurdwara Choha Sahib Ji before the restoration was started by Ranjit Nagara USA August 2020.

The Khalsa Panth had a considerable loss of its heritage with the British's partition of Punjab in August 1947. The maharani Bamba Duleep Singh, the granddaughter of Maharaja Ranjit Singh and the daughter of Maharaja Duleep Singh, was in Lahore and was a representative of the Khalsa Panth. She refused the proposal of the British to divide Punjab. The British were in power during 1947 and cleverly made false leaders announce Punjab's division. This book is about restoration; therefore, I will only discuss restoration in this book.

Gurdwara Choha Sahib Ji's building condition worsened with the climate and human detriment after the partition of Punjab in 1947 AD. The Rohtas residents used the Gurdwara Choha Sahib Ji prominent building of high religious priorities as an animal shelter, animal food storage after the partition. It provides a significant detriment to the building and its beauty. The water supply department of Rohtas also put a water pump inside the main building by making holes in the beautiful heritage building. Nowadays, the water supply department made an illegal forcefully made water pump room on the land of Gurdwara sahib's front side. The water supply department uses the Choha, which Guru Nanak Dev Ji started to sell the water to Rohtas village. The Choha (water source) began in the early 16th century by the Guru Nanak Dev Ji is continuing the primary water source for the whole Rohtas area in the 21st century.

History

Gurdwara Choha Sahib Ji was built because Guru Nanak Dev Ji started a water source in the Rohtas area. This water source in Punjabi is called Choha, and Bhai Kahan Singh Nabha authenticates this name, spelling Choha in Mahan Kosh. After visiting the Rohtas area, Guru Nanak Dev Ji was named famous as the Nanak Sarkar (Government) in the Pothohar region. The name is still renowned as Nanak Sarkar in the 21st century. The residents give Guru Nanak Dev Ji this name to express their devotion and love toward Guru Nanak Dev Ji. Guru Nanak Dev Ji is the first Sikh Guru and started a pure path today called Khalsa Panth.

Bhai Bhagtu was appointed as the first caretaker of the place and started facilitating the whole region with free food and water for everyone in approximately 1521 AD. Bhai Bhagtu was a permanent resident of Rohtas at that time. Bhai Ramu Bassi, the son of Bhai Bhagtu, was a great devotee of the Guru Nanak Dev Ji and Guru Gobind Singh Ji. Bhai Ramu Bassi was the second caretaker of the sacred place after his father and facilitated the whole Rohtas area with free food and water as needed. Bhai Ramu Bassi is the father of the Mother of Khalsa Panth Mata Sahib Kaur (Deva) Ji.

The Gurdwara Choha Sahib became famous for providing strangers, pilgrims, and needier shelter. Visitors stop at Gurdwara Choha Sahib Ji and take free food, water, and other necessary facilities without any cost. The services were provided to all without discrimination of caste, religion, race, gender, and age.

It is heard that Sri Guru Hargobind Sahib Ji visited Gurdwara Choha Sahib Ji during his visit to Rasul Nagar. Gurdwara Choha Sahib is approximately 43 miles away toward the North of Rasul Nagara.

During the first Sikh empire established by Baba Banda Singh Bahadar 1708 to 1716 AD

The saint and soldier Baba Banda Singh Bahadar blessed from Guru Gobind Singh Ji

Baba Banda Singh Bahadar was the one who stopped the bureaucracy in land use. He provided the land to the farmers and told them they had the full right and ownership. The prosperity and happiness in all social levels were spread in Punjab during the first Khalsa empire in 1708 to

76

1716 AD. He visited Gurdwara Choha Sahib Ji and Gurdwara Janam Asthan Mata Sahib Kaur Ji, but the actual dates need more research. Baba Banda Singh Bahadar did construction for Gurdwara Choha Sahib and Janam Asthan Mata Sahib Kaur Ji, but also need more research for the details.

Sardar Charat Singh Sukerchakia, son of Sardar Naudh Singh and Sardarni Lal Kaur born in 1732 AD. Rohtas Pothohar region was under the regime of Sardar Charat Singh. He started the construction of the present building of the Gurdwara Choha Sahib. He also made a free dispensary, free kitchen, and free-living rooms (Sra). Misl Sukerchakia was the powerful and robust Misl in the Khalsa empire of Misls. The general people feel pleased, prosper, and protected. He was a great leader and farsighted.

Sardar Charat Singh

Sardar Charat Singh made the boundary walls of the Gurdwara Choha Sahib and allotted land on the name of Gurdwara Choha Sahib Ji. The earnings from the Gurdwara Choha Sahib's land are used to facilitate for free to everyone, including medical aid, food, water, and shelter without any discrimination of caste, religion, gender, race, and designations. Everyone used the water from the water source (Choha) as sacred water. Seven-day celebrations were organized on the first Vaisakh of every year to celebrate the Inauguration Day of the Khalsa Panth. The value of Gurdwara Choha sahib was very high from the early 16th century.

Sardar Maha Singh

Sardar Maha Singh son of Sardar Charat Singh and Sardarni Desa Kaur in 1756 AD. He also expanded and continued the construction of the Gurdwara Choha Sahib Ji building and Sarovar. He developed the boundary wall, and free kitchen (Langer) area also built some rooms to facilitate the pilgrim and visitors. Expand the service of free medical aid to the needy. The people in his regime were delighted and entirely devoted to his kingdom. He was an ideal leader, saint, and soldier of his area.

Maharaja Ranjit Singh Son of Sardar Maha Singh and Sardarni Raj Kaur. He is well known by the name of Sher-e-Punjab and the Lion of Punjab. He united the Sikh Misls and established a third Khalsa empire from 1790 to 1849 AD after the second Khalsa empire of Sikh Misls in Punjab from 1732-1790 AD. He completes the current building and Sarovar Sahib at Gurdwara Choha Sahib Ji. He hired the best architects, constructors, designers, and best quality material to build the Gurdwara Choha Sahib Ji. The material he chose to use was very technical and robust, and the Gurdwara Choha Sahib Ji building structure has been solid since today. The current building was completed under his supervision in 1834. He devoted his whole life to Khalsa Panth, and today the world knows him as the maker of the emperor and kingdoms.

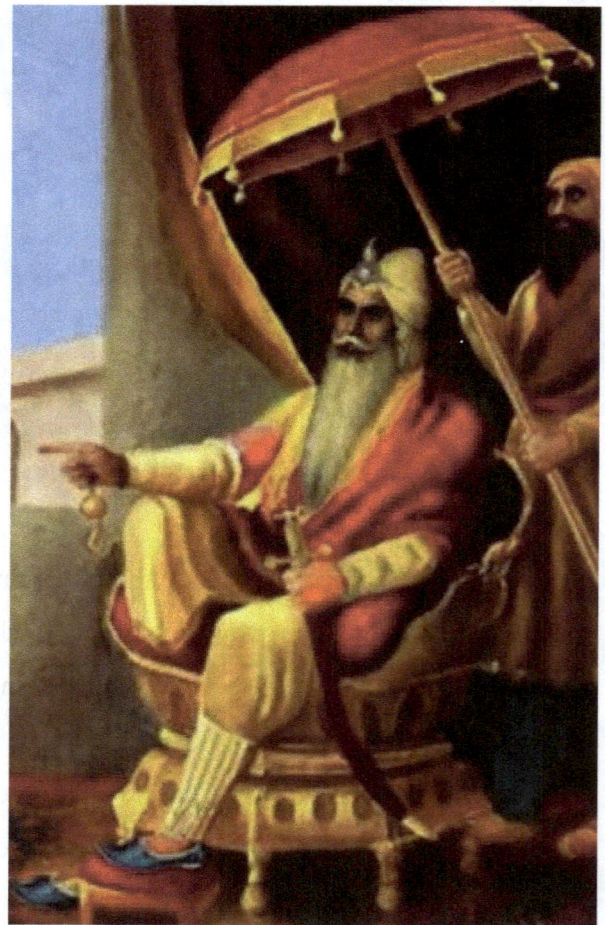

Maharaja Ranjit Singh Ji

Maharaja Ranjit Singh Ji allotted the permanent land 216 Kanal (1,176,120 Square feet) to Gurdwara Choha Sahib Ji Rohtas, Jhelum Punjab. It was the first time the land was officially recorded on the name of Gurdwara Choha Sahib Ji and documented. The land is still in the name of Gurdwara Choha Sahib Ji in the government department, Ranjit Nagara USA able to get the land of the Gurdwara Choha Sahib Ji Possession in August 2021.

The land was 1,176,120 square feet, but only 916,990 square feet of land is acquired back in the presence of Deputy Commissioner Rao Pervaiz Akhtar, Rohtas journalist Raja Waqar and other adjacent land acquirers. The red and black line represented the acquired land back to the Gurdwara Choha Sahib Ji in August 2021.

Gurdwara Choha Sahib Ji's land demarcation of the boundary is completed with the latest satellite technology and the map of 1908 AD available in the government of west Punjab in the presence of all government local and archeology department officials. The picture on this page clearly states the exact area of the Gurdwara Choha Sahib Ji in August 2021.

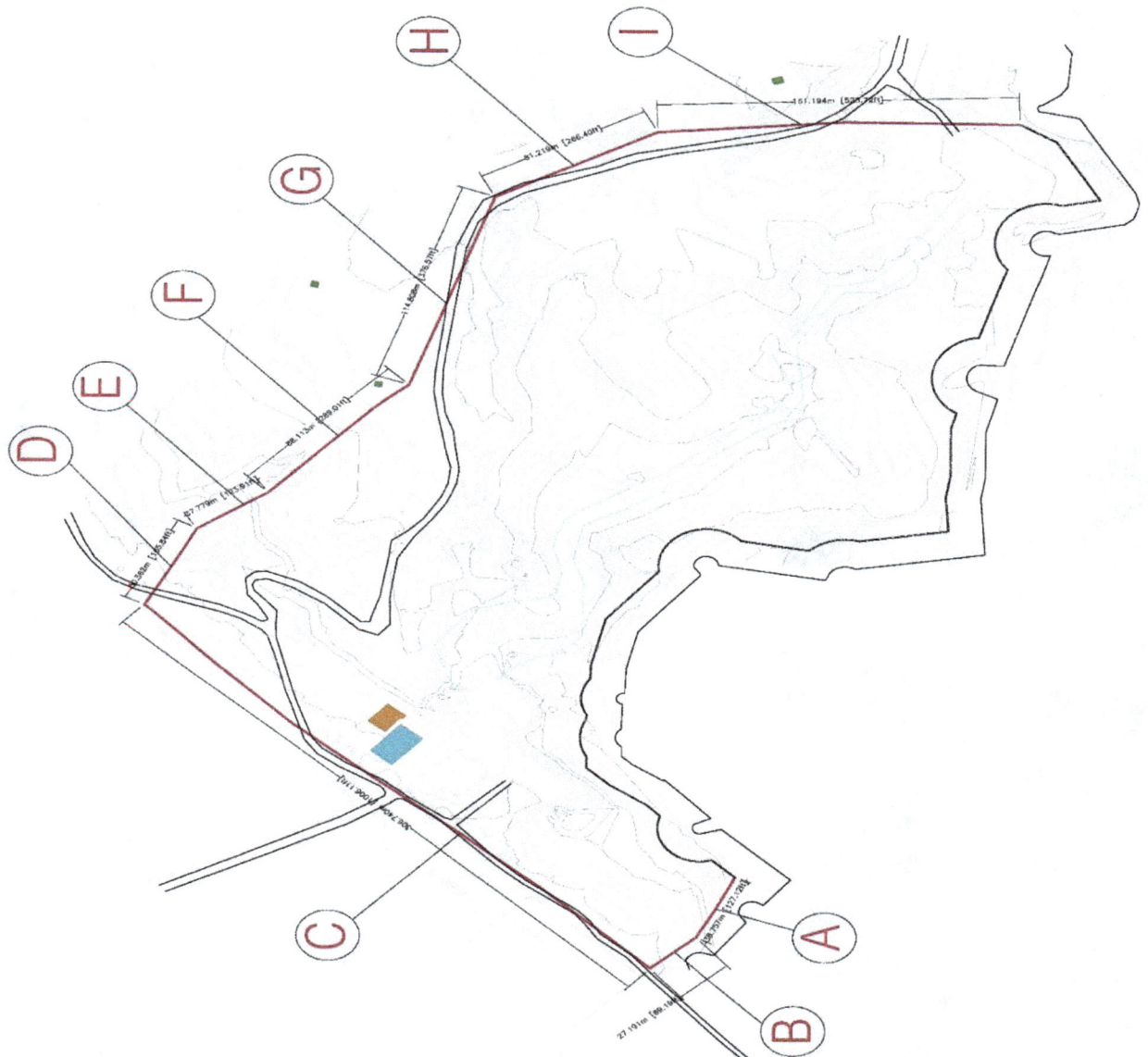

The red line represents the currently occupied area by Ranjit Nagara USA for the Gurdwara Choha Sahib Ji. This line is inside the actual boundary because the land is occupied by the local resident in august 1947 after the partition of Punjab by demolishing the actual boundary walls. However, the current demarcation completed in august 2021 has been shown in the picture.

It is also heard from the local Rohtas residents that Sher-e-Punjab Maharaja Ranjit Singh also allotted another land of 410 kanals (2,232,450 square feet) of the orchard (the land planted with fruit trees) in the nearby village on the name of the Gurdwara Choha Sahib Ji. But, further research is required.

Gurdwara Choha Sahib Ji is a very religious, historical, and heritage building in the Khalsa Panth. The main building and the Sarovar, and the surrounding area were restored by Ranjit Nagara USA from August 2020 to February 2022 AD in the same way Maharaja Raja Ranjit Singh did in 1834. The Gurdwara Choha Sahib Ji was handed back to Evacuee Trust Property Board (ETPB) and Pakistan Sikh Gurdwara Prabandhak Committee (PSGPC) on February 28, 2022. Now, the restored Gurdwara Choha Sahib Ji is in the care of ETPB and PSGPC. The future of this historically significant building depends on the care and handling of ETPB and PSGPC. Ranjit Nagara USA offered to take care of the continued expenses of the Gurdwara Choha Sahib Ji even after the restoration. But both ETPB and PSGPC promised that they would take care of themself.

Gurdwara Choha Sahib Ji Before starting the restoration

Gurdwara Choha Sahib Ji was thoroughly inspected and analyzed in detail. Ranjit Nagara USA prepared an appraisal report under the supervision of Satpreet Singh by the architect and restorer hired for the Restoration of Gurdwara Choha Sahib Ji. These initial inspections were completed on August 07, 2020 and forwarded to Satpreet Singh on August 13, 2020. The purpose of preparing this report was to find the current condition of the abandoned Gurdwara Choha Sahib Ji because many detriments were found after the partition of Punjab in 1947.

Northwest side of Gurdwara Sahib

The initial inspections were started on August 03, 2020 and completed on August 07, 2020. This report was divided into two parts as per the recommendation of Ranjit Nagara USA director Satpreet Singh.

The first part of the report consists of the current condition or state of the Gurdwara Choha Sahib Ji to determine the human detriment and nature detriment over time. The second part contains the recommendation for the work plan by Ranjit Nagara Hired contractors. The second part also includes the initial step to follow the restoration plan and process.

Condition of Gurdwara Choha Sahib Ji on August 07, 2020

Initial review

The observation found in part one was further divided into sub-parts: Context and Landscape, Current condition of the Gurdwara Sahib. This Gurdwara was abandoned during the partition of Punjab in August 1947. The current situation or state of the Gurdwara Sahib was regrettable.

Southwest façade with the mountain on the back

Access to the Gurdwara Choha Sahib was through an ad hoc zig-zag road composed of mud and unsettled stones, and it was not suitable even for regular traffic or regular material loads. A drainage system with the unprepared route and a tubewell illegally built along with an ad-hoc road on the land of Gurdwara Choha Sahib Ji was found in immediate surroundings. There was no current boundary wall exists that suggests the extent of the land in which the Gurdwara was found.

The remaining part of the entry gate of Gurdwara

Remains of earlier buildings were found in the surrounding of the Gurdwara Choha Sahib. According to both on-ground research and historical literature, a free operational dispensary, free-living rooms, and a free kitchen existed in the Gurdwara's surroundings before the partition of Punjab. It is still unknown who demolished the previous structure of Gurdwara Choha Sahib Ji, or it was natural whether related. It looks like is more human detriment because the main building of Gurdwara Sahib was still present. However, further research and investigations are required.

The remains were discovered with both the layers of earth as well as unplanned vegetation in the current state of the Gurdwara Sahib. The unwanted vegetation seen in the picture has a wall remain that is still present. British-style brick proves that the amendments were made on this Gurdwara Sahib between 1849 to 1947. As per

Remains of the surrounding buildings that were built before 1947

Mahan Kosh of Bhai Kahan Singh Nabha, there were seven days of Khalsa Panth festival performed on Vaisakhi every year before partition.

The Gurdwara Choha Sahib Ji has some unplanned landscape done unprofessionally. A three-fourth broken arch of the entrance gate has been found on the front of the Gurdwara Sahib at northwest façade. This broken entrance gate arch was also made after 1849 during the British era. Both nature and humans made the detriment after the abandonment of the Gurdwara Sahib.

Northeast Plantation on the historical remains of the Gurdwara Sahib

Some citrus trees have been planted on the northeast side of the Gurdwara Sahib. These citrus trees were planted after 2015 with the help of the Sikhs from the USA and Canada. There are signs of the construction during the period of Maharaja Ranjit Singh between 1790-1834. Ranjit Nagara USA team has handed over those remains to the PSGPC and ETPB authorized person in Gurdwara Choha Sahib Ji. Those remains were carefully removed without any harm to the citrus trees. It is also unfortunate that the plantation is made where Khalsa Panth-related historical remains were present. There was a lot more area present where the plantation was possible. Still, the current location of this plantation provides significant damage to the historical artifacts that tell the story before the abandonment of this Gurdwara Sahib.

The southeast side of the Gurdwara Sahib has unplanned and unwanted, nature-made vegetation because of the abandonment. The half-height of the southeast wall becomes part of the hill because of the detriment after August 1947. The mountain also shows the remains of the construction that also need further research and investigation. The details and accurate observation were not possible initially because of obstacles created by nature and significant detriments, and it requires more analysis. The outdoor floor of the Gurdwara Sahib was wade with the Nanak Shahi brick with the material of lime plaster made of Kach-Chuna Giri. Details of the material are given in the material section of this book. The bricks shown below in the picture of Sarovar are British-style bricks used in the British era in Punjab.

Sarwar on the west side of the Gurdwara Choha Sahib Ji

Towards the southwest of the Gurdwara Sahib faces the Choha (Sarovar), where unplanned and unwanted vegetation on a hill is visible. This hill also shows remains of earlier construction which require further investigation

The current state of the main building built and completed by Maharaja Ranjit Singh Ji in 1834 AD has three floors. The initial review of foundations was further divided into three parts: First floor, Second floor, and Third floor with the classification of interior and exterior. There was also some modification after 1849 AD. Some portions of Gurdwara material authenticate the construction of the British era between 1849 Ad to 1947 AD. But the exact time for the amendments is unavailable.

Lime-based plaster has been used throughout the main building of the Gurdwara Choha Sahib Ji. This material was used on most of the Sikh Gurdwaras during the period of the Khalsa empire and misls in Punjab between 1732 AD – 1849 AD. Some political differences were present in Sikh Misls, but they all united to save history for the coming generations. The exterior and interior pictures have apparent cracks across the wall's structure. The plinth protection of these parts is also missing completely.

Missing detail tells the story of the negligence in the care of the Gurdwara Sahib after 1947 AD. The picture on the left side shows the missing and broken details. The trifold arches found on the first and second floors were absent. Watering and biofilms were also found overall the facades on the ground floor.

Ranjit Nagara USA found Inappropriate interventions over time in the form of cement work. These interventions are harmful over the long term since the cement, and lime-based plasters are distinct. Their use together, in proximity, can result in further deterioration to the building façade.

Inappropriate interventions in the form of steel windows over the entrances to the Gurdwara using cement mortar. The southeast door to the Gurdwara has been closed with bricks and mortar.

It was a significant detriment and tried to destroy the Gurdwara and deter its current history

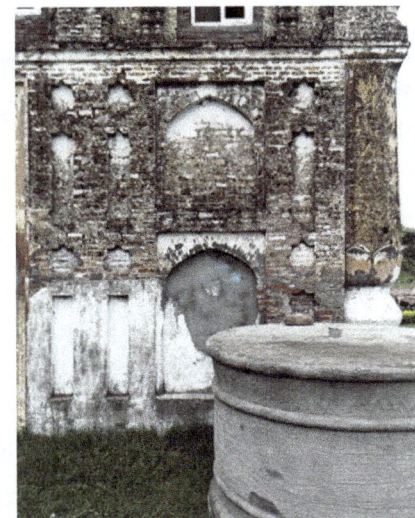

The incomplete front at northwest façade on the ground floor has significant

negligence and unprofessional work at Gurdwara Sahib to remove the historical significance. It also becomes a source of water seepage to damage the existing building.

The interior of the ground floor suggested interventions that have taken place over time. Ranjit Nagara USA found successive layers of paint, cement mortar, and terrazzo work inside. The current condition was critical, and cracks in the arches were seen clearly. The inappropriate material to the lime-base material like gypsum cement, low-quality paint, and unprofessional worker cause the significant detriment to the originality and historical look of the Gurdwara Choha Sahib Ji.

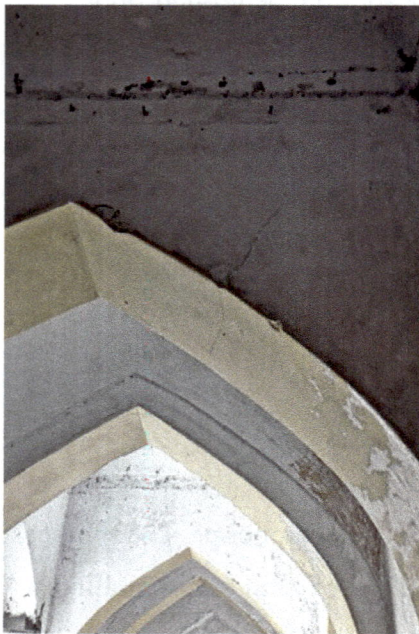

The cracks found in the pointed arches show the damage to the structure. Ranjit Nagara USA completed further investigation and research to determine the nature and extent of the damage.

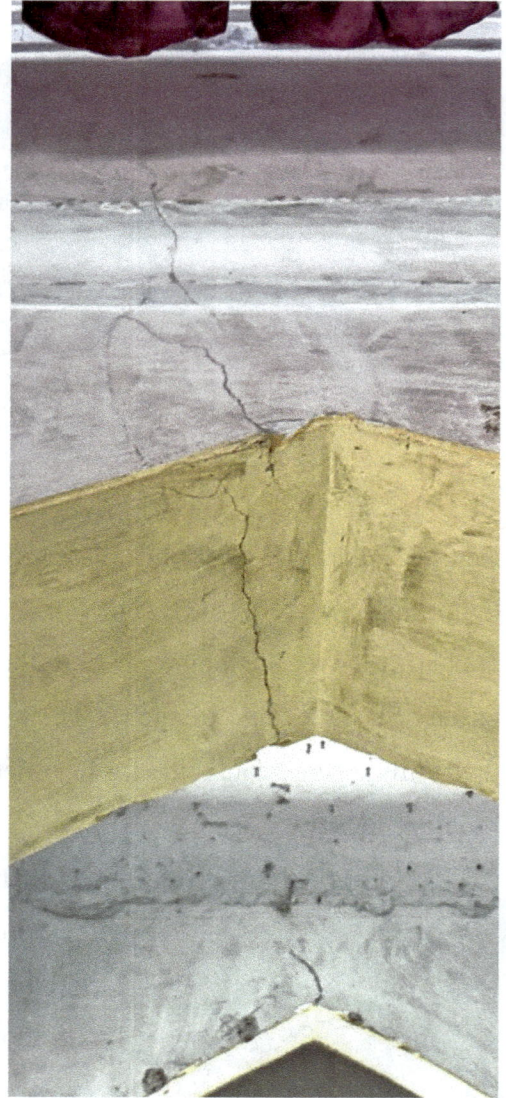

The leading cause of the detrimental destruction of the main Gurdwara Sahib building and floors suggested by cement work after 1947, whether 2016, 2019, or before. The big nails hammered into the structure of the domes on the ground floor were causing damage to the existing structure of the building. The structural and cosmetic beauty of the Gurdwara Sahib is greatly affected by these interventions.

Gurdwara Choha sahib has four accessible doors like all other Gurdwaras. But with the time and irregular, unauthorized, and unprofessional interventions were closed the three doors, and only one entry on the northwest side was left open. During restoration, Ranjit Nagara USA has opened all four doors and made them accessible to the pilgrims and public.

| NW main entrance door | SE right side door closed | SE back Door closed | NE left side door closed |

The above is the interior view of all four doors of the existing main structure of the Gurdwara Choha Sahib Ji. Below is the exterior view of the same four doors of the Gurdwara Choha Sahib Ji before Restoration. All doors were opened after restoration and are accessible now. The building condition and detriment are visible.

| NW main entrance door | SE right side door closed | SE back Door closed | NE left side door closed |

The exterior of the first floor was weathering and biofilm found on overall facades, windows were blocked with brick and mortar after 1947 AD, woodwork and details are broken and missing. The broken and loose window caused the water inside the first floor and damaged the existing structure of the building.

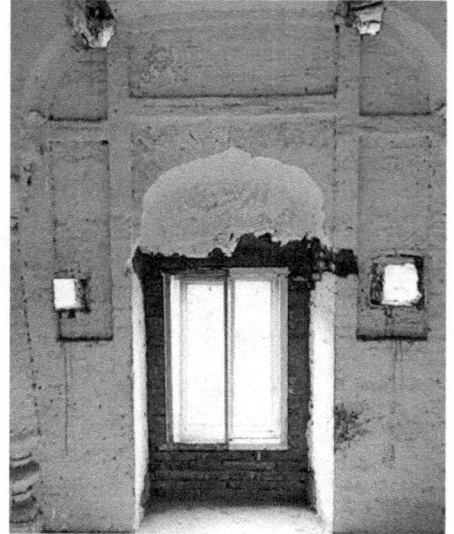

The unauthorized, unprofessional, and unskilled work were performed overtime after 1947 AD to the interior of the first floor of the Gurdwara Sahib. The successive layer of very low-quality paint and cement mortar after 1947 AD damaged the historical artifacts and significant beauty made by the Sikhs before the partition of Punjab. Cracks in the building were found, and Ranjit Nagara USA appointed a structure engineer to determine the extent of the structural damage. The significant detriment to the building was found with the floor finishes and cement work interventions after the abandonment of the Gurdwara Choha Sahib Ji. The first floor was cracked, and biofilm was discovered in certain interior portions of the floor. Open ventilation holes and windows cause the rainwater inside the first floor that causes the damages and other detriments.

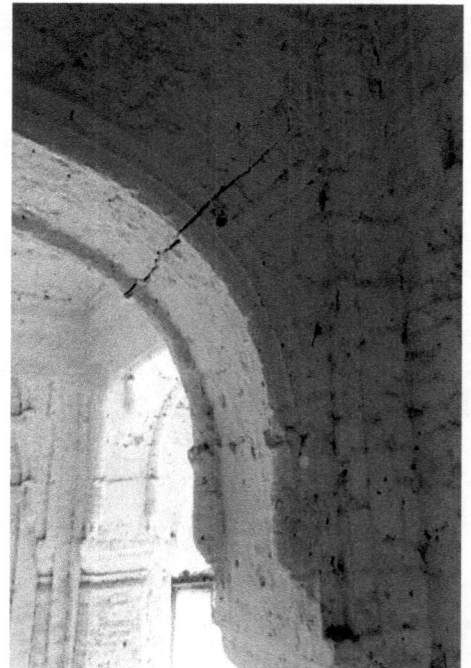

The second floor of Gurdwara Choha Sahib's exterior was weathering, and biofilm was discovered all over the facades. The artwork, Nanak Shahi brick, and woodwork were missing. The windows were damaged and opened without any protection. It acted as a significant egress source for water and other elements inside the floor.

Cracks on the floor of a small room on the second floor

Ranjit Nagara USA discovered the unauthorized, unprofessional by unskilled workers' interventions to the interior of the second floor. The low-quality cement and paint were used after 1947 AD and look like it was done intentionally to the building. Cracks were found on the interior arches of the second floor.

Cement work intervention on the second floor damaged the historical art, paintings, and beauty of the Gurdwara Sahib. Deterioration and inappropriate interventions were found in the interior of the central dome in the Gurdwara Sahib. The Infestation of bats and bees was found on the second floor.

The settlement sink was found on the top floor of the Gurdwara Choha Sahib Ji. It was used to

drain the water from the top floor to the ground outside the southeast side of the Gurdwara Sahib. The wrong intervention to the building after the partition of Punjab damaged the top floor and caused the block to the existing drain system.

Biofilm was found all over the floor and on the dome's exterior. The low-quality cement and unmatched material intervention

were found to cause extensive damage to the historic dome made in 1834 AD. The illegal and unauthorized interventions damage the waterproofing of the top floor causes to become source egress for water inside the building.

Geotechnical Condition of Gurdwara Choha Sahib Ji

Gurdwara Choha Sahib was an abandoned Gurdwara since the partition of Punjab in August 1947. There was a significant detriment to the Gurdwara buildings after 1947 partitions by both humans and weather. Dispensary, Free kitchen hall, accommodation, and boundary walls were demolished, and encroachment by the Rohtas and Jhelum residents was made after August 1947. The current condition of the prominent Gurdwara and Sarovar was very critical. The photo below was taken in February 2021 after cleaning around the Gurdwara Choha Sahib Ji.

To do the boundary wall, Langer hall (free kitchen for everyone), and accommodation of the Gurdwara. The Geotechnical investigation was required to evaluate the surficial and subsurface conditions at the site, select appropriate geotechnical parameters, and get recommendations for the design and construction of the foundation, including the selection of the most suitable foundation type, foundation depth, and the allowable bearing pressure for the creation of the foundation. The report on geotechnical investigation covers all the reporting requirements stipulated in the scope of work. The report contains the main text together with tables, figures, borehole logs, and plates.

The request to proceed on 17th June 2021 Geo Associates commenced the field investigation campaign on 18th June 2021 concurrent with field activities, selected representative subsurface samples obtained from the boreholes were tested at Geo Associates Laboratories Lahore.

This report presents the description of the site, a general geotechnical assessment of the project area, details of the investigation performed, an appreciation of the subsurface conditions, and recommendations and conclusions concerning the foundation design for the proposed structure investigation results. The report also includes suggestions on earthwork, including grading, excavation, fill, and compaction.

The scope of work for Geotechnical report

The goal of the geotechnical investigation was to determine the subsoil conditions for the construction buildings at Gurdwara Choha Sahib Ji, located near Rohtas Fort, Dina, District Jhelum, Punjab, and to evaluate the subsoil parameters for use in the design of the foundation. Specifically, the scope of work included:

- Field exploration, in-situ testing, and sampling.
- Laboratory testing
- Analyses of data gathered through field and laboratory investigations and preparation of report including recommendations for:

    a. Bearing capacity for the proposed foundation.
    b. Modulus of subgrade reaction
    c. Coefficients of lateral Pressure inactive, passive, and at rest states
    d. Chemical characteristics (recommendations for using an appropriate type of cement in constructing sub-structures).
    e. Construction aspects

Drilling of Boreholes

The field investigation included drilling ten boreholes at the locations suggested by the Ranjit Nagara. The areas of the boreholes were marked in Figure No 1. Boreholes were drilled to a depth ranging from 1 m (3 ft) to 2 m (6 ft) below ground level.

Exploratory borings of diameter 100 mm (4 inches) were drilled using manual percussion. It was initially planned that Standard Penetration Tests (SPTs) would be performed at a 1 m depth interval or refusal up to 10 m below the existing ground surface. However, the ground conditions were not suitable for hand percussion and performance of SPTs because of the presence of gravel, cobbles, and construction debris. Several trials were made at different locations, but the same conditions were encountered (i.e., soil mixed with gravels, cobbles, and construction debris). At some of the areas at shallow depth, Standard Penetration Tests (SPTs) were performed in accordance with ASTM D- 1586. SPT-Resistance values (N values) are shown on boring logs attached in the Appendix. Figure No 2 represents legends and symbols used on boring logs. The plates attached in the Appendix show the drilling activity at the site.

The disturbed samples recovered through the SPT spoon sampler were preserved in polythene bags and placed in plastic containers. All the samples were transported to the Geo Associates Laboratory at Lahore for testing.

Estimates of relative density of granular soils and consistency of the cohesive soils given on the boring logs, in general, are based on the SPT resistance as recommended by Terzaghi and shown in Table No 1.

Excavation of Test Pits

Test pits were excavated at all the borehole locations (ten test pits were excavated). Test pits were excavated manually to a depth where refusal conditions were encountered (presence of boulders, buried foundations, and construction debris). The testpits were excavated to a depth ranging from 1 m (3 ft) to 2.2 m (7 ft) below the existing ground surface. Insitu density tests were

97

performed wherever possible, and the geotechnical consultant physically inspected test pits. Test pit logs showing the description of material encountered during excavation and other features like the presence of old buried foundations, construction debris, roots, etc., are also mentioned in the test pit logs. The plates attached in the Appendix show different views of test pits and Sand Replacement Tests performed in the pits.

Laboratory Testing

Selected soil samples from each borehole/test pit were tested in the our laboratory at Lahore for the classification and determination of strength and chemical characteristics. All laboratory tests were performed per Standard ASTM procedures. The laboratory tests on selected soil samples included the following:

a. Grain Size Analysis
b. Direct Shear Tests
c. Chemical Tests on representative soil samples.

Table 2 and Table 2a at the end of this report represent the summary of the laboratory test result.

The Subsurface Condition at Gurdwara Choha Sahib Ji

Current Condition

At present Gurdwara building exist at the site. The site is uneven, and the level difference between the highest and lowest point is about 5 ft. The lowest point is at track level. The plates attached at the end depict the site conditions.

Subsoil Condition (Stratigraphy)

The field investigations have revealed the presence of soil mixed with gravels and cobbles of variable sizes. The soil consists of mostly Silt / silty Sand. Boulders were encountered at depths varying from 1 m (3 ft) to 2 m (6 ft). At some locations, buried foundations were also discovered at depths ranging from 1 m (3 ft) to about 2 m (6 ft) below the current ground level. Tree roots were also seen up to a depth of about 1.5 m (5 ft) below the existing ground surface. The subsoil consists of soil (Silt / sandy Silt / Sand) mixed with gravels and cobbles of variable sizes. The natural subsurface stratum exists in a loose to very dense condition of compactness.

Groundwater

The groundwater was not encountered up to the maximum investigated depth of about 2.2 m (7 ft) below the current ground level during a drilling operation conducted in June 2021.

Foundation Design Consideration

General

For the foundations to be safe, the load-carrying strata must be competent to sustain the imposed loading without undergoing shear failure. At the same time, any settlements of the foundations must not exceed the tolerable limits. Therefore, the load-carrying characteristics of the strata must be evaluated from these two considerations.

Selection of Foundation Type

Considering the competence of the strata, as evaluated from the investigation results and the type of structures to be constructed, any shallow foundation (Isolated, Strip, or Mat) can be used for the foundation design of building construction. However, if isolated foundations are used, the foundations must be tied at two levels to reduce the chances of differential settlement. Deep foundations (piles) will not be required.

The preference of a type of shallow foundation over the other for a particular structure must be carefully evaluated, considering the resistance of a foundation type to the shear stresses and deformation characteristics of the bearing soils and consideration for the economy of construction.

The settlement of a structure is also a function of the type of foundation system adopted, among other factors. A spread footing is more sensitive to the variations in the subsurface conditions. Therefore, it may settle more than a strip footing, which can bridge over the relatively weaker zones between adjacent columns and, thereby, add a significant rigidity foundation system. The mat foundation provides even more advantages in this respect.

Depth of Foundation and Allowable Bearing Capacity

Regardless of the foundation type adopted for a particular structure, the foundations must be laid at a sufficient depth, below the depth of the seasonal variation zone of the subsoil. The depth of foundation, among other factors, was also governed by the lateral stability requirements and presence of surficial debris, organic matter, and chemically harmful materials, all of which is within the zone of influence of foundation, must be replaced by a competent material and the foundations be placed well below such materials so that these can transmit the Pressure directly onto the competent load-bearing strata. In the present case, it is understood that the building structures will consist of single-story buildings without a basement. The geotechnical investigation has revealed the presence of heterogenic soil, buried foundations, deep tree roots, etc. Based upon the field test results and physical inspection of the site following recommendations are suggested for the foundation design of the structures:

- Excavate and remove the existing soil to a minimum depth of 1.5 m (5 ft) below the current ground level at the foundation's footprint. Deep excavation will be required at the locations where buried foundations/construction debris will be encountered (in specific areas only). The foundation should be placed on natural soil.

- Compact the bottom of the excavation to 95% of the dry density obtained by the Modified AASHTO compaction test (ASTM D1557).

- Raise the level to 1 m (3 ft) depth below the existing ground level by using well compacted/dense roller compacted concrete (50% sand + 50% gravel + 4% cement).

100

- Foundation can be placed on compacted/dense roller-compacted concrete at a depth of 1 m (3 ft) below the current ground level.

- Any type of shallow foundation (Isolated, Strip, or Mat) can be used for building structure foundation design. However, if isolated foundations are used, the foundations must be tied at two levels to reduce the chances of differential settlement.

- Because of the heterogenic nature of the soil, difficult geotechnical conditions, presence of old construction debris, and the existence of deep tree roots, it is strongly recommended that a senior geotechnical engineer should certify that excavation at the footprint of the foundations has reached the recommended depth (natural subsoil).

- It is strongly recommended that a senior geotechnical engineer certify that compaction and foundations works have been accomplished according to recommendations.

Settlement and Allowable Bearing Pressures

The allowable bearing pressure for the design of foundations must not exceed more than the allowable bearing capacity of the load-carrying soil concerning shear failure. At the same time, the settlement corresponding to the permissible bearing pressure must not exceed the maximum permitted limit of settlement for the particular foundation/structure system. In the present case, it is the allowable settlement criteria and not the shear failure, which will determine the allowable bearing pressure for the design of foundations. In order to recommend permissible bearing pressure for the design of foundations, it is first necessary to establish the permissible settlement criteria for the structures to be constructed at the site.

The total allowable settlement for structures reported in the literature varies between the classical Terzaghi criteria of 25 mm to more than 100 mm. Generally, 50 mm total settlement is recommended format foundation. However, it is noted that it is usually the differential settlement rather than the total settlement that is of concern in the design of foundations. State-of-the-art criteria for fair settlements are developed based on the distortion that a structure can tolerate, which is then related to the differential and total settlements which a structure can tolerate depending

101

upon various loading conditions and subsurface characteristics. Typical soil parameters used for the calculations of settlement and bearing pressure for foundations are presented in Table 3.

Settlement Calculations

The settlement calculations for isolated and strip footings of variable dimensions placed at 1 m (3 ft.) depth on well-compacted soil have been calculated using the following relationship given by Timoshenko and Goodier and later on refined by Bowles. (Ref: Foundation Analysis & Design by J.E. Bowles):

$$\Delta H = q_a B' \left(\frac{1 - 0.3^2}{E_s} \right) I_f \, (I_s \times 4)$$

Where

ΔH	=	Allowable Settlement
Qa	=	Allowable Bearing Pressure
B'	=	Least lateral dimension of the foundation
If	=	Influence factor for reduction of settlement when foundation is placed at some depth "D" in the ground.
Is	=	Influence factor which depends upon L/B, thickness of stratum H and Poisson's ration 0.3.
Es	=	Elastic soil parameter.

The results of settlement analysis for isolated and strip footings are presented in Tables No 4 and 5 for foundations placed at 1 m (3 ft.) depth below the existing ground level on improved soil.

The settlement of Mat foundation placed at 1 m (3 ft) depth below the existing ground level on the improved ground has been calculated using the following relationship given by Meyerhof,

$$s = \frac{3.13 \, q}{N} (C_w C_D)$$

Where

102

q   =   Applied foundation pressure (kPa).

N   =   Blow count corrected for the effect of water table.

Water Table Factor:

$$C_w = 2 - 0.5[D_w / B] \leq 2.0$$

Depth factor:

$$C_D = 1 - 0.25[D / B]$$

The results of the settlement analysis of Mat foundation of different least lateral dimensions placed at 1 m (3 ft) depth below the existing ground level are presented in Table No 6.

Shear Strength Consideration

The safe bearing capacity for different widths of square and strip footings and mat foundations has been calculated using the following general bearing capacity equation and factors suggested by Vesic (Joseph E. Bowles: Foundation Analysis and Design 5th Edition):

$$q_{ult} = cN_c S_c I_c D_c + \gamma D_f N_q S_q I_q D_q + 0.5\gamma BN_\gamma S_\gamma I_\gamma D_\gamma$$

Where:

c = cohesion

B = width of foundation D_f =
depth of foundation

N_c, N_q and N_γ are bearing capacity factors S_c, S_q
and S_γ are shape factors

I_c, I_q and I_γ are inclination factors D_c, D_q and
D_γ are depth factors

The results of safe bearing capacity calculations for different widths of square and strip footing and mat foundation placed at 1 m (3 ft) depth are presented in Tables 7 to 9, respectively. A factor of safety of 3 has been applied to the calculated ultimate bearing capacity values to measure the safe bearing capacity of the soil.

Allowable Bearing Capacity

The allowable bearing capacity is smaller than the safe bearing capacity (foundation should not fail in shear), and the bearing capacity is calculated based on a fair settlement. Therefore, the load-carrying characteristics of the strata must be evaluated from these two considerations. The width of the foundation, along with other factors, generally controls the allowable bearing capacity; as the width of the foundation increases, it is the permissible settlement of the foundation rather than the shear failure of the ground which will govern the assignment of the allowable bearing pressure for the design of the foundation.

Charts 1 to 3 shows the comparison of the bearing capacity obtained by shear strength and allowable settlement criteria for square, strip, and mat foundations, respectively. Generally, the permissible settlement for framed building structures supported on square/strip footing is taken as 25mm. In the case of mat foundations, a larger magnitude of settlement, up to 50mm, can be allowed. Charts 1 to 3 can be used to select allowable bearing pressure for any particular foundation width in the case of square, strip, and mat foundations, respectively.

With consideration of the above-described criteria, the net allowable bearing pressure has been calculated at 1 m (3 ft) depth below the existing ground surface for square, strip, and mat foundations, respectively. The recommended allowable bearing pressure values, in general, are as follows:

Type of Foundation	Depth of Foundation (m)	Least lateral Dimension of Foundation (m)	Net Allowable Bearing Pressure (kPa)
Square	1.0	1.5	100
		2.0	102
		2.5	100
		3.0	95
		3.5	90
Strip	1.0	1.0	87
		1.5	92
		2.0	90
		2.5	85
		3.0	80
Mat	1.0	10.0	148
		15.0	170
		20.0	160
		25.0	150
		30.0	150

The actual net bearing pressure value for any particular width of the square, strip, and Mat foundation can be seen from Charts 1 to 3, respectively.

Elastic Shear Modulus

The Shear Modulus relates shear strain to shear force. This modulus, also referred to as Modulus of Rigidity, is determined by the following relationship (Ref: Foundation Analysis and Design by J.E. Bowles)

$$\text{Shear Modulus } G = \frac{E}{2(1+\mu)}$$

Where, E   = Modulus of Elasticity

μ = Poisson's Ratio

In the Gurdwara Choha Sahib case, using SPT' N' values empirical correlations available in the literature, the elastic modulus for sandy soils from the depth below five ft. can be taken as 12 MPa. Taking 'E, as 12 MPa and $\mu = 0.3$, the Shear Modulus is estimated as 4.61 MPa.

Modulus of Subgrade Reaction (KS)

Vertical Modulus of Subgrade Reaction (Ks), also referred to as soil "spring" constant or coefficient of subgrade reaction, is defined as the deformation induced in the soil per unit application of Pressure. This modulus is frequently used to design mat foundations and rigid pavements. Its magnitude is a function of the stiffness of the foundation supporting strata, but it depends on the foundation size and its rigidity. The Modulus of Subgrade Reaction can be approximately measured using the following relationship (Ref.: Foundation Analysis and Design by J.E. Bowles).

$$Ks = 20 \text{ (FOS) qa for 50 mm settlement}$$

The value of Ks for silty sand has been estimated as 10,000 kN/m3.

Coefficients of Earth Pressure

The coefficients of earth pressures for granular soils are essential functions of the angle of internal friction (Ø). In the case of heterogeneous soils, such as those occurring at the site, the

106

estimation of coefficients of earth pressures should be based on the shear strength parameters along the weakest planes in the soil mass. Therefore, the adopted Ø value of 16 degrees is considered realistic for earth pressure calculations. Accordingly, the coefficients of active, passive, and at rest pressures are estimated as follows:

(a) Coefficient of

Active Earth Pressure (Ka) $= \dfrac{1 - Sin\text{Ø}}{1 + Sin\text{Ø}} = 0.57$

(b) Coefficient of

Passive Earth Pressure (Kp) $= \dfrac{1 + Sin\text{Ø}}{1 - Sin\text{Ø}} = 1.77$

(c) Coefficient of

"At rest" Earth Pressure (Ko) $= 1 - Sin\text{Ø} = 0.72$

In the case of backfill materials, it is considered that as recommended in the subsequent section, the materials shall be granular and compacted to a dry density of not less than 95% of the maximum Modified Proctor Density (ASTM D 1557) in case of the structural fill, and not less than 90% in case of general backfill. The granular backfill materials compacted to this recommended density will develop an angle of friction of the order of 35 degrees. Therefore the coefficients of Earth Pressures for the well-compacted engineering fill will be as under:

Active Earth Pressure (Ka) $= 0.27$

Passive Earth Pressure (Kp) $= 3.69$

$$\text{At rest Earth Pressure (Ko)} \quad = 0.43$$

Chemical Parameter

Chemical tests were performed on representative soil samples collected from boreholes. The tests included the determination of Sulphates and Chloride. The results of the Tests are presented in Table 2a.

Seismic Factor

The project site is located in an earthquake zone "2B". The ground accelerations due to earthquakes in such a zone have been reported up to 0.24 g. Earthquake motion always results in lateral force. This lateral force may act on the structures in any horizontal direction. The effect of this lateral force may be evaluated according to the Uniform Building Code for different earthquake zones.

The Earthwork

Clearing, Grubbing, Leveling, and Grading

Before any construction activity at the site, all debris and surface vegetation must be cleared. Graders/dozers can carry this out. Stakes should be installed on a grid marked by surveying Crews for leveling and grading. The required levels to be attained through a cut or fill at the grid points must also be identified.

The leveling and grading can be passed out by normal earth moving machine. As predominantly silty and sandy soils will be encountered in excavation throughout the project area, no particular problems are anticipated in excavating and moving these soils with excavators, scrapers, and dozers.

Excavations

The excavations for building foundations, other substructures, or trenches for utility lines can be made using conventional earthmoving machinery, including scrapers, dozers, trenchers, etc. All the excavations should be sloped appropriately or supported to avoid any stability failure and movement in the adjacent structures. After reaching the designed foundation level and placing the foundation, the soil should be well compacted using an appropriate roller or equivalent.

Fill Material

General Fill

The on-site materials obtained from excavation of the topsoil can not be used as a general backfill. The backfill material should be granular, and the quantities of fines should limit to the recommended values.

Structural Fill

The fill to support the structural foundations or floors must comprise only the "select materials." The "select fill material" must be free of organic and other harmful substances. The material must be granular in texture and be 100 percent passing 10cm sieve and not more than 20 percent passing Number 200 sieve. The portion of the material passing No. 40 sieve shall have a maximum liquid limit of 35 percent and a maximum plasticity index of 10.

Backfill for Utility Trenches and around Substructures

The soils used for backfilling the trenches and around substructures must be free draining when impermeability is not required, when free drainage is desired or when perfect bedding or foundations of low compressibility are desired. Tractor compacted fill or fills compacted by consolidating processes, and the materials used must be free draining sandy and gravelly soils. When good bedding is required under and around the concrete pipe, the material can easily be made to flow and compact to high density in the critical wedge under the pipe and between the pipe and trench surfaces, providing proper procedures are used for wetting and vibrating the material.

Placement and Compaction

It is recommended that structural fill be placed so that it can extend a minimum distance beyond the outer perimeters of structural foundations equal to twice the average foundation width. Permanent slopes beyond width should not be steeper than one vert: 3 Horz. All fill materials must be placed in layers not exceeding 20 cms in a loose state. In the case of general fill, each layer should be compacted to a dry density not less than 90% as determined by Modified Proctor Compaction Tests (ASTM D 1557) or to a minimum relative density of 70 percent. In the case of structural fill, the compacted density must not be less than 95% determined based on Modified Proctor Compaction Tests (ASTM D-1586) or not less than 75% of the relative density.

All compaction should be carried out at moisture content, within a tolerable range of -2 to + 2 percent of optimum. To verify that the specified degree of compression has been achieved in-place density tests per ASTM D-1556 or D-2922 should be taken after each fill lift and performed at least on lift thickness below the compacted surface. At least one in-situ density should be performed for every 1000 square meters section of each compacted layer in general fill and 500 square meters section for each compacted layer of structural fill, including fill for supporting machine foundations. At least one in-situ density test should also be performed in every case whenever there is significant suspicion of a change in the quality of moisture control or efficiency of compaction.

The compaction can be efficiently carried out using a suitable vibratory roller. Hand-operated tampers may be used for backfilling, trenches, and other areas of limited accessibility. In cases where tampers are used, the loose lift thickness should be restricted to 10 cms instead of 20 cms.

It is recommended that before compaction of the fill materials, field test sections be made by placing the earth materials in layers and compacting the same using the intended compacting equipment. The test section's in-situ density of each layer should be checked to verify if the intended compaction is achieved using the test placement and compaction methodology. The experience on the construction, quality control, and performance of the test section will serve as a quality control guide for the field earthwork involving selecting materials, placement, and compaction.

Erosion Protection

All the earth fill surfaces and slopes must be protected against wind and erosion. This can be done using several methods: placement of sweet soil and plantation, cement/bitumen stabilization, gravel/stone pitching, or paving the area. Adopting a suitable approach for the project site will depend on the landscape planning, availability of materials, and cost of construction of such an erosion protection system. All areas surrounding the structures should be graded away to a surface drainage system. Water must not be allowed to "pond up" at any place.

Soil Corrosivity

Protection of Concrete against Corrosion

The chemical tests performed on on-site soils indicate a low degree of deleterious salts; therefore, ordinary Portland cement can be used for foundation works. A layer of bitumen coating should be applied to the exterior of all the foundation and other concrete coming in contact with soil.

Protection of Utilities

All utility lines (water, sewage, oil pipelines, cobbles, etc.) must be protected against corrosion due to harmful salts in the soil materials used for backfilling utility trenches. Such protection can be provided by coating all the utility lines with bitumen/ epoxy paint. For protection required explicitly for certain underground utilities, the manufacturer's specifications of such utility should be followed.

Construction Aspects

The following measures are recommended for the long-term stability of the structures.

- Compact the bottom of the excavation to not less than 95% of the dry density obtained by AASHTO Modified Test (ASTM D1557) using appropriate compaction equipment (such as tamping plates).

- A pad of at least 6 inches of 1:4:8 PCC (well compacted) should be placed on the prepared ground before placing the foundations.

- Engineering fill (A-1-a, A-1-b, or A-3) should be backfill material. The commonly available backfill material is A-3 (sand).

- Plinth protection slabs sloping away from the buildings should be provided around the structure to reduce water ingress to foundation soils.

- Proper surface drainage should be provided in the project area, and the site should be graded to keep the surface runoff away from the structure. The ingress of water from any source should be avoided.

Recommendation based on Geotechnical Investigation

Type of Foundation

Any shallow foundation (Isolated, Strip, or Mat) can be used to design foundations; however, if isolated foundations are used, the foundations must be tied to reduce the chances of differential settlement.

Minimum Depth of the Foundation

The foundation should be placed at a minimum depth of 1 m (3 ft.) below the existing ground surface on well-compacted improved soil. Foundations should not be placed on loose soil/fill.

Bearing Pressure: The general bearing pressure values are tabulated below

Type of Foundation	Depth of Foundation (m)	Least lateral Dimension of Foundation (m)	Net Allowable Bearing Pressure (kPa)
Square	1.0	1.5	100
		2.0	102
		2.5	100
		3.0	95
		3.5	90
Strip	1.0	1.0	87
		1.5	92
		2.0	90
		2.5	85
		3.0	80
Mat	1.0	10.0	148
		15.0	170
		20.0	160
		25.0	150
		30.0	150

The actual net bearing pressure value for any particular width of the square, strip, and Mat foundation can be seen from Charts 1 to 3, respectively.

General view on Geotechnical Condition

- Considering the heterogenic nature of the soil, difficult geotechnical conditions, the presence of old construction debris, and the existence of deep tree roots, it is strongly recommended that a senior geotechnical engineer should certify that excavation at the footprint of the foundations has reached the recommended depth (natural subsoil).

- The bottom of the excavation must be compacted to not less than 95% of the dry density obtained by the AASHTO Modified Test (ASTM D1557) using appropriate compaction equipment (such as tamping plates).

- Ordinary Portland cement can be used for the foundation works. However, a thick layer of rich concrete should be provided to steel coming in contact with soil.

- Special precautions should be observed during excavation.

- The slopes of the hills, especially the slope of the hill supporting the fort's walls, must be appropriately stabilized using a suitable slope stability technique.

- A senior geotechnical engineer should certify that the compaction and foundations works have been accomplished according to recommendations.

Ground Water

The groundwater was not encountered up to the maximum investigated depth of 2.2 m (7 ft.) below the current ground level during the drilling operation conducted in June 2021.

All tables and charts referenced in the geotechnical condition are given on the following pages in order:

- Tables

- Charts

- Figures

- Bore Hole and test Pit Logs

- Plates

Table 1: Empirical value for ϕ, q_u, D_r and unit weight of soils based o the SPT

GRANULAR SOILS					
Description	Very Loose	Loose	Medium	Dense	Very Dense
Relative Density, D_r	0–0.15	0.15–0.35	0.35–0.65	0.65–0.85	0.85–1.00
Standard Penetration Test value, N	0–4	5–10	11–30	31–50	51–UP
Approximate angle of internal friction, ϕ (degree)	25–28	28–30	30–35	35–40	38–43
Approximate range of moist unit weight, γ (pcf)	70–100	90–115	110–130	110–140	130–150
Submerged unit weight, γ_{sub}	60	55–65	60–70	65–85	75

COHESIVE SOILS						
Description	Very Soft	Soft	Firm	Stiff	Very Stiff	Hard
Unconfined compressive strength, q_u (tsf)	0–0.25	0.25–0.5	0.5–1.0	1.0–2.0	2.0–4.0	4.0–UP
Standard Penetration Test value, N	0–2	3–4	5–8	9–16	17–32	33-UP
Approx. range of saturated unit weight, γ_{sat} (pcf)	100–120		100–130		120–140	130^+

Table 2: Summary of Laboratory Results

BH # Test Pit	Depth (ft)	Sieve Analysis			Atterberg Limits		Direct Shear Test		Unconfined Compression Test (kPa)
		Gravel (%)	Sand (%)	Silt & Clay (%)	LL (%)	PI	c (kPa)	$\phi°$	
BH/TP-1	3.0	00	57	43	-	-	3.4	26.9	-
	6.0	07	54	39	-	-	3.7	27.3	-
BH/TP-2	3.0	00	68	32	-	-	-	-	-
	6.0	Soil mixed with gravels and construction debris			-	-	-	-	-
BH/TP-3	3.0	00	79	21	-	-	2.8	25.6	-
	6.0	Soil mixed with gravels and construction debris			-	-	-	-	-
BH/TP-4	3.0	01	53	46	-	-	-	-	-
	6.0	Soil mixed with gravels and construction debris			-	-	-	-	-
BH/TP-5	3.0	28	43	28	-	-	3.5	28.4	-
	6.0	Soil mixed with gravels and construction debris			-	-	-	-	-
BH/TP-6	3.0	28	25	47	-	-	-	-	-
	6.0	Soil mixed with gravels and construction debris			-	-	-	-	-
BH/TP-7	3.0	00	60	40	-	-	3.5	27.4	-
	6.0	Soil mixed with gravels etc.			-	-	-	-	-
BH/TP-8	3.0	28	50	21	-	-	-	-	-
	6.0	Soil mixed with gravels etc.			-	-	-	-	-
BH/TP-9	3.0	55	37	07	-	-	-	-	-
	6.0	Soil mixed with gravels etc.			-	-	-	-	-
BH/TP-10	3.0	30	38	32	-	-	4.2	24.9	-
	6.0	Soil mixed with gravels and construction debris			-	-	-	-	-

Table 2a: Chemical Analysis of Soil Samples

BH/TP No	DEPTH (m)	SULPHATES %	CHLORIDES %
BH/TP – 1	1.0	0.14	0.34
BH/TP – 1	2.0	0.10	0.18
BH/TP – 3	1.0	0.12	0.17
BH/TP – 5	1.0	0.10	0.13
BH/TP – 6	2.0	0.09	0.10
BH/TP – 10	1.0	0.17	0.18

Table 3: Parameters used for the analysis of settlement and bearing pressure

DESCRIPTION OF PARAMETER	VALUE OF PARAMETER
Bulk unit weight of topsoil	18 kN/m^3
Bulk unit weight of soil below 1 m	20 kN/m^3
Corrected average N-value	15 blows/300mm
The angle of internal friction of topsoil	20°
The angle of internal friction of soil below 5 ft depth.	25°

Table 4: Estimated settlement of square footing

	Least Width B (M)	ESTIMATED SETTLEMENT IN MM					
		CONTACT PRESSURE IN kN/m2					
		50	75	100	125	150	175
	1.50	-10.54	-15.82	-21.09	-26.36	-31.63	-36.90
	2.00	-12.27	-18.41	-24.55	-30.68	-36.82	-42.96
	2.50	-12.48	-18.73	-24.97	-31.21	-37.45	-43.69
	3.00	-12.84	-19.26	-25.68	-32.10	-38.52	-44.94
	3.50	-13.19	-19.78	-26.37	-32.96	-39.56	-46.15

The above calculations are based on the following:

- o H= qB(1-ϖ2) Is*If/ Es (Ref: Foundation Analysis & Design-J.E. Bowels) where, H=Settlement, q=contact pressure at foundation level, B=width of foundation
- The thickness of the compressible layer has been taken as
  - o Two times the width of the foundation.
- Modulus of Elasticity 'E' has been calculated using the following relation given by Foundation Analysis and Design by J. E. Bowels;
  - o E = 300 (N + 6) and 500 (N + 15) , where N is the average SPT value
- Poissons ratio=0.3, Depth of Footing = 1.0 M below the EGL on improved soil

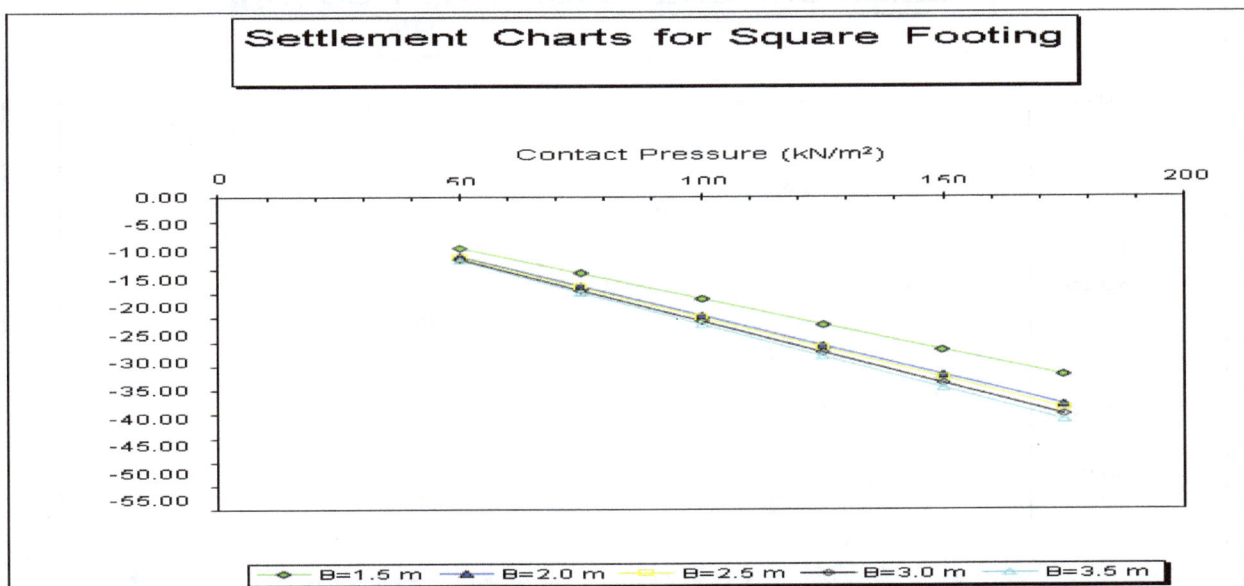

119

Table 5: Estimated settlement of strip foundation

Least Width B (M)	ESTIMATED SETTLEMENT IN MM					
	CONTACT PRESSURE IN kN/m2					
	50	**75**	**100**	**125**	**150**	**175**
1.00	-11.79	-17.68	-23.58	-29.47	-35.36	-41.26
1.50	-12.63	-18.95	-25.27	-31.59	-37.90	-44.22
2.00	-14.19	-21.29	-28.39	-35.48	-42.58	-49.67
2.50	-14.67	-22.01	-29.35	-36.68	-44.02	-51.36
3.00	-15.66	-23.49	-31.32	-39.15	-46.98	-54.81

The above calculations are based on the following:

$H = qB(1-\varpi 2) Is*If/ Es$ (Ref: Foundation Analysis & Design-J.E. Bowels) where,

H=Settlement, q=contact Pressure at foundation level, B=width of foundation

- The thickness of the compressible layer has been taken as
    Four times the width of the foundation.

- Modulus of Elasticity 'E' has been calculated using the following relation given by Foundation Analysis and Design by J. E. Bowels;

    $E = 300 (N + 6)$ and $500 (N + 15)$, where N is the average SPT value

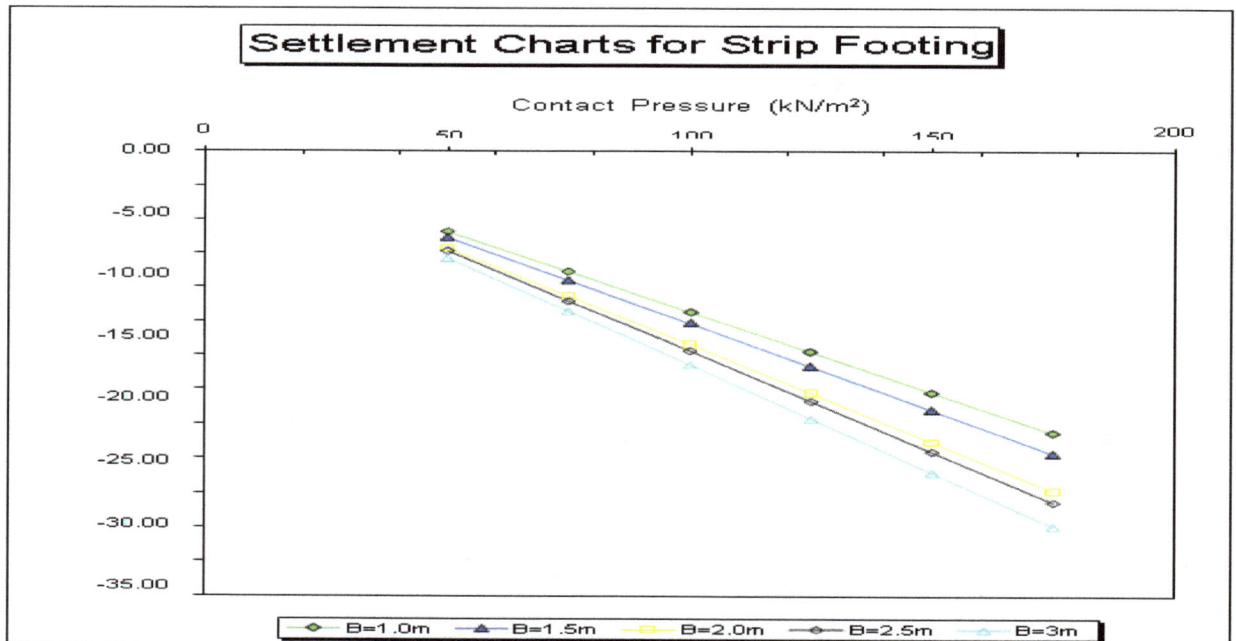

Settlement Charts for Strip Footing

Table 6: Net allowable bearing pressure for foundation

Depth Below Existing Ground Level (m)	Width of Foundation (m)	Net Allowable Bearing Pressure (kN\m²)	Predicted Settlement (mm)
	10.0	180	49.08
	12.5	175	47.96
	15.0	170	46.75
	17.5	165	51.98
1.0	20.0	160	48.33
	22.5	155	50.01
	25.0	150	50.87
	27.5	150	52.90
	30.0	150	54.60

Table 7: Bearing Capacity (Shear Strength Consideration)

Type of Foundation =	Square
Unit Weight of Soil (kN/m3) =	20
Depth of foundation (m) =	1
Cohesion (kPa) =	0
Angle of Internal Friction (degree) =	20
Nc =	14.83
Nq =	6.40
Nr =	5.40
Factor of safety	3
Sc	1.43
Sq	1.36
Sr	0.60

Dc	Dq	Dr
1.27	1.21	1.00
1.20	1.16	1.00
1.16	1.13	1.00
1.13	1.11	1.00
1.11	1.09	1.00

Width of Footing (m)	Ultimate Bearing Capacity (kPa)	Safe Bearing Capacity (kPa)		Net Safe Bearing Capacity (kPa)
1.5	259.84	86.61		99.95
2.0	266.87	88.96		102.29
2.5	277.57	92.52		105.86
3.0	290.10	96.70		110.03
3.5	303.68	101.23		114.56

Table 8: Bearing Capacity (Shear Strength Consideration)

Type of Foundation =   Strip

Unit Weight of Soil   (kN/m3) =   20

Depth of foundation (m) =   1

Cohesion (kPa)   =   0

Angle of Internal Friction   (degree) =   20

Nc =   14.83

Nq =   6.40

Nr =   5.40

Factor of safety   3

Sc   1.00
Sq   1.00
Sr   1.00

Dc	Dq	Dr
1.40	1.32	1.00
1.27	1.21	1.00
1.20	1.16	1.00
1.16	1.13	1.00
1.13	1.11	1.00

Width of Footing	Ultimate Bearing Capacity	Safe Bearing Capacity	Net Safe Bearing Capacity
(m)	(kPa)	(kPa)	(kPa)
1.0	222.34	74.11	87.45
1.5	235.89	78.63	91.96
2.0	256.17	85.39	98.72
2.5	279.14	93.05	106.38
3.0	303.45	101.15	114.48

Table 9: Bearing Capacity (Shear Strength Consideration)

Type of Foundation =	Mat
Unit Weight of Soil (kN/m3) =	20
Depth of foundation (m) =	1
Cohesion (kPa) =	0
Angle of Internal Friction (degree) =	20
N_c =	14.83
N_q =	6.40
N_r =	5.40
Factor of safety	3
S_c	1.43
S_q	1.36
S_r	0.60

D_c	D_q	D_r
1.04	1.03	1.00
1.03	1.02	1.00
1.02	1.02	1.00
1.02	1.01	1.00
1.01	1.01	1.00

Width of Footing	Ultimate Bearing Capacity	Safe Bearing Capacity	Net Safe Bearing Capacity
(m)	(kPa)	(kPa)	(kPa)
10.0	504.06	168.02	148.02
15.0	664.23	221.41	201.41
20.0	825.31	275.10	255.10
25.0	986.76	328.92	308.92
30.0	1148.40	382.80	362.80

Chart No 1: Comparison of Net Allowable Bearing Pressure Based on Shear Strength and Settlement Considerations   **Square Footing**   **Foundation Width (m).**

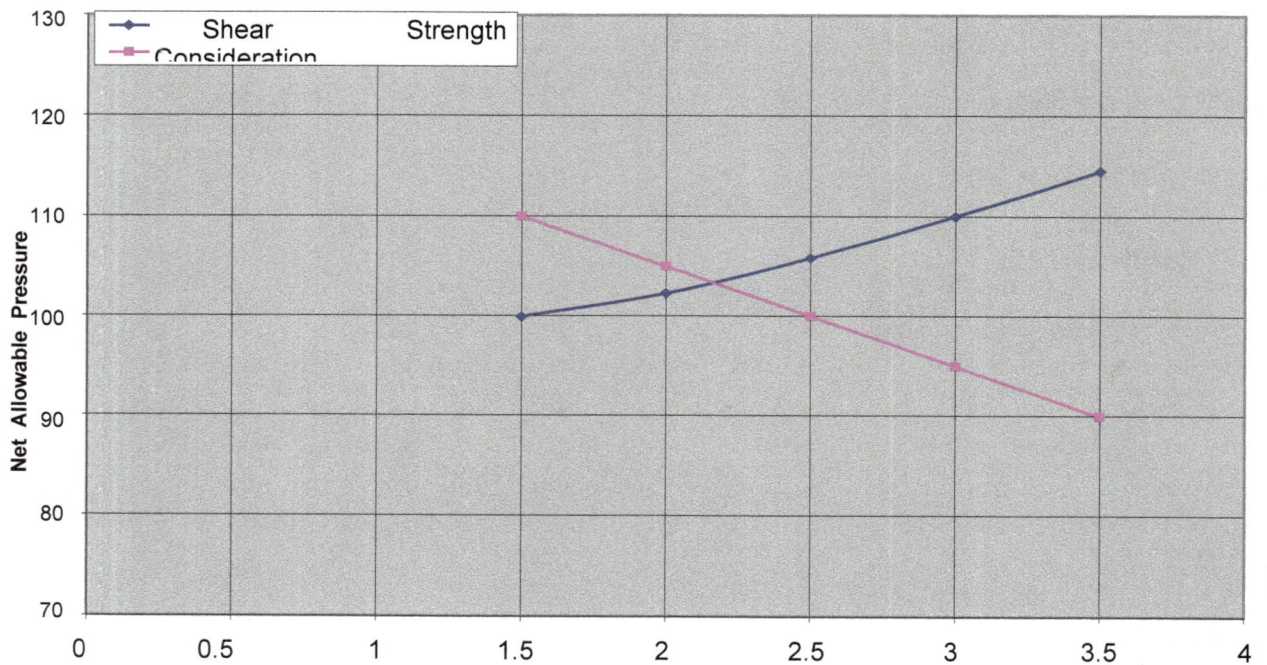

Chart No 2: Comparison of Net Allowable Bearing Pressure Based on Shear Strength and Settlement Considerations   **Strip Footing**   **Foundation Width (m)**

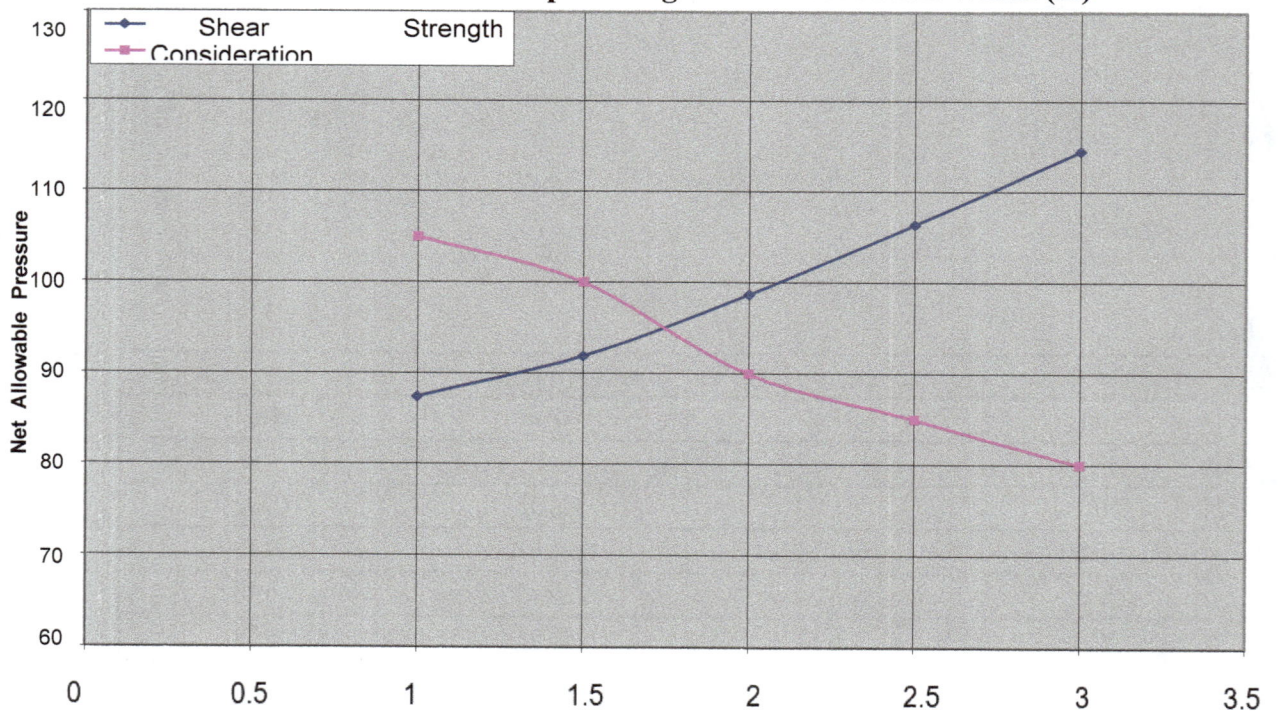

Chart 3: Comparison of Net Allowable Bearing Pressure Based on Shear Strength and Settlement Considerations   Mat Foundation   Foundation Width (m)

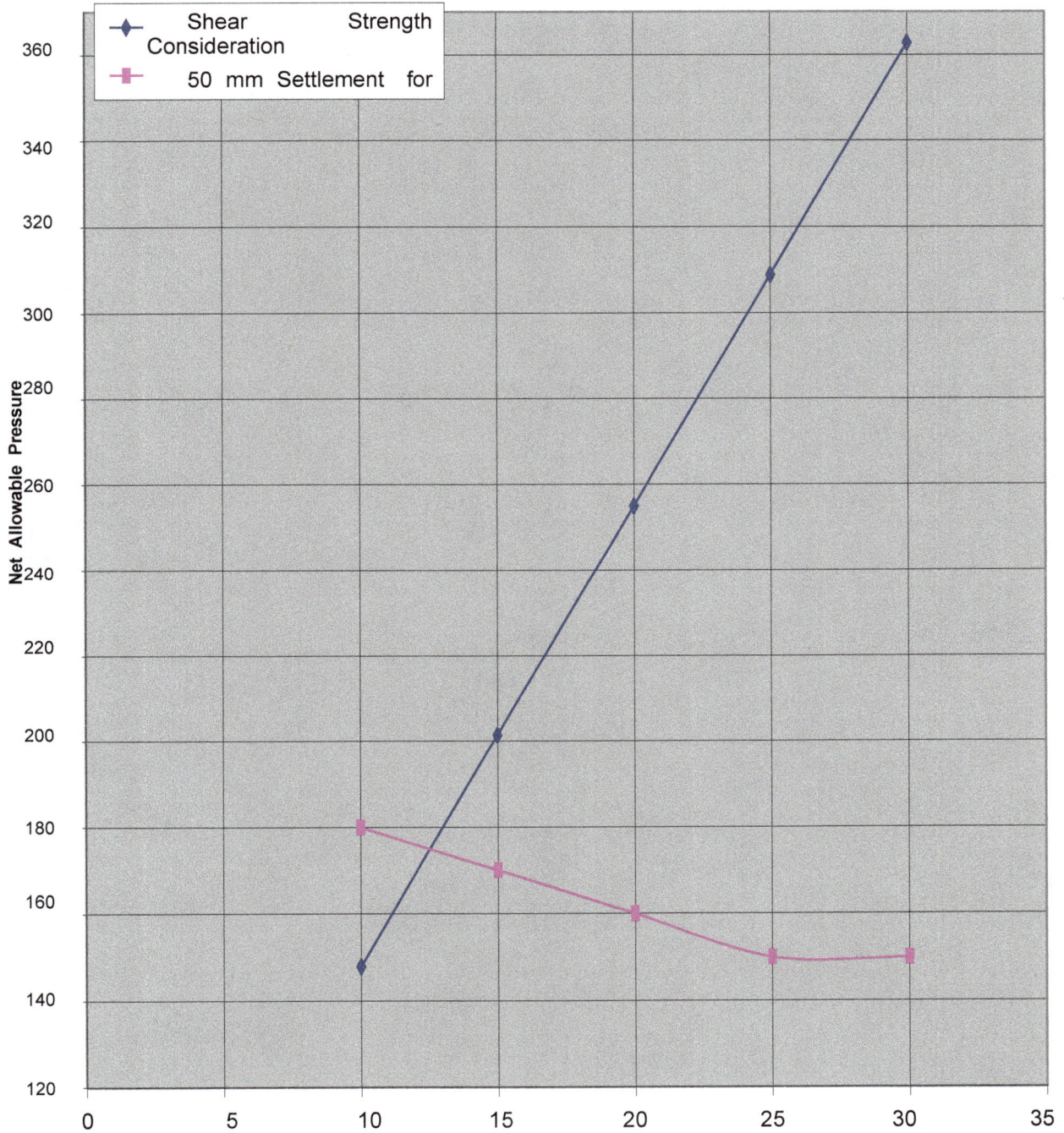

Figure 1: Bore Hole Locations

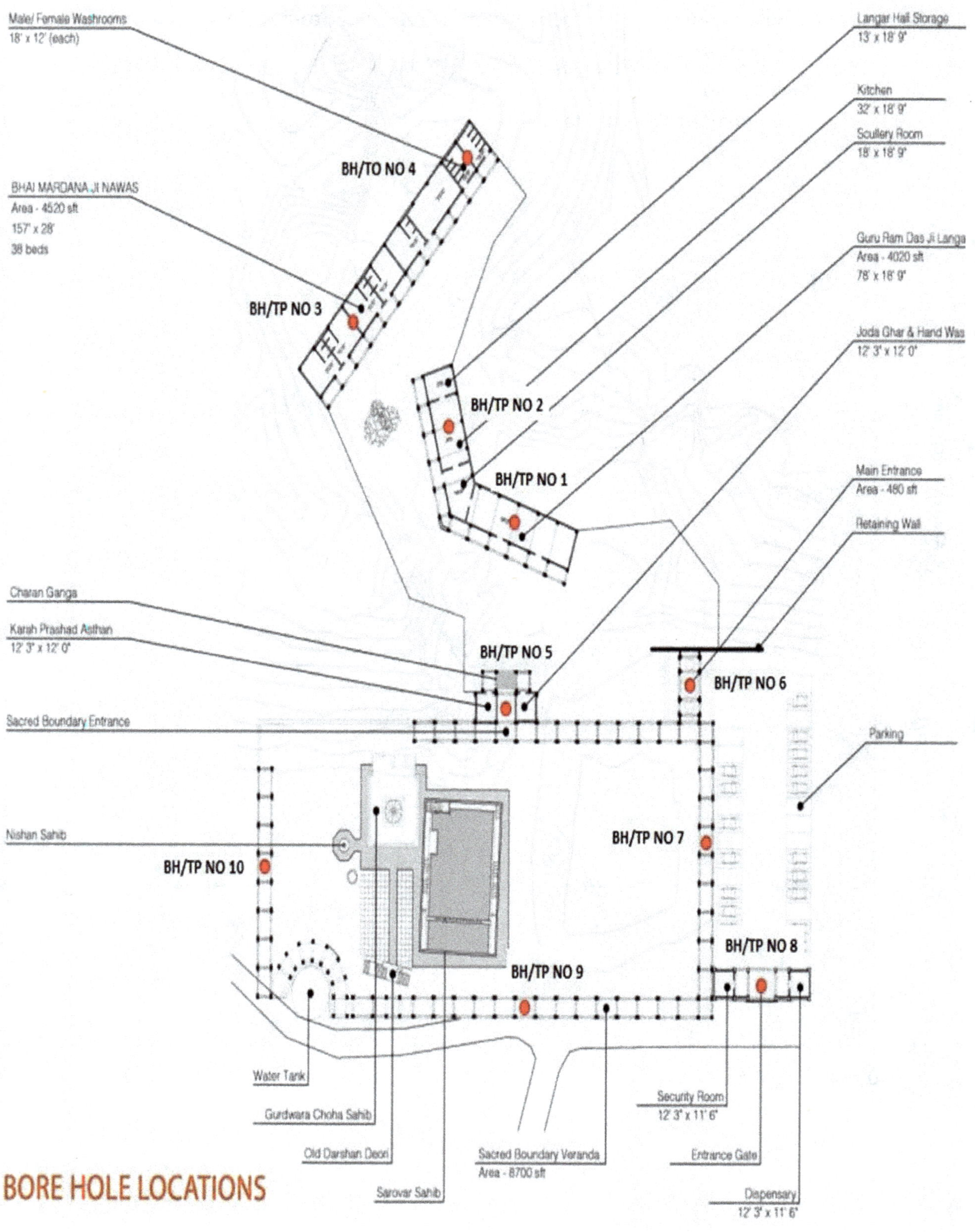

Male/ Female Washrooms
18' x 12' (each)

Langar Hall Storage
13' x 18' 9"

Kitchen
32' x 18' 9"

Scullery Room
18' x 18' 9"

BHAI MARDANA Ji NAWAS
Area - 4520 sft
157' x 28'
38 beds

Guru Ram Das Ji Langa
Area - 4020 sft
78' x 16' 9"

Joda Ghar & Hand Was
12' 3" x 12' 0"

BH/TO NO 4

BH/TP NO 3

BH/TP NO 2

BH/TP NO 1

Main Entrance
Area - 480 sft

Retaining Wall

Charan Ganga

Karah Prashad Asthan
12' 3" x 12' 0"

BH/TP NO 5

BH/TP NO 6

Sacred Boundary Entrance

Parking

Nishan Sahib

BH/TP NO 7

BH/TP NO 10

BH/TP NO 8

BH/TP NO 9

Water Tank

Gurdwara Choha Sahib

Security Room
12' 3" x 11' 6"

Old Darshan Deori

Sacred Boundary Veranda
Area - 8700 sft

Entrance Gate

BORE HOLE LOCATIONS

Sarovar Sahib

Dispensary
12' 3" x 11' 6"

Figure 2: Symbols and Legends

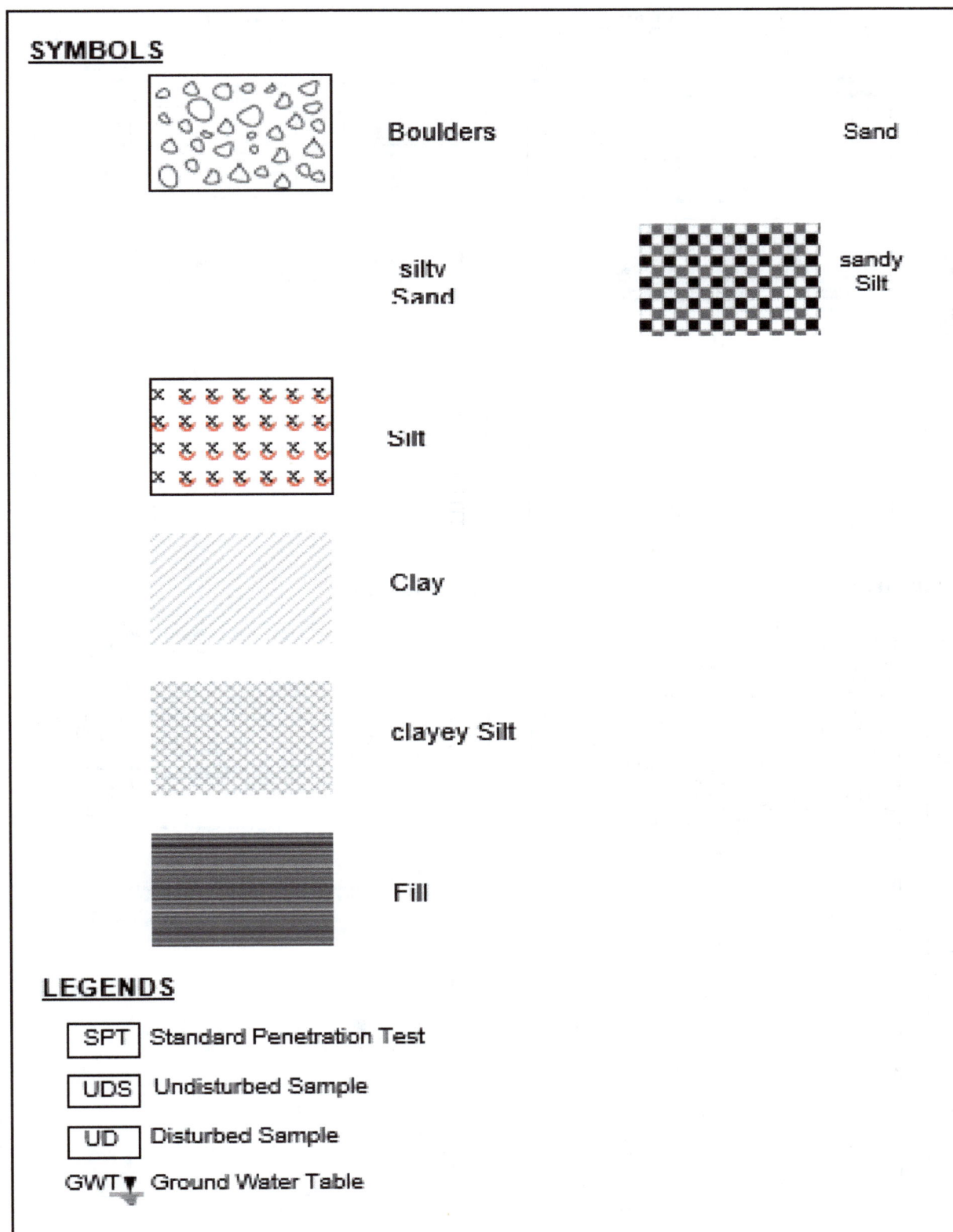

SYMBOLS

Boulders

Sand

silty Sand

sandy Silt

Silt

Clay

clayey Silt

Fill

LEGENDS

SPT	Standard Penetration Test
UDS	Undisturbed Sample
UD	Disturbed Sample
GWT▼	Ground Water Table

Figure 3

Geo Associates Defence Lahore					
Surface Exploration Borehole/Test pit Log	BH - 1	Test Pit No 1	Figure - 3		

Project: _Construction of Gurdwara Choha Sahib Ji Kila Rotas Dina District Jhelum_
Type of Boring: _Augering_   Test Pit: _Manual Excavation_
Dia of casing/hole: _4 inch_   Depth: _5 ft above track level_
Ground Water Table: Not Encountered Inspector: Mohabat Dated: _18-06-2021_

Depth (ft)	NMC (%)	Sample #	Legend	Symbol	DESCRIPTION OF MATERIAL	SPT Blows / ft	Bulk Density PCF	Remarks
3	3.38	SPT-1			Light brown dense silty Sand trace gravel	●32	87.36	
6	6.60	SPT-2			Light brown dense silty Sand with gravel	●34	131.04	

Refusal because of gravels and boulders
TEST PIT NO 1

Test Pit was excavated to a depth of 6.5 ft below the existing ground level. The test pit was physically inspected and insitu density tests were performed. soil mixed with gravel and cobbles was encountered at different depth horizons and tree roots were observed upto a depth of about 5 ft below the existing ground level.

Figure 4

Geo Associates Defence Lahore					
Surface Exploration Borehole/Test pit Log	BH - 2	Test Pit No 2	Figure - 4		

Project: _Construction of Gurdwara Choha Sahib Ji Kila Rotas Dina District Jhelum_
Type of Boring: _Augering_   Test Pit: _Manual Excavation_
Dia of casing/hole: _4 inch_   Depth: _5 ft above track level_
Ground Water Table: Not Encountered Inspector: Mohabat Dated: _18-06-2021_

Depth (ft)	NMC (%)	Sample #	Legend	Symbol	DESCRIPTION OF MATERIAL	SPT Blows / ft	Bulk Density PCF	Remarks
3	4.15	SPT-1			Brown loose silt with sand, gravel and brick pieces / Brown loose silty Sand with gravel and construction debris	Refusal ●	99.22	

Refusal because of gravels and boulders
TEST PIT NO 2

Test Pit was excavated to a depth of 3.5 ft below the existing ground level. The test pit was physically inspected and insitu density test was performed. Soil mixed with gravel and cobbles was encountered. Buried foundation and construction debris were encountered.

Figgure 5

Geo Associates Defence Lahore					
Surface Exploration Borehole/Test pit Log	BH - 3	Test Pit No 3	Figure - 5		

Project: _Construction of Gurdwara Choha Sahib Ji Kila Rotas Dina District Jhelum_
Type of Boring: _Augering_   Test Pit: _Manual Excavation_
Dia of casing/hole: _4 inch_   Depth: _5 ft above track level_
Ground Water Table: Not Encountered Inspector: Mohabat Dated: _18-06-2021_

Depth (ft)	NMC (%)	Sample #	Legend	Symbol	DESCRIPTION OF MATERIAL	SPT Blows / ft	Bulk Density PCF	Remarks
3	5.88	SPT-1			Brown loose sandy Silt with gravel / Brown loose silty Sand with gravel and construction debris	Refusal ●	82.37	

Refusal because of gravels and boulders
TEST PIT NO 3

Test Pit was excavated to a depth of 3.5 ft below the existing ground level. The test pit was physically inspected and insitu density test was performed. Soil mixed with gravel and cobbles was encountered.

Figure 6

Geo Associates Defence Lahore					
Surface Exploration Borehole/Test pit Log	BH - 4	Test Pit No 4	Figure - 6		

Project: _Construction of Gurdwara Choha Sahib Ji Kila Rotas Dina District Jhelum_
Type of Boring: _Augering_   Test Pit: _Manual Excavation_
Dia of casing/hole: _4 inch_   Depth: _5 ft above track level_
Ground Water Table: Not Encountered Inspector: Mohabat Dated: _18-06-2021_

Depth (ft)	NMC (%)	Sample #	Legend	Symbol	DESCRIPTION OF MATERIAL	SPT Blows / ft	Bulk Density PCF	Remarks
3	6.34	SPT-1			Brown loose silt with sand, gravel and brick pieces / Brown dense silty Sand with gravel and construction debris	Refusal ●	136.66	

Refusal because of gravels and buried piller
TEST PIT NO 4

Test Pit was excavated to a depth of 3.5 ft below the existing ground level. The test pit was physically inspected and insitu density test was performed. Soil mixed with gravel and cobbles was encountered. Buried foundation and construction debris were encountered.

Figure 7

Geo Associates Defence Lahore								
Surface Exploration Borehole/Test pit Log					BH - 5	Test Pit No 5		Figure - 7

Project: Construction of Gurdwara Choha Sahib Ji Kila Rotas Dina District Jhelum
Type of Boring: Augering   Test Pit: Manual Excavation
Dia of casing/hole: 4 inch   Depth: 5 ft above track level
Ground Water Table: Not Encountered Inspector: Mohabat Dated: 18-06-2021

Depth (ft)	NMC (%)	Sample #	Legend	Symbol	DESCRIPTION OF MATERIAL	SPT Blows / ft	Bulk Density PCF	Remarks
3	3.45	SPT-1			Brown loose silt with sand, gravel and brick pieces. Brown very dense silty Sand with gravel and debris	Refusal ●	151.63	

Refusal because of gravels and buried piller

TEST PIT NO 5

Test Pit was excavated to a depth of 3.5 ft below the existing ground level. The test pit was physically inspected and insitu density test was performed. Soil mixed with gravel and cobbles was encountered. Buried foundation and construction debris were encountered.

Figure 8

Geo Associates Defence Lahore								
Surface Exploration Borehole/Test pit Log					BH - 6	Test Pit No 6		Figure - 8

Project: Construction of Gurdwara Choha Sahib Ji Kila Rotas Dina District Jhelum
Type of Boring: Augering   Test Pit: Manual Excavation
Dia of casing/hole: 4 inch   Depth: 5 ft above track level
Ground Water Table: Not Encountered Inspector: Mohabat Dated: 19-06-2021

Depth (ft)	NMC (%)	Sample #	Legend	Symbol	DESCRIPTION OF MATERIAL	SPT Blows / ft	Bulk Density PCF	Remarks
3	14.4	SPT-1			Light brown dense sandy Silt with gravel. Light brown dense silty Sand with gravel and debris	●30	106.08	

Refusal because of gravels, boulders and construction debris

TEST PIT NO 6

Test Pit was excavated to a depth of 5.5 ft below the existing ground level. The test pit was physically inspected and insitu density test was performed. soil mixed with gravel, cobbles and construction debris was encountered at different depth horizons and tree roots were observed upto a depth of about 5 ft below the existing ground level.

Figure 9

Geo Associates Defence Lahore								
Surface Exploration Borehole/Test pit Log					BH - 7	Test Pit No 7		Figure - 9

Project: Construction of Gurdwara Choha Sahib Ji Kila Rotas Dina District Jhelum
Type of Boring: Augering   Test Pit: Manual Excavation
Dia of casing/hole: 4 inch   Depth: 3 ft above track level
Ground Water Table: Not Encountered Inspector: Mohabat Dated: 19-06-2021

Depth (ft)	NMC (%)	Sample #	Legend	Symbol	DESCRIPTION OF MATERIAL	SPT Blows / ft	Bulk Density PCF	Remarks
3	15.48	SPT-1			Brown medium dense silt with sand trace gravel. Brown medium dense silty Sand with gravel and tree roots	Refusal ●	121.68	

Refusal because of gravels and boulders

TEST PIT NO 7

Test Pit was excavated to a depth of 4 ft below the existing ground level. The test pit was physically inspected and insitu density test was performed. Soil mixed with gravel and cobbles was encountered. Tree roots were also encountered.

Figure 10

Geo Associates Defence Lahore								
Surface Exploration Borehole/Test pit Log					BH - 8	Test Pit No 8		Figure - 10

Project: Construction of Gurdwara Choha Sahib Ji Kila Rotas Dina District Jhelum
Type of Boring: Augering   Test Pit: Manual Excavation
Dia of casing/hole: 4 inch   Depth: 2 ft above track level
Ground Water Table: Not Encountered Inspector: Mohabat Dated: 19-06-2021

Depth (ft)	NMC (%)	Sample #	Legend	Symbol	DESCRIPTION OF MATERIAL	SPT Blows / ft	Bulk Density PCF	Remarks
3	5.58	SPT-1			Brown medium dense silty Sand with gravel. Brown medium dense silty Sand with gravel and cobbles	Refusal ●	117.94	

Refusal because of gravels cobbles and boulders

TEST PIT NO 8

Test Pit was excavated to a depth of 5 ft below the existing ground level. The test pit was physically inspected and insitu density test was performed. Soil mixed with gravel and cobbles was encountered.

Figure 11

Geo Associates Defence Lahore

| Surface Exploration Borehole/Test pit Log | BH - 9 | Test Pit No 9 | Figure - 11 |

Project: Construction of Gurdwara Choha Sahib Ji Kila Rotas Dina District Jhelum

Type of Boring: Augering   Test Pit: Manual Excavation
Dia of casing/hole: 4 inch   Depth: 3 ft above track level
Ground Water Table: Not Encountered Inspector: Mohabat Dated: 19-06-2021

Depth (ft)	NMC (%)	Sample #	Legend	Symbol	DESCRIPTION OF MATERIAL	SPT Blows / ft	Bulk Density PCF	Remarks
3	1.61	SPT-1			Brown loose sandy Silt with gravel	Refusal ●	109.82	
					Brown loose silty Sand with gravel and cobbles			

Refusal because of gravels and boulders

TEST PIT NO 9

Test Pit was excavated to a depth of 4 ft below the existing ground level. The test pit was physically inspected and insitu density test was performed. Soil mixed with gravel and cobbles was encountered.

Figure 12

Geo Associates Defence Lahore

| Surface Exploration Borehole/Test pit Log | BH - 10 | Test Pit No 10 | Figure - 12 |

Project: Construction of Gurdwara Choha Sahib Ji Kila Rotas Dina District Jhelum

Type of Boring: Augering   Test Pit: Manual Excavation
Dia of casing/hole: 4 inch   Depth: 4 ft above track level
Ground Water Table: Not Encountered Inspector: Mohabat Dated: 19-06-2021

Depth (ft)	NMC (%)	Sample #	Legend	Symbol	DESCRIPTION OF MATERIAL	SPT Blows / ft	Bulk Density PCF	Remarks
3	3.13	SPT-1			Brown loose silt with sand, gravel and brick pieces	Refusal ●	104.21	
					Brown loose silty Sand with gravel and construction debris			

Refusal because of gravels and buried piller

TEST PIT NO 10

Test Pit was excavated to a depth of 4 ft below the existing ground level. The test pit was physically inspected and insitu density test was performed. Soil mixed with gravel and cobbles was encountered. Buried foundation and construction debris were encountered.

Plate 1

Plate 2

130

Plate 3

Plate 4

Plate 5

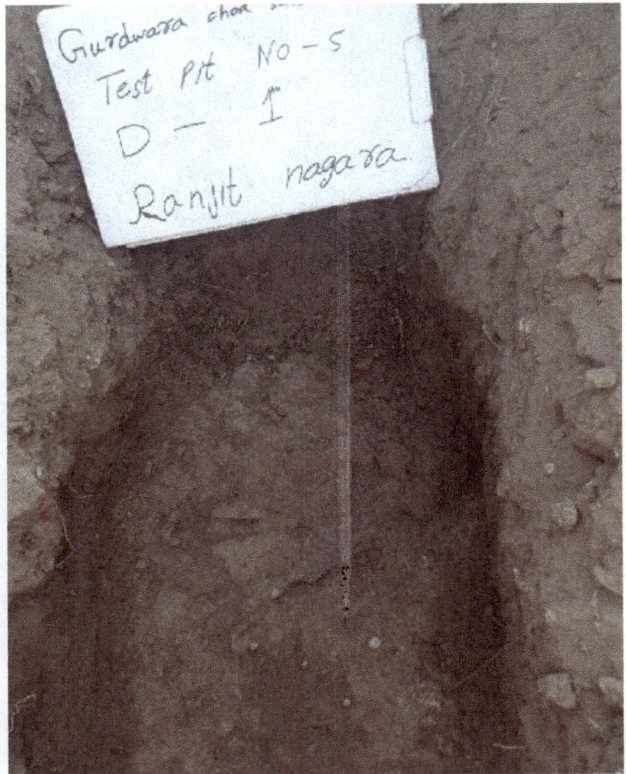

Plate 6

Plate 7

Plate 8

Plate 9

Plate 10

132

Master Plan of

Gurdwara

Choha Sahib Ji

Master Plan of Gurdwara Choha Sahib Ji, Rohtas

The master plan of Gurdwara Choha Sahib Ji, Rohtas, Jhelum, Punjab includes the main building restorations per the original construction of 1834. The surroundings of the main building and Sarovar were empty. Therefore, the free kitchen (Langer Hall), free-living rooms (Sra), sacred boundary wall, Car parking, Main entrance gate, outer boundary wall, the bathroom will be under new construction. Ranjit Nagara USA also proposed merging the new building with the Gurdwara Choha Sahib Ji history. The Langer Hall name is selected as Guru Ramdas Ji langar hall, and Sra name is selected as Bhai Mardana Ji Niwas.

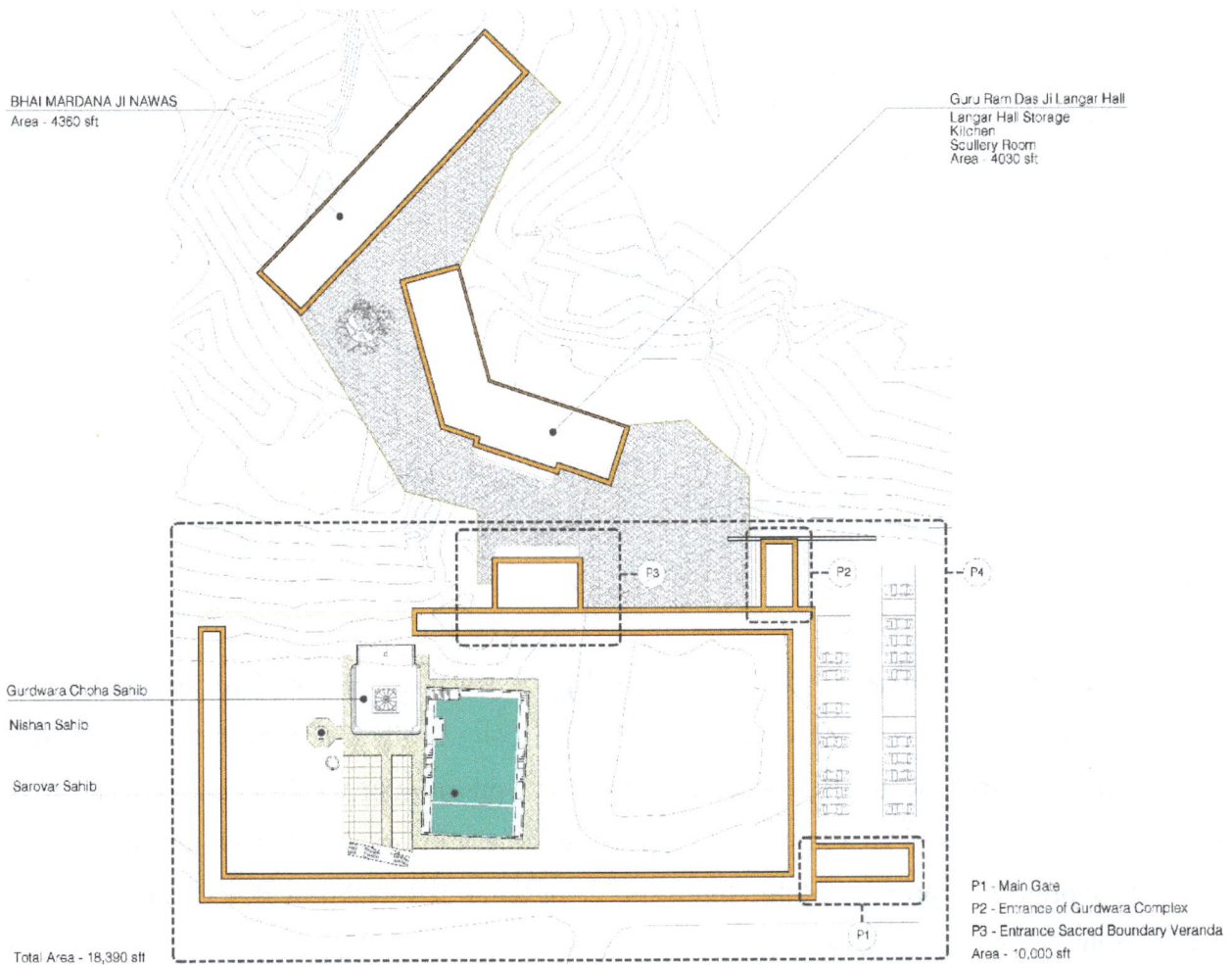

BHAI MARDANA JI NAWAS
Area - 4360 sft

Guru Ram Das Ji Langar Hall
Langar Hall Storage
Kitchen
Scullery Room
Area - 4030 sft

Gurdwara Choha Sahib
Nishan Sahib
Sarovar Sahib

Total Area - 18,390 sft

P1 - Main Gate
P2 - Entrance of Gurdwara Complex
P3 - Entrance Sacred Boundary Veranda
Area - 10,000 sft

Master proposed plan of Gurdwara Choha Sahib Ji, Rohtas, Jhelum, Punjab

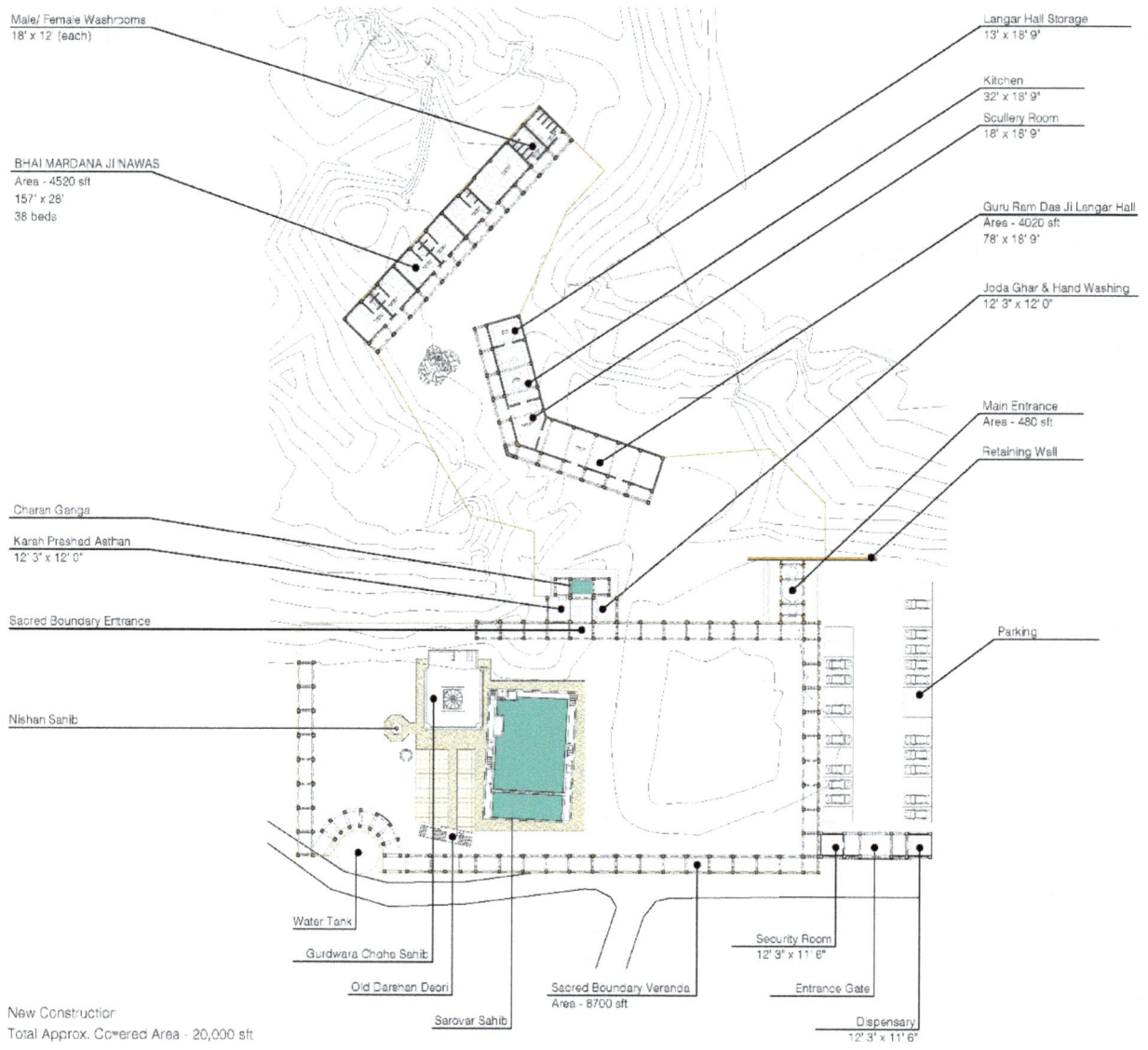

Male/ Female Washrooms
18' x 12' (each)

BHAI MARDANA JI NAWAS
Area - 4520 sft
157' x 28'
38 beds

Langar Hall Storage
13' x 18' 9"

Kitchen
32' x 18' 9"

Scullery Room
18' x 18' 9"

Guru Ram Das Ji Langar Hall
Area - 4020 sft
78' x 18' 9"

Joda Ghar & Hand Washing
12' 3" x 12' 0"

Charan Ganga

Karah Prashad Asthan
12' 3" x 12' 0"

Main Entrance
Area - 480 sft

Retaining Wall

Sacred Boundary Entrance

Nishan Sahib

Parking

Water Tank

Gurdwara Choha Sahib

Old Darshan Deori

Sacred Boundary Veranda
Area - 8700 sft

Security Room
12' 3" x 11' 6"

Entrance Gate

Sarovar Sahib

Dispensary
12' 3" x 11' 6"

New Construction
Total Approx. Covered Area - 20,000 sft

The master plan includes all the facilities and places required in any Gurdwara Sahib. The dispensary near the main entrance of the Gurdwara Choha Sahib Ji shown in the picture will provide free medical aid to the resident, visitors, and pilgrims in the Rohtas area. The Sikh population in the Rohtas area is minimal; therefore, a security room or check-in room is also designed to protect the property of the Gurdwara Choha Sahib Ji. It will provide safety and security and keep the count of the visitors inside the Gurdwara Sahib. It was the requirement to design this room because of the current circumstances and situations in the Rohtas area.

Further, the parking lot is decided near the sacred boundary (veranda), so the pilgrims and visitors can see the Gurdwara sahib from the entrance. Old darshan deori will be the main entrance to the Parkash Asthan in the historical building of Gurdwara Choha Sahib Ji. The water tank marked area is a room built by the water supply department on the land of Gurdwara Choha Sahib Ji to supply the water to the Rohtas area from the Sarovar.

The new construction layout is shown below. The Guru Ram Das Ji Langer hall has a big hall, pot cleaning room, kitchen, and storage area. Bhai Mardana Ji Niwas include rooms with attached washrooms, a big hall, and separate male-female restrooms.

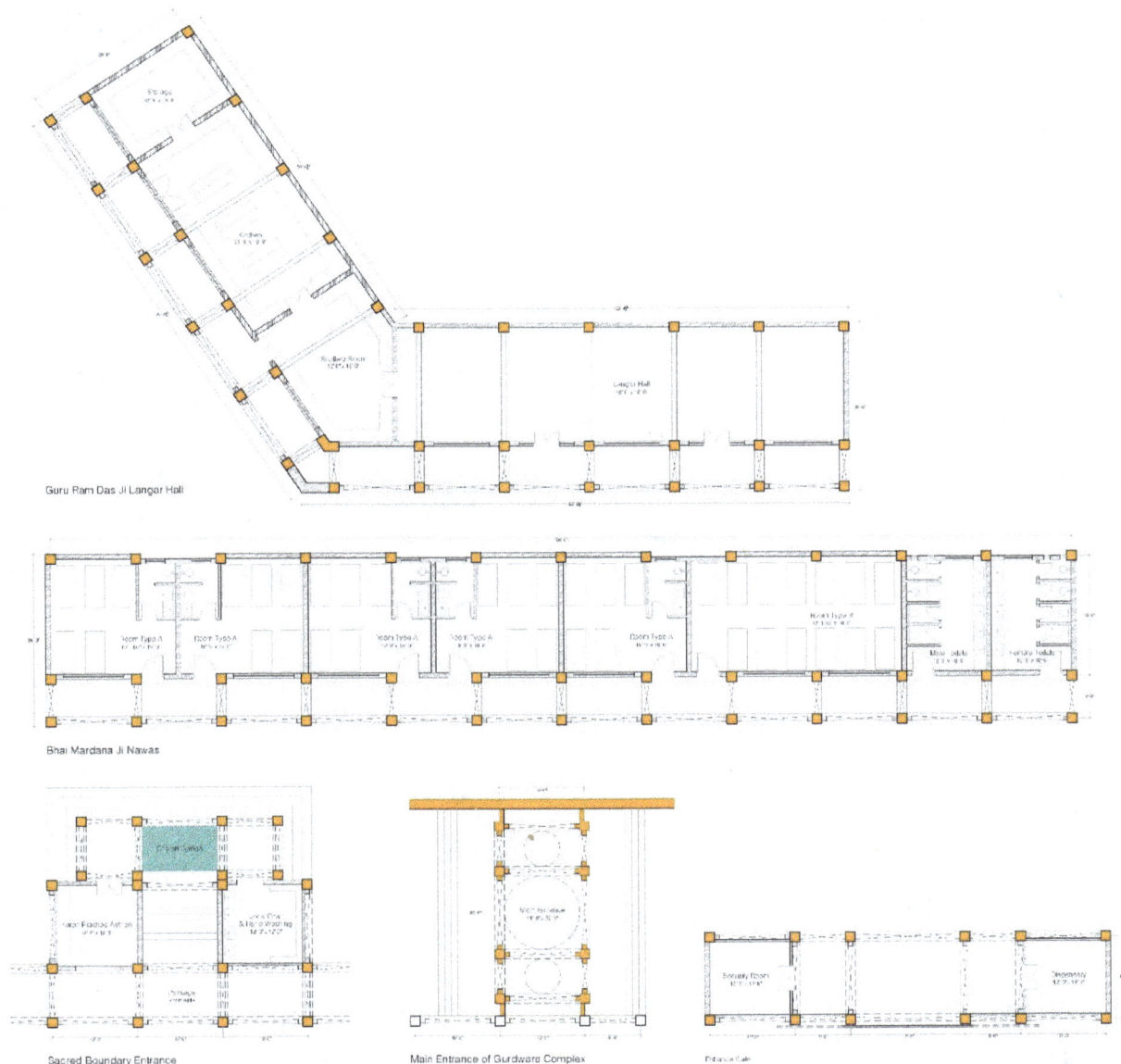

Proposed new construction at Gurdwara Choha Sahib Ji

137

Gurdwara Choha Sahib Ji is in a mountainous area; therefore, Ranjit Nagara has leveled the land needed for the new construction. Surveys are completed, and all information is available in the Ranjit Nagara's head office in Manteca, California, USA.

As we know, the Gurdwara Choha Sahib was an abandoned Gurdwara after the partition of Punjab in August 1947. There was no structure available except the main building and the Sarovar. Therefore, the first challenge that Ranjit Nagara faced was how the Sewadars and labor would accommodate for the restoration of Gurdwara Choha Sahib Ji. The rooms, langer area, kitchen, and washroom were immediately made within approximately 20 days to facilitate architects, restorers, Sewadars, and labor.

Ranjit Nagara USA built rooms to facilitate the restoration work of Gurdwara Choha Sahib Ji.

Washrooms built by Ranjit Nagara USA in November 2020

Temporary Langar Hall and dimensions made by Ranjit Nagara during the process of restoration of Gurdwara Choha Sahib Ji. The langer is open to all including labor, Sewadars, architects, restorers, and visitors.

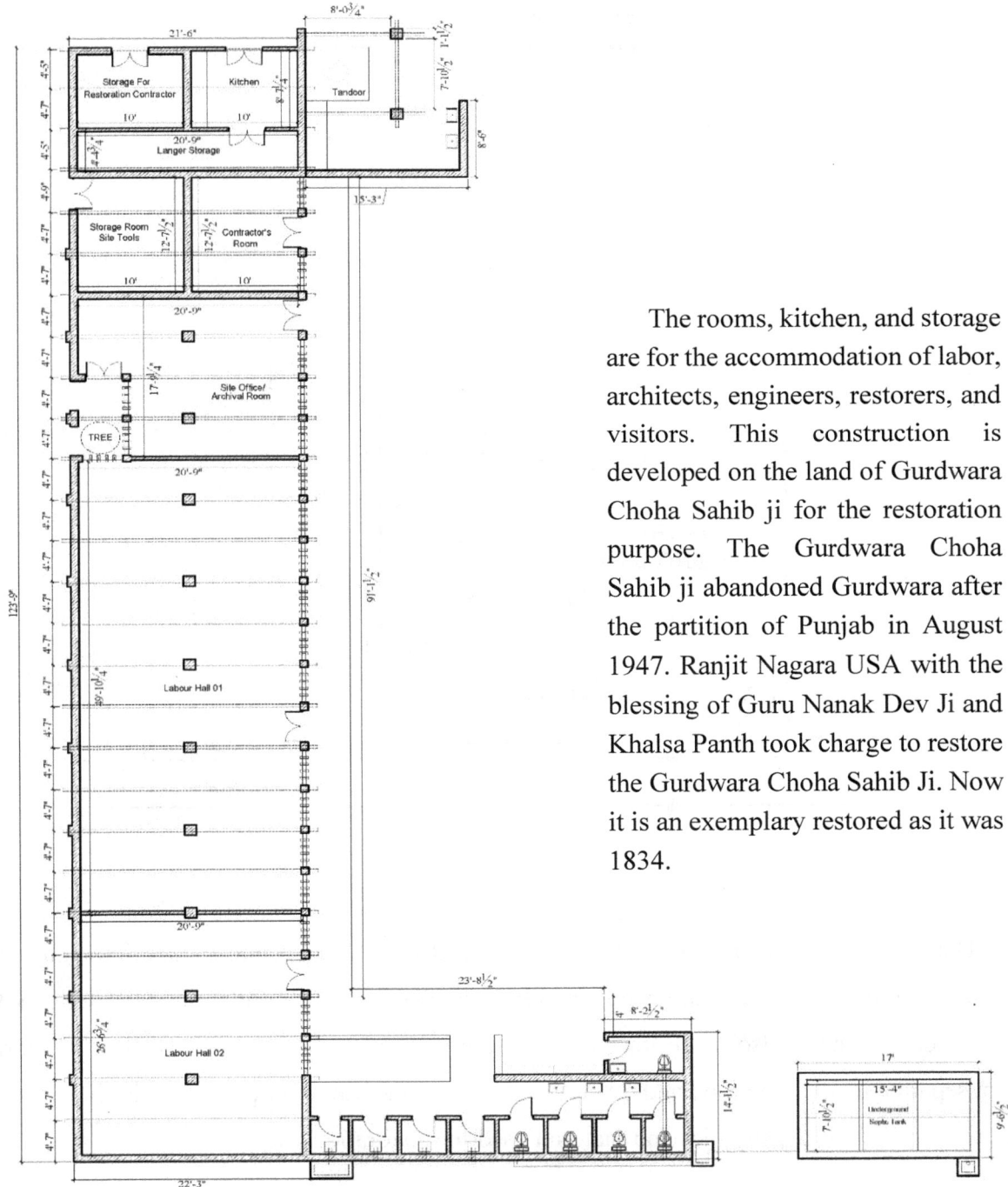

The rooms, kitchen, and storage are for the accommodation of labor, architects, engineers, restorers, and visitors. This construction is developed on the land of Gurdwara Choha Sahib ji for the restoration purpose. The Gurdwara Choha Sahib ji abandoned Gurdwara after the partition of Punjab in August 1947. Ranjit Nagara USA with the blessing of Guru Nanak Dev Ji and Khalsa Panth took charge to restore the Gurdwara Choha Sahib Ji. Now it is an exemplary restored as it was 1834.

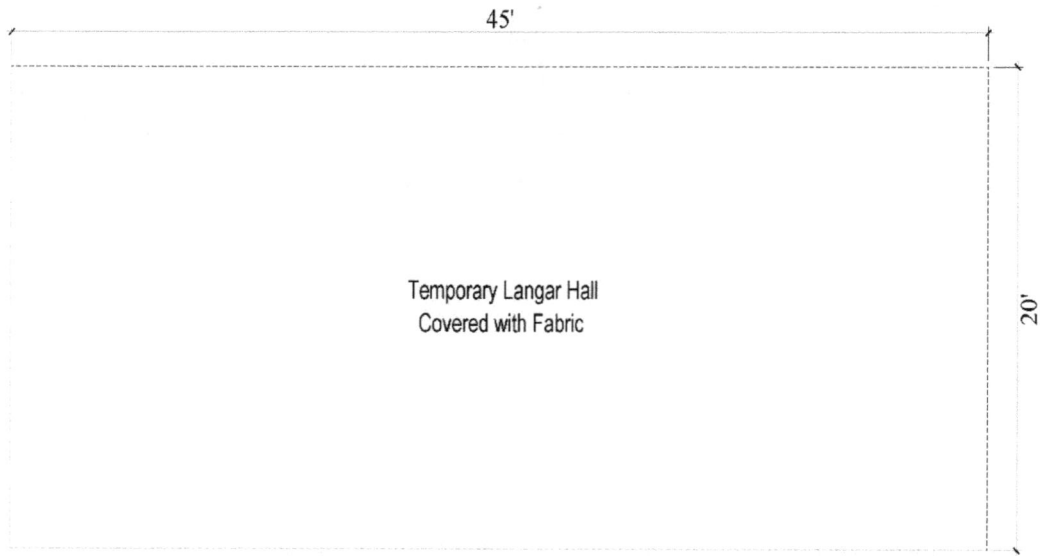

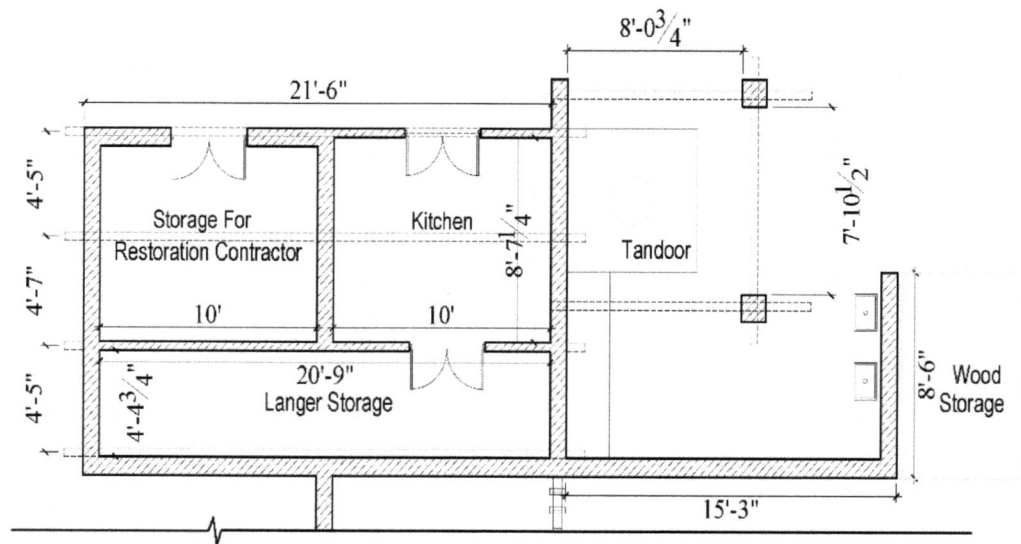

The temporary langer hall is 45 feet by 20 feet and covered with fabric from all sides. A separate room is established to keep the kitchen supplies, and Tandoor is installed with a kitchen. The wood storage is also made for baking food at Gurdwara Choha Sahib Ji. Langer storage is kept separate to store the food and other vegetables for the use of langer. There is also on separate room designed for the supplies and material used for restoration purposes.

140

The shower area and the washrooms are on the side of the road, away from the Gurdwara Sahib sacred boundary. The septic tank is made by lining with brick and plastering that none of the water seepages to the ground. The shower and the other water directly go to the other side of the road outside the Gurdwara Sahib boundary. The temporary accommodation, langer hall, kitchen, storage, and washrooms become very beneficial during the restoration of Gurdwara Choha Sahib Ji.

Material Used for the Restoration of Gurdwara Choha Sahib Ji

The material used for the restoration of Gurdwara Choha Sahib Ji

Ranjit Nagara USA used the same material on the Gurdwara Choha Sahib Ji used during the Khalsa empire and Sikh Misls empire from 1732 AD to 1849 AD. Some material was also used from 1850 AD to 1947 AD, like British-style bricks in Sarovar. The details of the material used at Gurdwara Choha Sahib Ji can be read in the material section of this book in Sikha's theory of restoration and construction. Here, only the material used on Gurdwara Choha Sahib Ji restoration is briefly explained as follow:

Bricks

The Nanak Shahi brick is made from lime plaster and is more resilient than any other type of brick. The usual size of the Nanak shahi brick is 6" x 4" x 1.25". Some different dimensions of Nanak Sahi bricks are also present depending on the area and era of use. The picture of Nanak Shahi brick is taken from the Gurdwara Anandgarh Sahib in the district of Sri Anandpur Sahib in east Punjab. Ranjit Nagara USA ordered the same Nanak Shahi bricks used on Gurdwara Choha Sahib Ji during the period of the Khalsa empire. Nanak Shahi bricks are specially made from the famous and specialized brick-making city Bhai Pheru in west Punjab.

The British-style bricks were used in the Sarovar of Gurdwara Choha Sahib Ji, and Ranjit

Nagara USA used the same brick style in the Sarovar. These bricks are also ordered with a clear face from the famous brick-making city Bhai Pheru in west Punjab. The British brick style has life is approximately five times less than Nanak Shahi bricks. The usual size of the British-style brick is 8" x 4" x 2.25". These bricks are also found in different sizes.

Lime

Lime is made from high-quality natural limestone. It is a vital source of material used to make historically significant buildings. Lime is a high-quality material with a high quantity of calcium oxide CaO. Lime is made from natural material and has a much longer life, and is very high quality than any other type of cement.

Raw lime   Lime Powder

Lime is also made with Curd, Milk, Gur, butter, Jute, Banana, Mango Pulp, Coconut, Moog dal, Maser Dal. The lime made with these materials is waterproof and non-shrinking. The Sikha theory of restoration and construction material section gives more details about lime.

Some samples of the brick mortar are given in the picture used during the Gurdwara Choha Sahih Ji restoration. The usual ratio of the brick mortar is 1:3 but also varies as per the region and area. The ratio can be adjusted as per the requirement of the building, structure, weather conditions, or circumstances.

Brick Mortar Samples

Kankar (Pebble)

Kankar is a small stone found in arid or semi-arid soil shaped by the natural worn and rounded by the natural flow of water. They are usually found in unfertilized or unproductive land. Kankar (pebble) shown in the picture are collected and then burned in on solid heat and then crushed to make the powder of Kankar to mix with lime.

Brick Crush

Crushed bricks into tiny pieces are used at Gurdwara Choha sahib Ji to strengthen the material and match the color with the existing material. The crushed bricks are used in various sizes, depending on their uses.

Jute

Jute is extracted from the Corchorus capsularis or Corchorus olitorius plant. It is soft, shiny, has long fiber, and is used in various ways. Jute is readily available in the east or west Punjab regions. It makes a strong connection between the building materials with longer sustainability.

Moong Dal

The material used at the Gurdwara Choha Sahib also includes the moong dal. It is also known as yellow split gram. Moong dal is usually used as a vegetable alternative in dishes and is very healthy for the human body. Moong dal is used in the building material to provide longer life. It is used in the small ratio in the building material as required.

Saffron

Saffron is the most expensive material rarely available in the market. Saffron is found in two colors, yellow and reddish-orange color. It changes the color of the material as required for the building. The use of the material by the Khalsa Panth in the Gurdwara building material provides a beautiful smell and beautiful experience.

Buffalo Milk

Milk is an opaque white fluid that is rich in fat and protein. Buffalo milk is more expensive than other types of milk and has more potent ingredients. The Sikh Misls and Khalsa empire era used milk for the building material of Gurdwara sahib building to make them waterproof and more substantial for a longer time. It also helps the building material to be white.

Seashells

Seashell is created by sea animals naturally and has a hard protective outer layer. The seashells are usually found on the shore of the sea. They are solid and used to strengthen the building material for a steady and extended time. They also help to stop the building material from shrinking over time. The seashells are crushed to make powder and mixed with the other material to build mortar.

149

Yogurt

Yogurt is made with milk high in protein, vitamins, calcium, and probiotics. Yogurt is beneficial for the bone of the human body and is also used as a source of protein. The use of yogurt in the building material strength the material for a long life span. It is used in little quantity in the building material depending on the building condition, weather, and environmental circumstances.

Jaggery

Jaggery is a non-centrifugal cane sugar made from the canes in the Punjab region. It is concentrated from the cane juice heated on high flame and then cold at an average temperature. It is also instrumental in the building material for strengthening the material. It is heated and mixed with other building materials per the required limit and demand.

Milk Cream (Malai)

Milk cream is made from milk by heating the milk at the required temperature. Then, milk is kept under the average temperature to get cream. The milk cream is used in cooking and pudding the fruit. The milk cream in the material helps joint and strengthen the other building materials. It is only used as required in the building material depending on the area's environmental conditions.

Indigo (Neel)

Indigo is called Neel in Punjabi. It is used as a color to dye clothes. It comes from the indigo tree, and the color made with indigo is usually permanent. Indigo is high in aluminum, sodium, and sulfides. It is readily available in Punjab. Indigo is used to make the blue color of the building to make it beautiful. The material color changes to blue and permanently provides longer life to the paint.

Milk Butter

Buffalo milk butter s also used in the building material to help stickiness. The use of milk butter in the building material makes it slippery and protects the building material from external dirt. It gives the feeling of marble finish in the building. Milk butter is only used as a building material and structure as per the requirement to protect it from water and weather-related damages.

151

Acacia gum is used to treat many wounds and is widely used in the pharmaceutical field. It helps remove or stop the harmful bacteria in the environment and remove the early deposition of plaque. The acacia gum is also used in the building material to make it sticky and non-shrinkable. It works like glue in the historically significant material to join the other part. It also stops the spread of bacteria inside the building.

Acacia Gum

Kali

Pakka Kali is a stone burnt in boiling water for days. It gets cools down in a few days the gets filtered with a cotton cloth. It has an excellent finish and is used in the Gurdwara Sahiban for the glossy look. It has solid white color and is used at the outer layers of the lime plaster for the final finish. The shades of Pakka kali are flat, stan, semi-gloss, and glossy depending on the building look and structure.

All the materials used at Gurdwara Choha Sahib Ji are the same as were used by the Mahara Ranjit Singh. The beauty of this material is that they have at least five times more life than the current 20th gypsum cement material. These materials are naturally made by nature and have many medical benefits to stop the spread of bacteria in the environment. The detail of these materials is given in this book's Sikha theory of restoration, renovation, and construction.

Material Testing

Gurdwara Choha Sahib Ji's main restoration building material is specially drilled and sent to Centralized Resource Laboratory at the University of Peshawar. It is situated in the capital of Khyber Pakhtunkhwa. The Khyber Pass area was fully closed for invaders by Sardar Hari Singh Nalwa under the command of Sher-e-Punjab (The Lion of Punjab) Maharaja Ranjit Singh. During the Sikh empire, all invaders were scared and permanently stopped to enter Punjab. It was the first large city toward South-Asia in ancient Punjab. Sardar Hari Singh Nalwa built the Jamrud fort approximately 15 miles away from Peshawar in 1823 AD in only 54 days.

Jamrud fort ariel view 1928

Approximately 800 Khalsa armies defeated more than 100,000 Afghan armies very severely in 1837 under Sardar Hari Singh Nalwa. Afghans stopped thinking about entering Punjab after this battle and started getting scared, even from the name of Sardar Hari Singh Nalwa and Maharaja Ranjit Singh Ji. Some historical names of Peshawar are Parshpur, Pushpapura. The Peshawar word represents itself as the place of the frontier.

The test report given below is the lime plaster testing material authentication for the exterior domes of the Gurdwara Choha Sahib Ji. The same material is prepared by Ranjit Nagara USA and used for the exterior dooms.

The test report of material used for the Nanak Sahi brick mortar at Gurdwara Choha Sahib Ji. The same mortar is prepared and used to restore the Gurdwara Choha Sahib Ji. These reports are prepared at the centralized resource laboratory in the University of Peshawar.

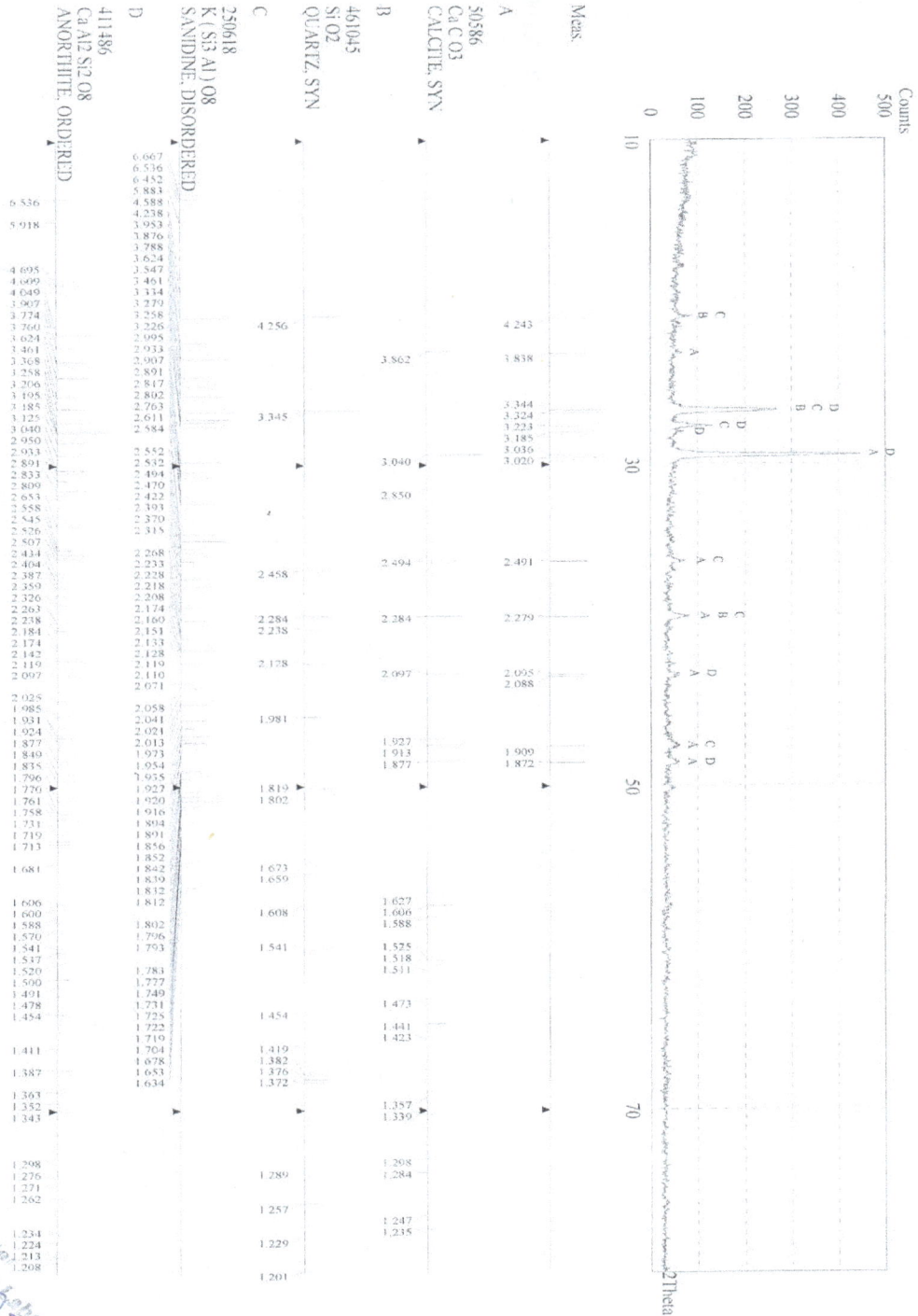

Meas.

A
50586
Ca C O3
CALCITE, SYN

B
461045
Si O2
QUARIZ, SYN

C
250618
K (Si3 Al) O8
SANIDINE, DISORDERED

D
411486
Ca Al2 Si2 O8
ANORTHITE, ORDERED

C:\DATA\(01112010)\2021\pVTRubab Chishti 11.jd\jd1 [Smoothing data]

155

The report for the material used for the Gurdwara Choha Sahib Ji floors. These reports are prepared to ensure the restoration is completed with the same material used by the Khalsa Panth during the Khalsa empire and Sikh Mils empire.

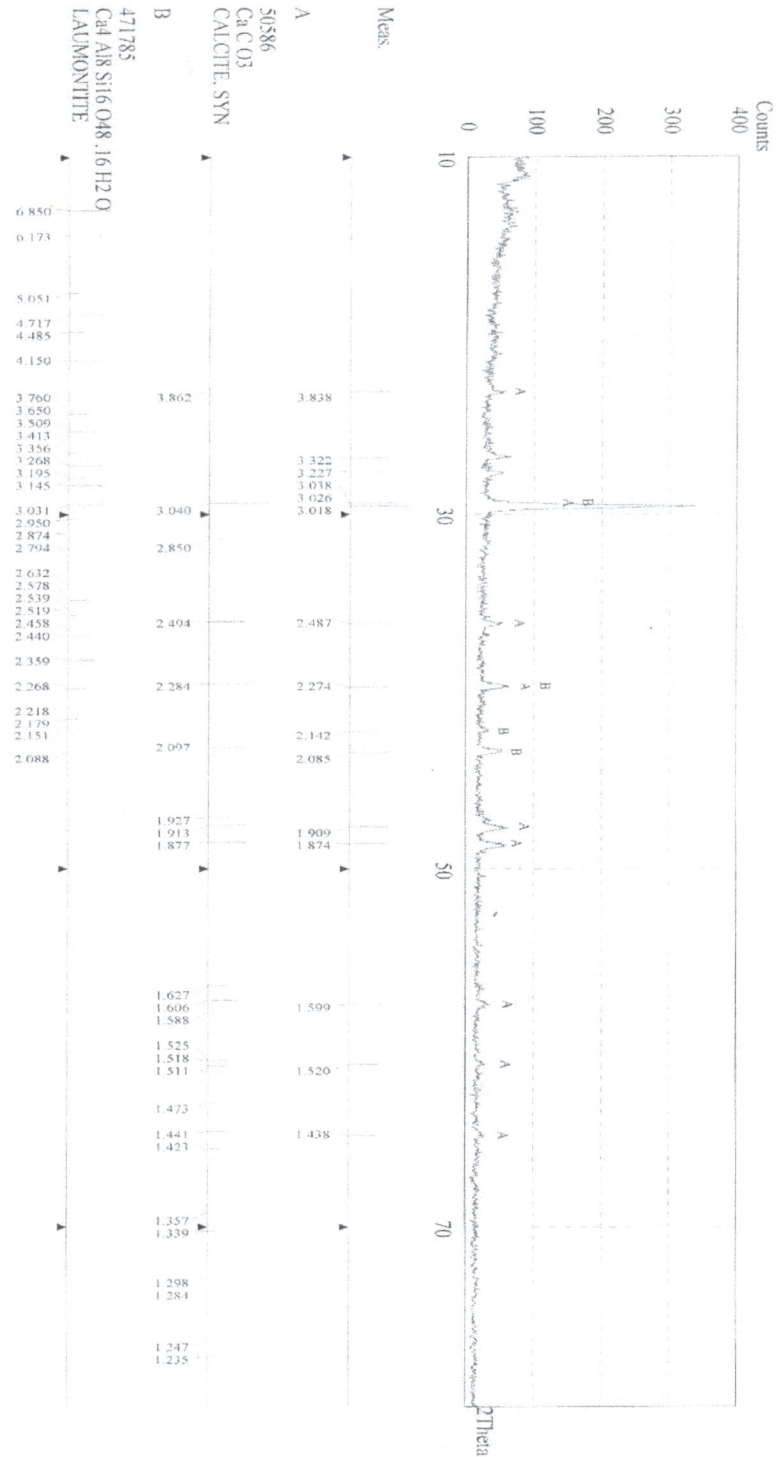

The material report shows the material used for the main centralized of the Gurdwara Choha Sahib Ji. The same material is used for the ceilings of the Gurdwara Sahib. Ranjit Nagara USA used the same material for restoration purposes.

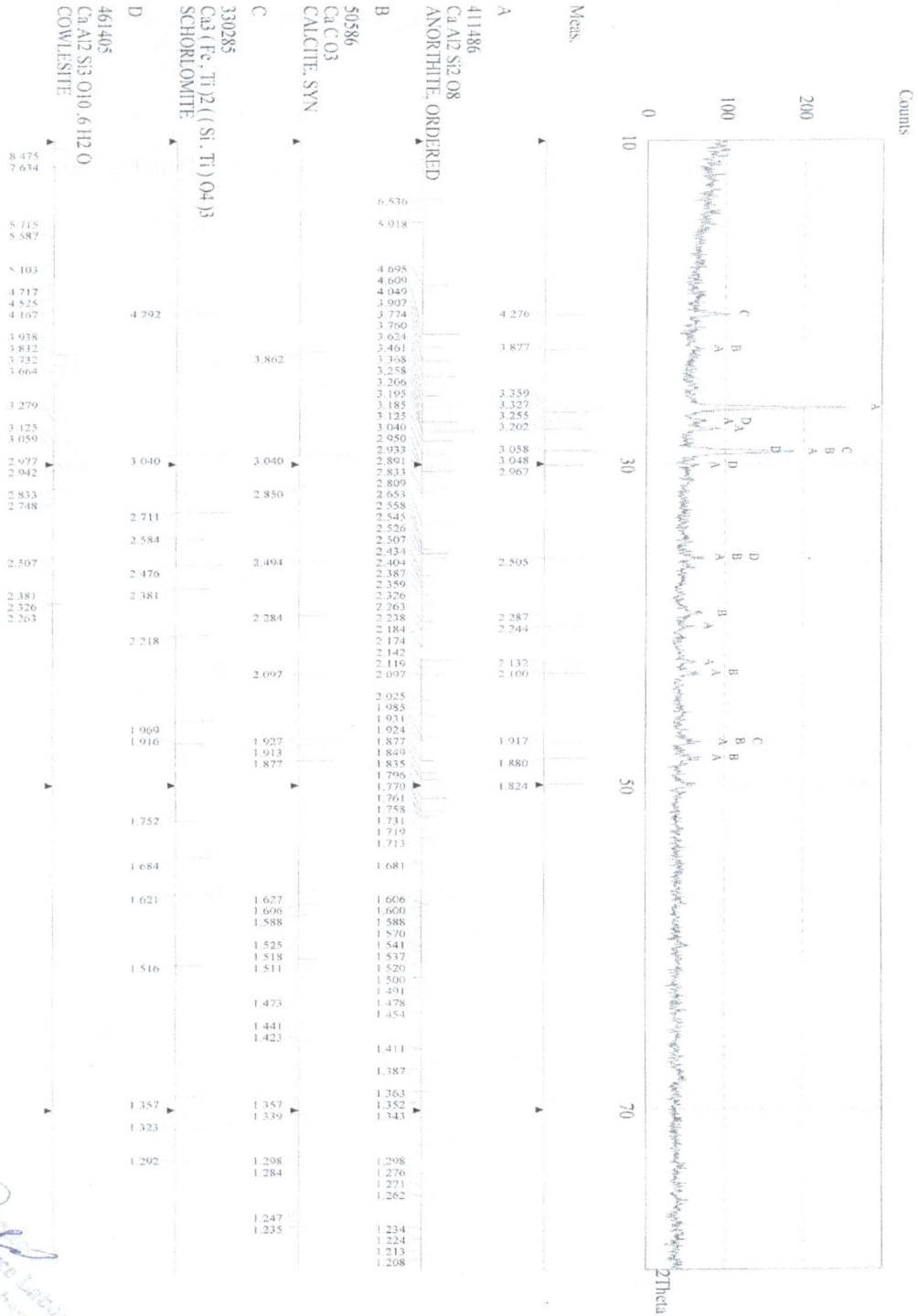

157

The reports are the copy of the actual reports prepared from the material used at the Gurdwara Choha Sahib Ji, Rohtas, Jhelum, Punjab during the Khalsa empire and Sikh Misls empire 1732-1849 AD. The Ranjit Nagara USA representative delivered this material personally to the Centralized resource laboratory in the University of Peshawar. The reports were also picked up personally by visiting the university laboratory. There are many reports were prepared from various parts of the building. Here only four reports are provided. The rest of the material testing reports are available at the head office of Ranjit Nagara USA, in Manteca, USA.

Choha
(Sarovar Sahib)
Of
Gurdwara
Choha Sahib Ji

Choha (Sarovar) of Gurdwara Choha Sahib Ji

Gurdwara Choha Sahib Ji's name was adopted from its Choha (Sarovar). Since its origination by Guru Nanak Dev Ji, the Sarovar has been present in the early 15th century. The Sarovar (Choha) is still a primary water source for the entire Rohtas area since its origination in the 15th century. The name Choha is witnessed by Mahan Kosh, written by Bhai Kahan Singh Naba in the late 18th and early 19th centuries. The abandonment of the Gurdwara Sahib during the partition of Punjab in August 1947 has affected the historically significant buildings of the Gurdwara Choha Sahib and the name of the Gurdwara Sahib. The name detriment started when some writers just started writing to get the fame of their name and write without reading the centuries back history. Those writers visit places or sites and write about them from the recent material like words from people or recently published pamphlets. They do not try to know history research history and are concerned about history.

These types of writers always create confusion and complexity for the coming generations. In the early 21st century, some writers try to change its name from Choha to Chowa or Choa. The detriment names change the meaning of the original word Choha completely. Details about the name detriment of Gurdwara Choha Sahib Ji are given in the name detriment section.

Sarovar condition on August 18, 2015

161

The condition of Choha originated by Guru Nanak Dev Ji became critical after the partition of Punjab in 1947. The unwanted and unplanted vegetation, foliage, and bushes provide vital damage to the Sarovar beauty and structure. The two pictures given below are, taken on August 18, 2015,

clearly show the condition of the Sarovar Sahib. The water supply department put water pump (motor) pump used for various purpose. But they never tried to clean the Sarovar; instead, plastic bags and empty plastic bottles were thrown by humans can be seen easily.

However, the condition of the Sarovar becomes critical because this historical Sarovar was originated by the Guru Nanak Dev Ji and attached to the name of the Sikhs. Sikhs were not present after the partition, and the Sarovar condition became worse even though it is a primary source of water for the entire Rohtas area continuously.

However, under the Supervision of Ranjit Nagara USA, a nonprofit Sikh organization, it cleaned the Sarovar, and its sounding were cleaned in 2020. The picture taken on October 05, 2020, is given below.

Sarovar condition on October 05, 2020

It takes proximally three months to clean the Sarovar and its surroundings by the Ranjit Nagara team under the supervision of experts hired by Ranjit Nagara USA. Nanak-Sahi bricks floor has been completed around the Sarovar and is well-maintained now. The complete restored Gurdwara has been handed over back to Evacuee Trust Property Board (ETPB) and Pakistan Sikh Gurdwara Prabandhak Committee (PSGPC) on February 28, 2022, by Ranjit Nagara USA. It is up to ETPB and PSGPC how they keep maintained and clean.

Procedure and method used: Layout and Main areas marking.

Paouna, the area of women's sacred bath in the Sarovar. It was covered before the partition of Punjab in 1947.

Remains of dividing wall in the open area and covered area.

Drainage outlet for the water flow.

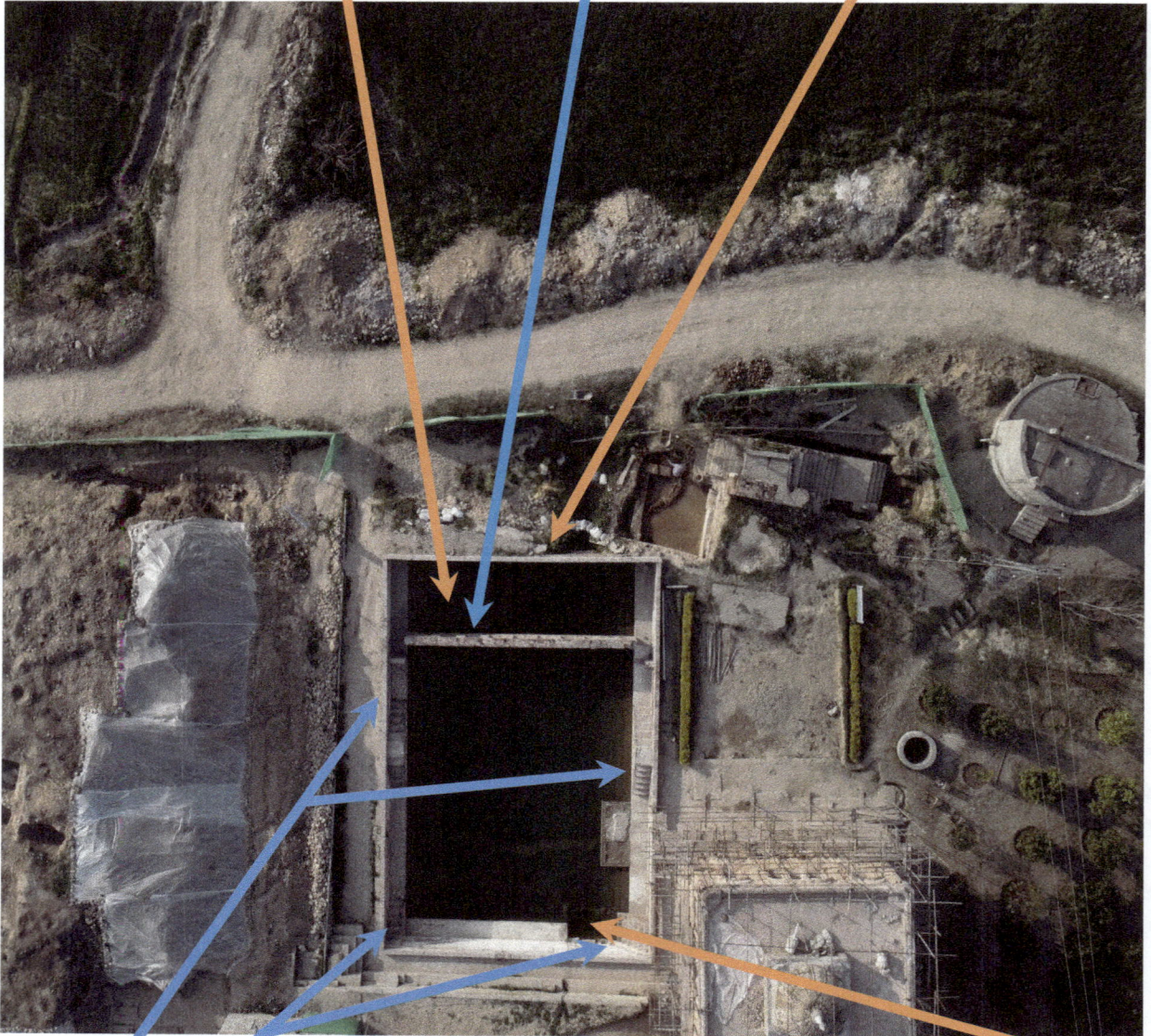

Two-way Stairs

One-way Stairs

Amrit Kund (Choha) originated by Guru Nanak Dev Ji in the early 15th century at the request of the residents because the entire area had no water. Even today, this Choha (water source) is the primary water source for daily life use. Even now, in 2022, water is not available in that area except this Choha.

Choha (water source), originated by Guru Nanak Dev Ji, is the primary water source for the whole Rohtas area from the early 15th century to the present day in the 21st century and continues. Ranjit Nagara first cleaned the central area of Choha:

1.   The first drainage of the Sarovar Sahib and cleaning of Amrit Kund (Choha) was completed in October 2020 after the partition of Punjab in 1947. Visual observation of the Choha brings forth that the water source within the Choha is from the natural rock of the mountain, and water flows into the Amrit Kund (Choha). Small walls around the Choha pour the water to the rest of the Sarovar.

The water flow is natural. Guru Nanak Dev Ji made a miracle to facilitate the Rohtas area with water. In 2018 AD, the Government of Pakistan government-sponsored project tried to dig 126 wells in the Rohtas area. Still, they were unsuccessful in getting water from anyone in their 126 excavated wells location. It was the kindness of Guru Nanak Dev Ji to get

satisfied the water shortage in the Rohtas area during his visit in the early 15th century.

The Rohtas fort and nearby villages water from this Gurdwara Choha Sahib Ji for their daily needs free of cost. Currently, the water supply department of Jhelum district also built a water pump (motor) room illegally

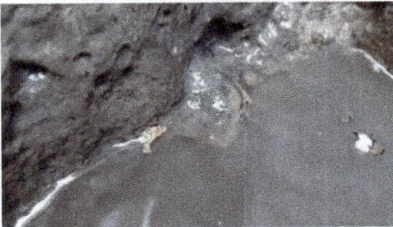

built on the land of Gurdwara Sahib to get the water from the Choha originated by Guru Nanak Dev Ji. Currently, It is used by the water supply department for the need of Rohtas residents

The first cleaning of the Sarovar after 73 years from the Partition of Punjab in August 1947 was completed by the Ranjit Nagara USA with the help of Sikh volunteers who came from Peshawar, Panja Sahib, Nankana Sahib, and Lahore with the supervision of experts present on

Gurdwara Choha Sahib. As per Khalsa Panth Maryada (code and conduct), at the very first stage, Ardas (Prayer) was made in front of Akal Purkh Guru Nanak Dev Ji, and the cleaning of the Sarovar was completed. The Ranjit Nagara USA team continuously cleaned the Sarovar for three months to make it beautiful again as before the partition of Punjab. The Sarovar walls were found to have suffered from bio-growth and have an even layer of biofilm over them. The clean the Sarovar, walls, and floor was completed by Sikh Volunteers and hired manual labor by Ranjit Nagara USA.

166

Electric System Design Proposal for Gurdwara Choha Sahib Ji

Electric System design for Gurdwara Choha Sahib Ji

The current era 21st century has the necessity of the electric system in every building. The electrical system provides the light and other facilities inside and outside the building. CCTV, AC, Speakers, and communication devices are all used with electric power. Electricity is also used to make and maintain a comfortable environment inside and surrounding of the building regarding heating, cooling, and air quality. Therefore, Electric power installation in all buildings, including historic ancient buildings, is essential.

Ranjit Nagara USA hired electrical engineers to design the electric design and structure of the Gurdwara Choha Sahib Ji. The method of the electric system is developed under the direct supervision of Ranjit Nagara USA. It was kept in mind that there must be no detriment to any part of the historic building and material. Therefore, most of the system is designed on floors instead of walls unless required. The proposed plan is divided into three different sections given below:

1. All the floors of the existing main building of Gurdwara Choha Sahib Ji.

2. Proposed building for the Guru Ramdas Ji Langar hall (free kitchen for everyone).

3. Proposed living quarters Bhai Mardana Ji Niwas (free-living quarters for the neediest and pilgrims)

Climate change is the primary concern of today's world, and electricity makes the environment required to facilitate the humans inside the building. The details are given in the following pages with clear views and locations. Gurdwara Choha Sahib Ji's main building is very energy efficient and environmentally friendly. The newly proposed Guru Ramdas Ji Langer Hall and Bhai Mardana Ji Niwas matched the existing building structure and style.

A separate electric room is set up on the northeast side of the Gurdwara Choha Sahib Ji to control the electricity with the main existing building.

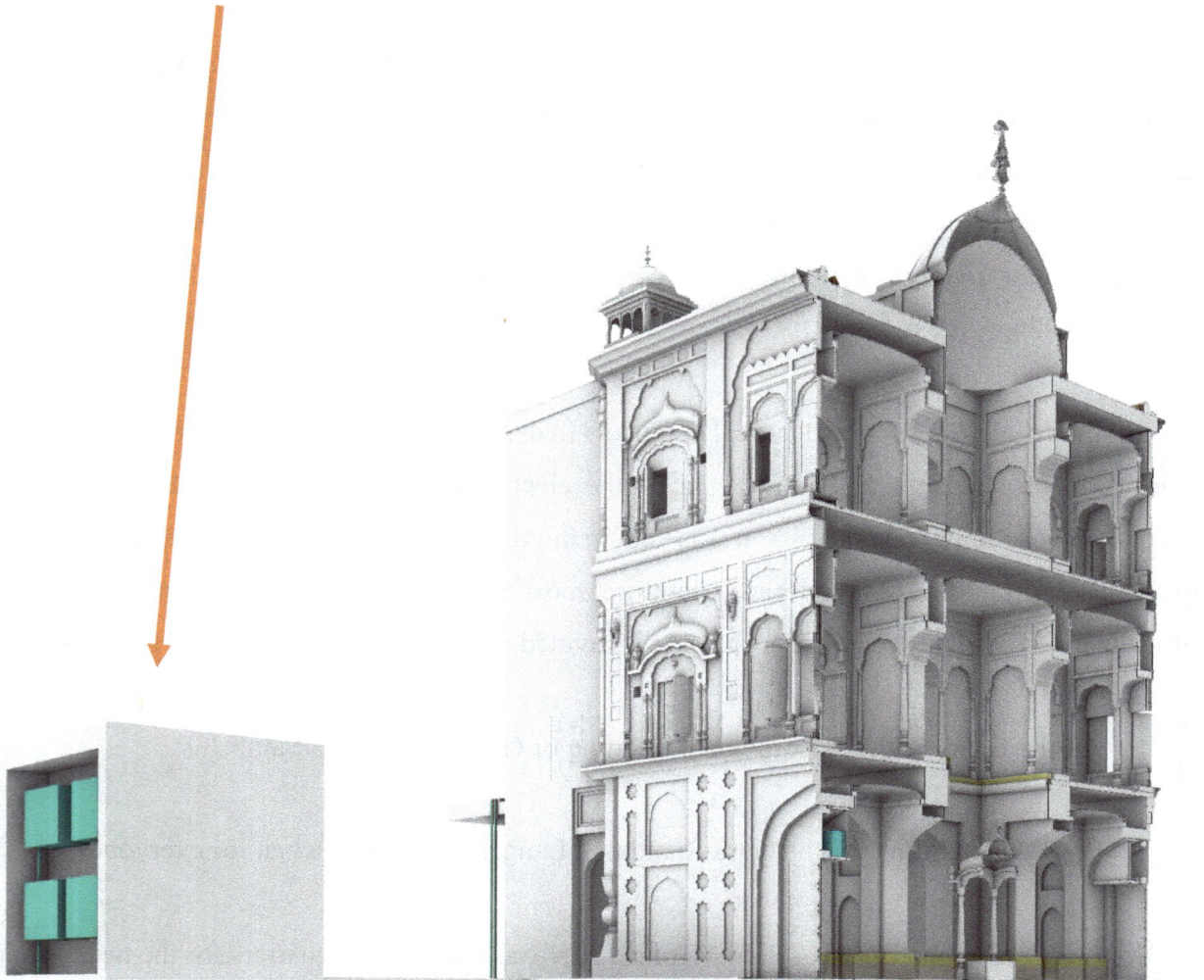

This room will have the master electric control and supply the electricity to all three-story buildings of the Gurdwara Sahib. Each floor has its connection and management for safety and protection. The electric room is designed a little far from the building to keep and maintain the traditional beauty of the Gurdwara Sahib. The actual implementation of the plan on site is waiting for some documentation from ETPB and PSGPC. Currently, it is on hold as of February 28, 2022. Ranjit Nagara USA team spend months developing a secure and protective electric plan for the historical building of the Gurdwara Choha Sahib Ji.

The complete electric function layout of the ground floor of the Gurdwara Choha Sahib Ji. Most of the wiring is designed through the ground instead of the walls.

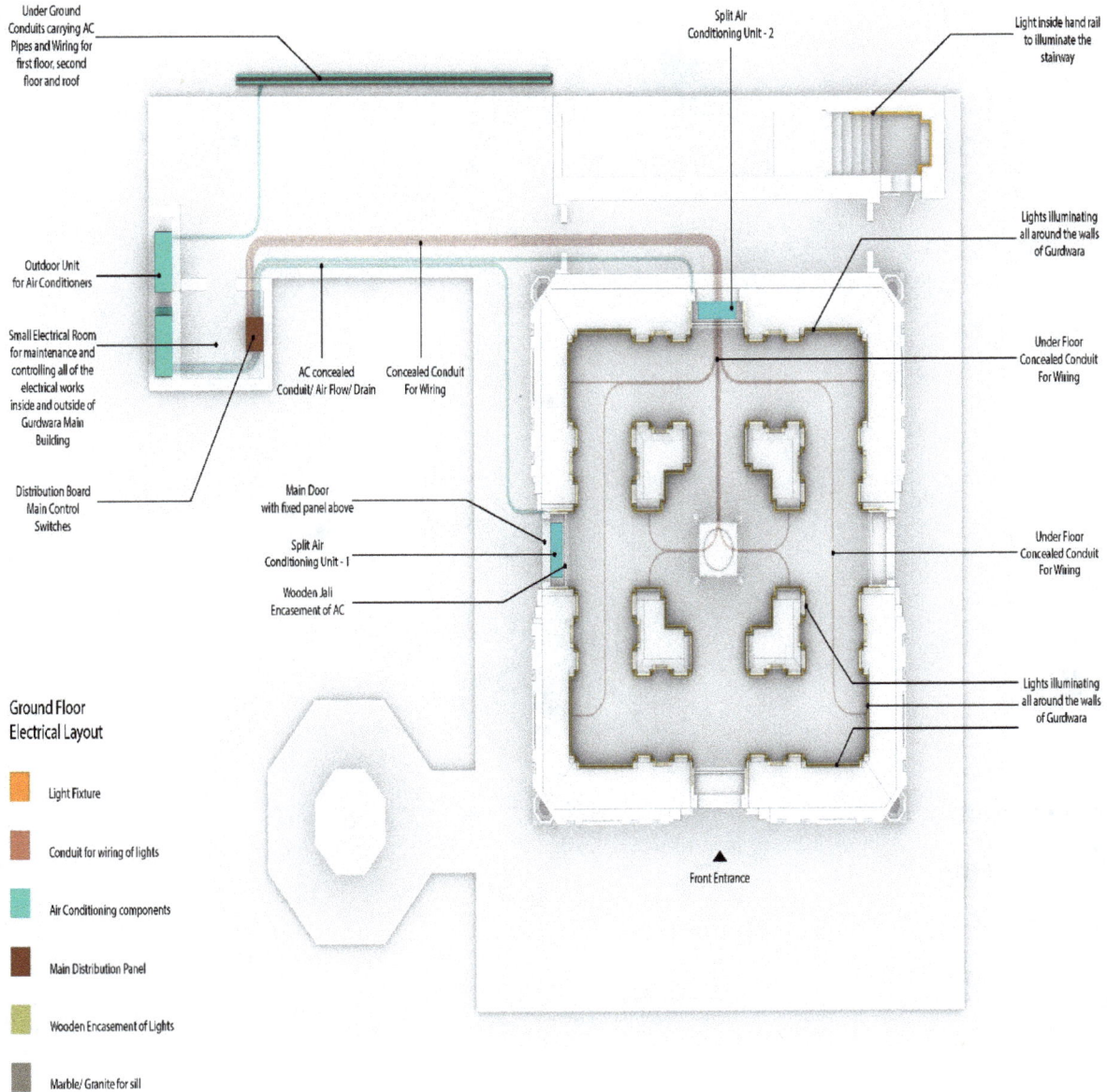

Under Ground Conduits carrying AC Pipes and Wiring for first floor, second floor and roof

Split Air Conditioning Unit - 2

Light inside hand rail to illuminate the stairway

Outdoor Unit for Air Conditioners

Small Electrical Room for maintenance and controlling all of the electrical works inside and outside of Gurdwara Main Building

Distribution Board Main Control Switches

AC concealed Conduit/ Air Flow/ Drain

Concealed Conduit For Wiring

Main Door with fixed panel above

Split Air Conditioning Unit - 1

Wooden Jali Encasement of AC

Lights illuminating all around the walls of Gurdwara

Under Floor Concealed Conduit For Wiring

Under Floor Concealed Conduit For Wiring

Lights illuminating all around the walls of Gurdwara

Front Entrance

Ground Floor Electrical Layout

Light Fixture

Conduit for wiring of lights

Air Conditioning components

Main Distribution Panel

Wooden Encasement of Lights

Marble/ Granite for sill

The different color square on the side explains the meaning of the wire and area of use. The ground floor design is developed without detriment to the existing building and beauty.

More detailed view of the electric plan at Gurdwara Choha Sahib Ji inside the main existing 1834 AD historic building.

Ground Floor
Electrical Layout

Light Fixture

Conduit for wiring of lights

Air Conditioning components

Main Distribution Panel

Wooden Encasement of Lights

Marble/ Granite for sill

The electric light pipe came through the grounds and entered the main building through the back door of the Gurdwara Sahib. The Nisan Sahib on the northeast side of the Gurdwara sahib also gets the electric power from the central control room via the ground.

The conduit for wiring is used under-floor and concealed by the floor. A 12mm transparent surface will pass the light to the building with LED linear light. The wooden back behind the LED linear will protect the electric circuit shoot.

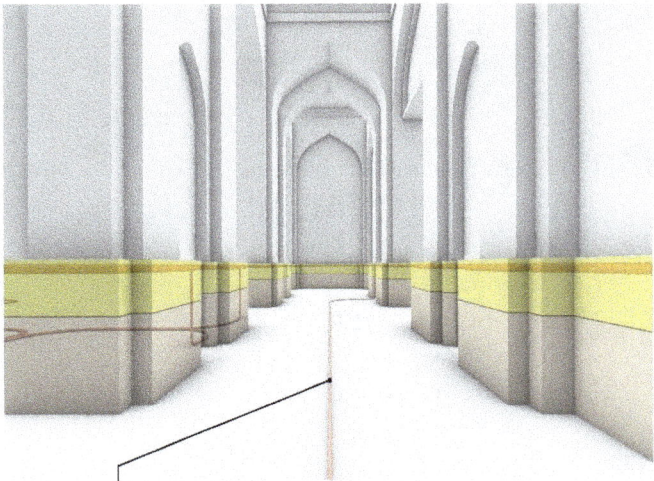

Under Floor Concealed
Conduit For Wiring

Glass @12mm
Transparent Surface to allow
light to pass through

LED Linear Light

3/4" Thick Wooden Back
Panel 6" High

1/2" Thick Wooden
Open-able Front Panel
6" High

Potential space for
switches/ sockets

2" Thick Marble/ Granite
@ 9" High from
Finish Floor Level

Channel Embedded in
floor screwed with
marble on top

Under Floor Concealed
Conduit For Wiring

Main Door
with fixed panel above

Split Air
Conditioning Unit - 1

Wooden Jali
Encasement of AC

AC Conduit concealed
in Door Frame (Chaughat)
Contains Air Flow Pipe,
Electric Supply & Drain

**Ground Floor
Conduit Concealing Strategies**

Light Fixture

Conduit for wiring of lights

Air Conditioning components

Main Distribution Panel

Wooden Encasement of Lights

Marble/ Granite for sill

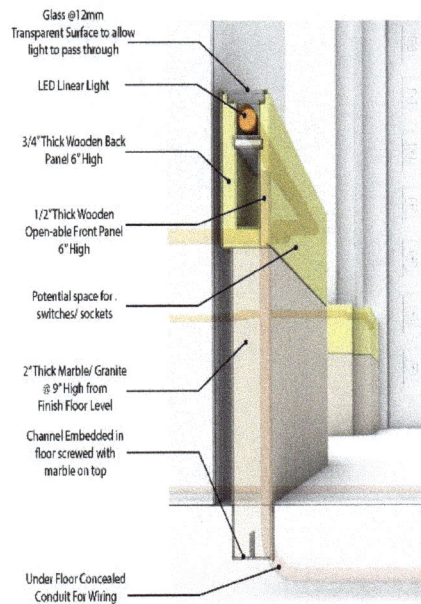

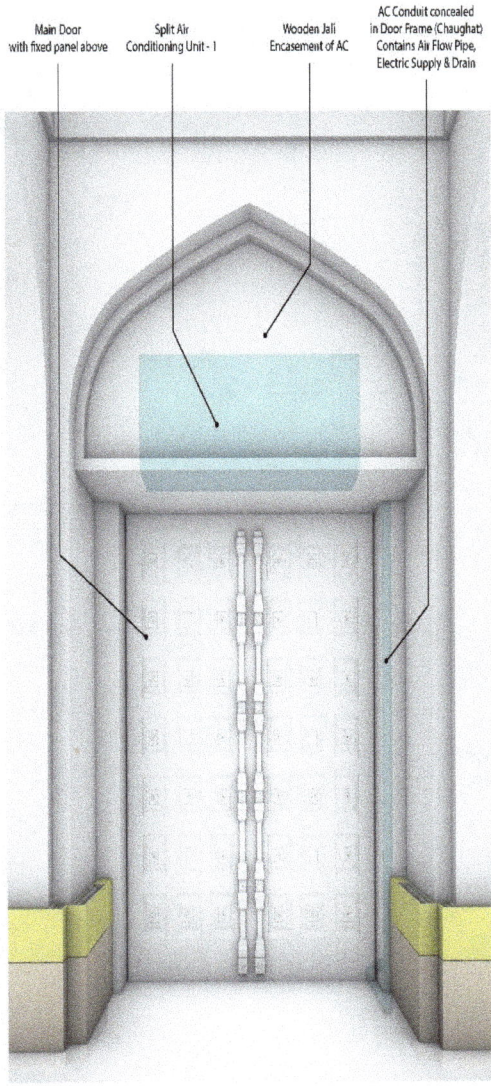

Electric engineers team makes the ground floor conduit concealing strategy under the supervision of Ranjit Nagara USA. The complete electric channel will cover screws from the ground for the stability of the lighting structure inside the ground floor of the Gurdwara Choha Sahib Ji.

First Floor Electric layout for the existing building of Gurdwara Choha Sahib Ji is given below. The first floor has many saved surface-mounted historical details. Linear light illuminating the double-height space in the center of the first floor will provide perfect lighting.

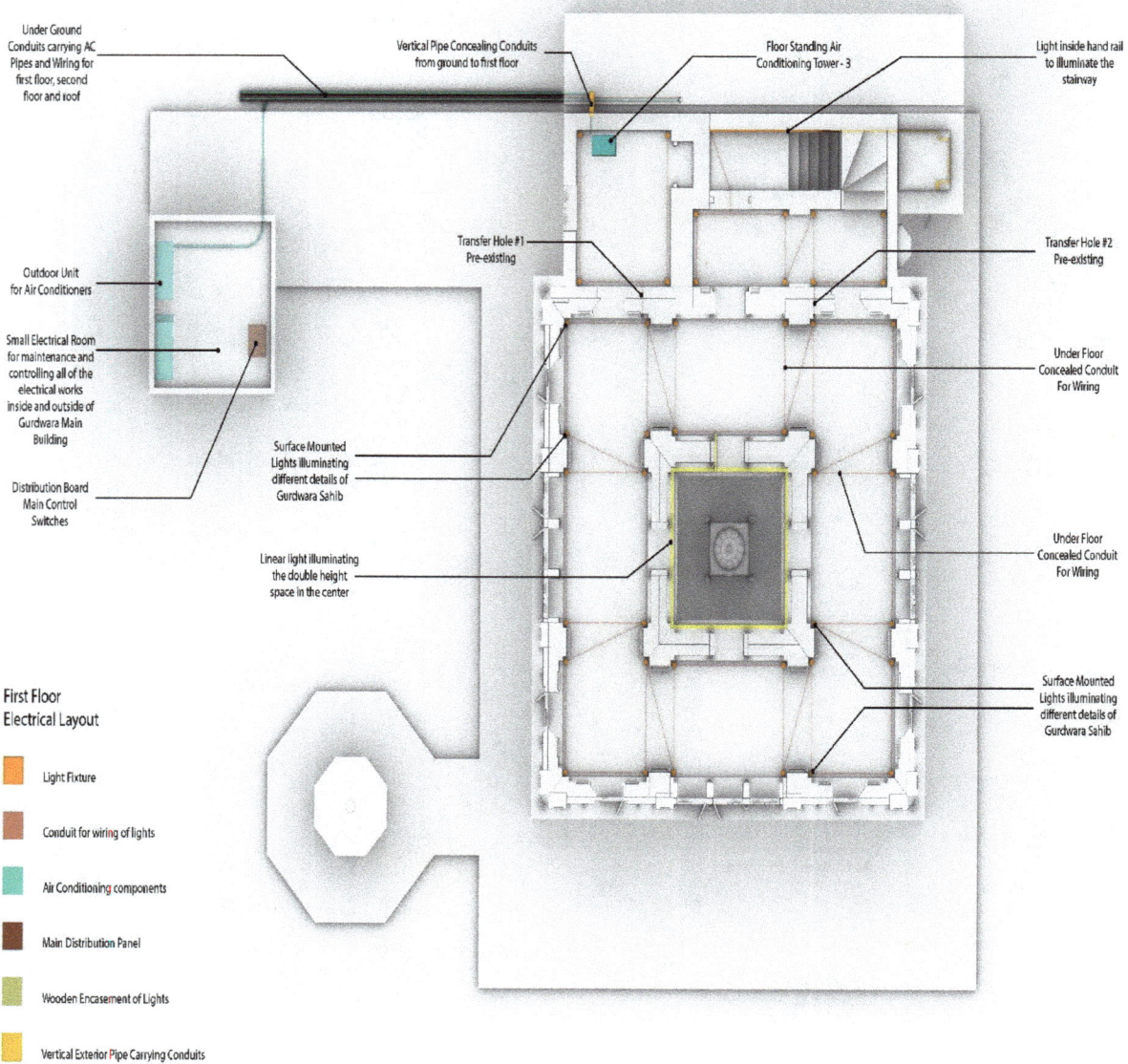

Under Ground Conduits carrying AC Pipes and Wiring for first floor, second floor and roof

Vertical Pipe Concealing Conduits from ground to first floor

Floor Standing Air Conditioning Tower - 3

Light inside hand rail to illuminate the stairway

Outdoor Unit for Air Conditioners

Small Electrical Room for maintenance and controlling all of the electrical works inside and outside of Gurdwara Main Building

Distribution Board Main Control Switches

Transfer Hole #1 Pre-existing

Transfer Hole #2 Pre-existing

Under Floor Concealed Conduit For Wiring

Surface Mounted Lights illuminating different details of Gurdwara Sahib

Linear light illuminating the double height space in the center

Under Floor Concealed Conduit For Wiring

Surface Mounted Lights illuminating different details of Gurdwara Sahib

First Floor Electrical Layout

Light Fixture

Conduit for wiring of lights

Air Conditioning components

Main Distribution Panel

Wooden Encasement of Lights

Vertical Exterior Pipe Carrying Conduits

The wiring conduit from the ground floor is ruing through a hole preexisted on the back of the building. The stairs to the first floor will get light from the handrail to illuminate.

The first-floor historically significant detail will be illuminated with the lighting through the concealed conduits. Every part of the first floor will be decorated with the central lighting method without detriment to the floor.

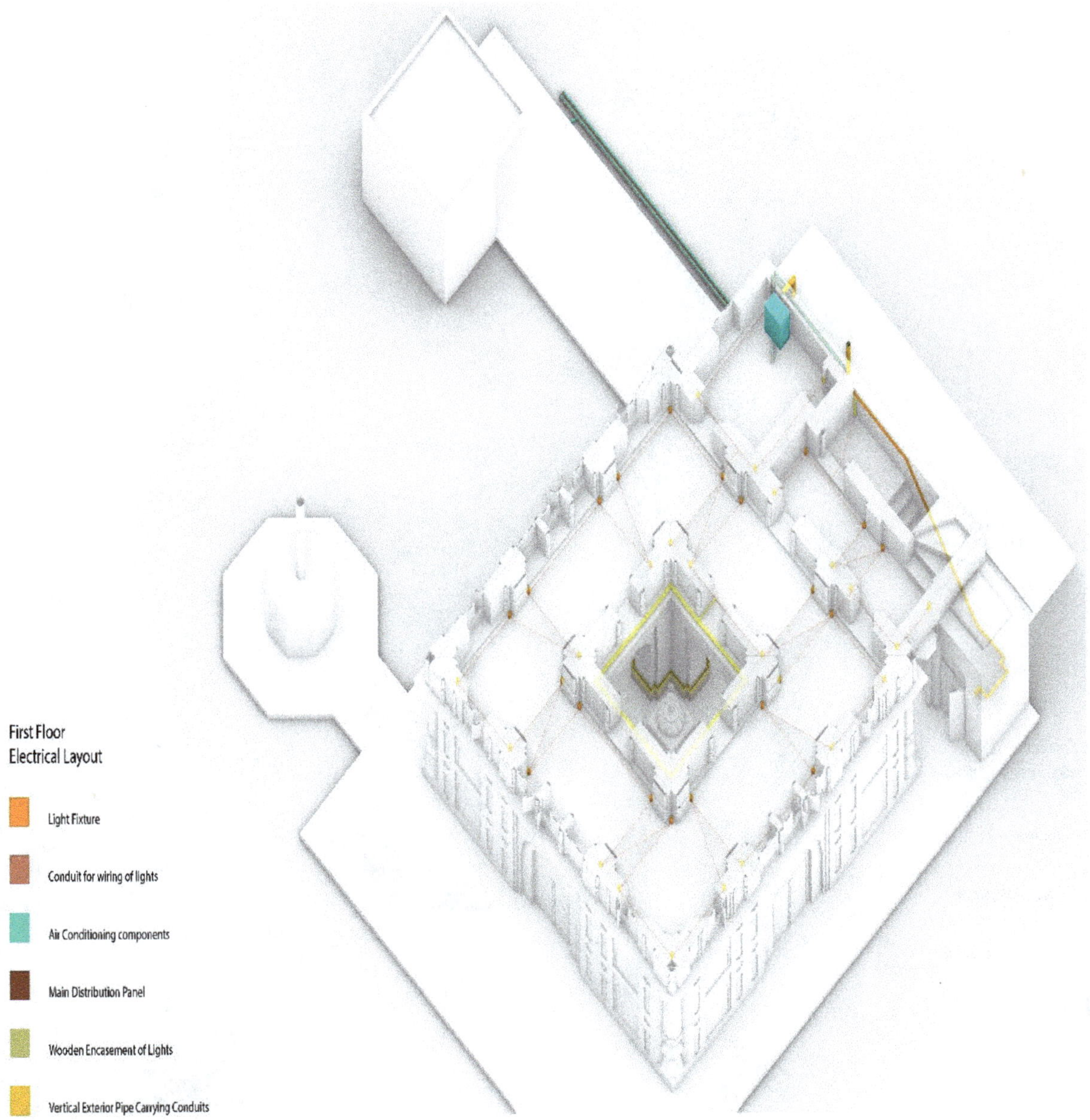

First Floor
Electrical Layout

Light Fixture

Conduit for wiring of lights

Air Conditioning components

Main Distribution Panel

Wooden Encasement of Lights

Vertical Exterior Pipe Carrying Conduits

The First floor of the Gurdwara sahib has an open area with the ground floor, and the proposed lighting plan will provide a beautiful look by indicating the historical details.

Underfloor concealed conduit for wiring is designed on the first floor. Surface-mounted lights illuminate the different details of the Gurdwara Choha Sahib Ji on the first floor.

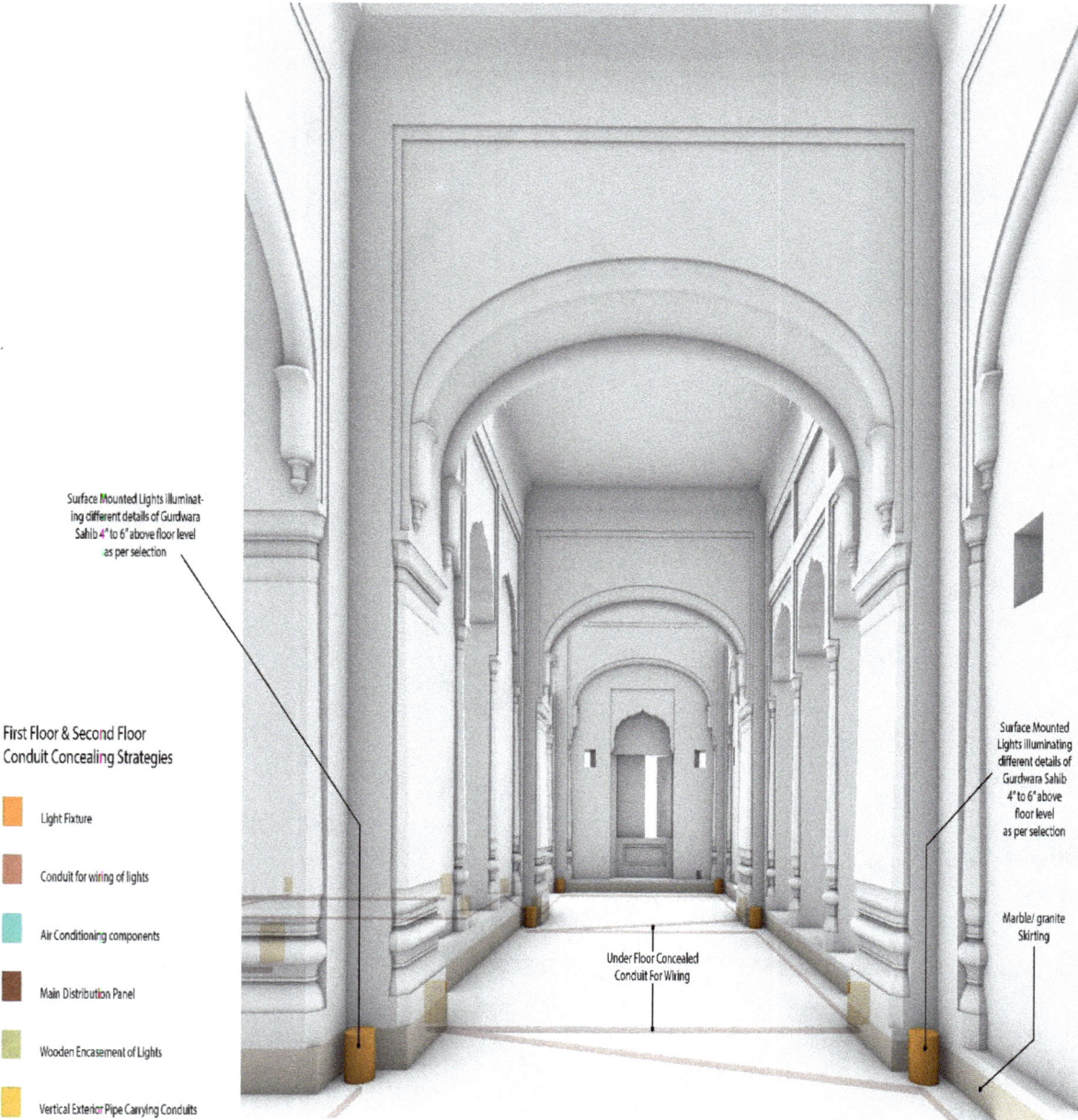

Surface Mounted Lights illuminating different details of Gurdwara Sahib 4" to 6" above floor level as per selection

Surface Mounted Lights illuminating different details of Gurdwara Sahib 4" to 6" above floor level as per selection

Marble/ granite Skirting

Under Floor Concealed Conduit For Wiring

First Floor & Second Floor Conduit Concealing Strategies

- Light Fixture
- Conduit for wiring of lights
- Air Conditioning components
- Main Distribution Panel
- Wooden Encasement of Lights
- Vertical Exterior Pipe Carrying Conduits

Marble or granite skirt will help beautify the Gurdwara Choha Sahib Ji's first floor.

The second-floor electric power design is like the first-floor design except for the air condition unit. Floor standing air conditioner is the best choice to save the historical values of the building. The second-floor details were damaged entirely after the partition of Punjab in August 1947 AD.

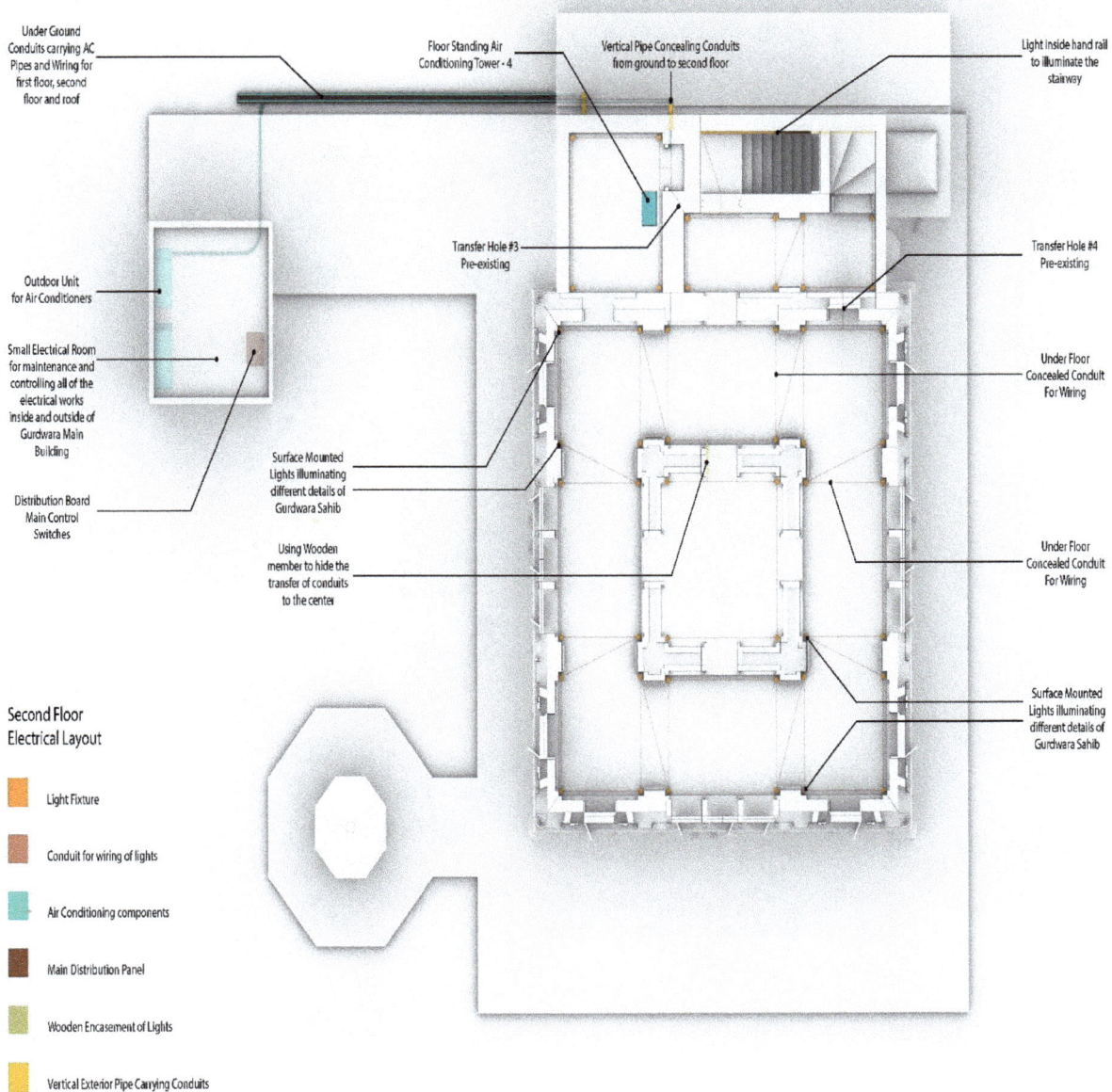

Under Ground Conduits carrying AC Pipes and Wiring for first floor, second floor and roof

Floor Standing Air Conditioning Tower - 4

Vertical Pipe Concealing Conduits from ground to second floor

Light inside hand rail to illuminate the stairway

Outdoor Unit for Air Conditioners

Transfer Hole #3 Pre-existing

Transfer Hole #4 Pre-existing

Small Electrical Room for maintenance and controlling all of the electrical works inside and outside of Gurdwara Main Building

Under Floor Concealed Conduit For Wiring

Distribution Board Main Control Switches

Surface Mounted Lights illuminating different details of Gurdwara Sahib

Under Floor Concealed Conduit For Wiring

Using Wooden member to hide the transfer of conduits to the center

Surface Mounted Lights illuminating different details of Gurdwara Sahib

Second Floor Electrical Layout

- Light Fixture
- Conduit for wiring of lights
- Air Conditioning components
- Main Distribution Panel
- Wooden Encasement of Lights
- Vertical Exterior Pipe Carrying Conduits

The second floor of the Gurdwara sahib will receive the electric power through the preexisting hole with a vertical pipe concealing the conduits from the ground.

177

The Ranjit Nagara USA team tries to design the damaged details similar to the first-floor details to keep the second floor's historical significance.

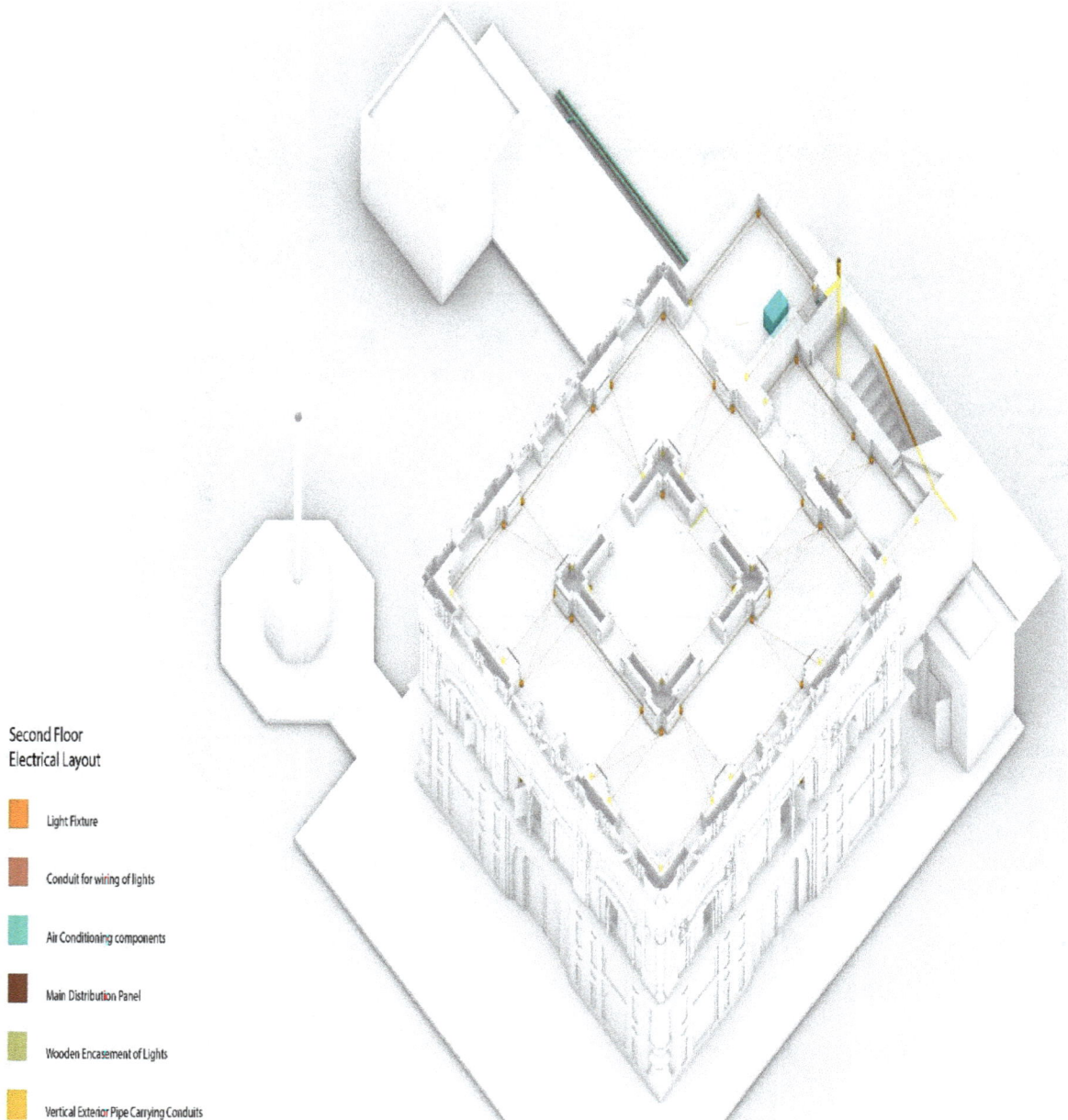

Second Floor
Electrical Layout

Light Fixture

Conduit for wiring of lights

Air Conditioning components

Main Distribution Panel

Wooden Encasement of Lights

Vertical Exterior Pipe Carrying Conduits

Wooden encasement of lights is used for the lightning on the second floor. The stair to the second floor will be illuminated through the handrail.

Rearview of the Gurdwara for the electric power supply. Vertical pipes 1 shown in the picture will light the first floor from the ground. Vertical pipe two will provide electricity to the second floor and roof of the Gurdwara Choha Sahib Ji. Both vertical pipes 1 and 2 enter inside the Gurdwara through the preexisting holes.

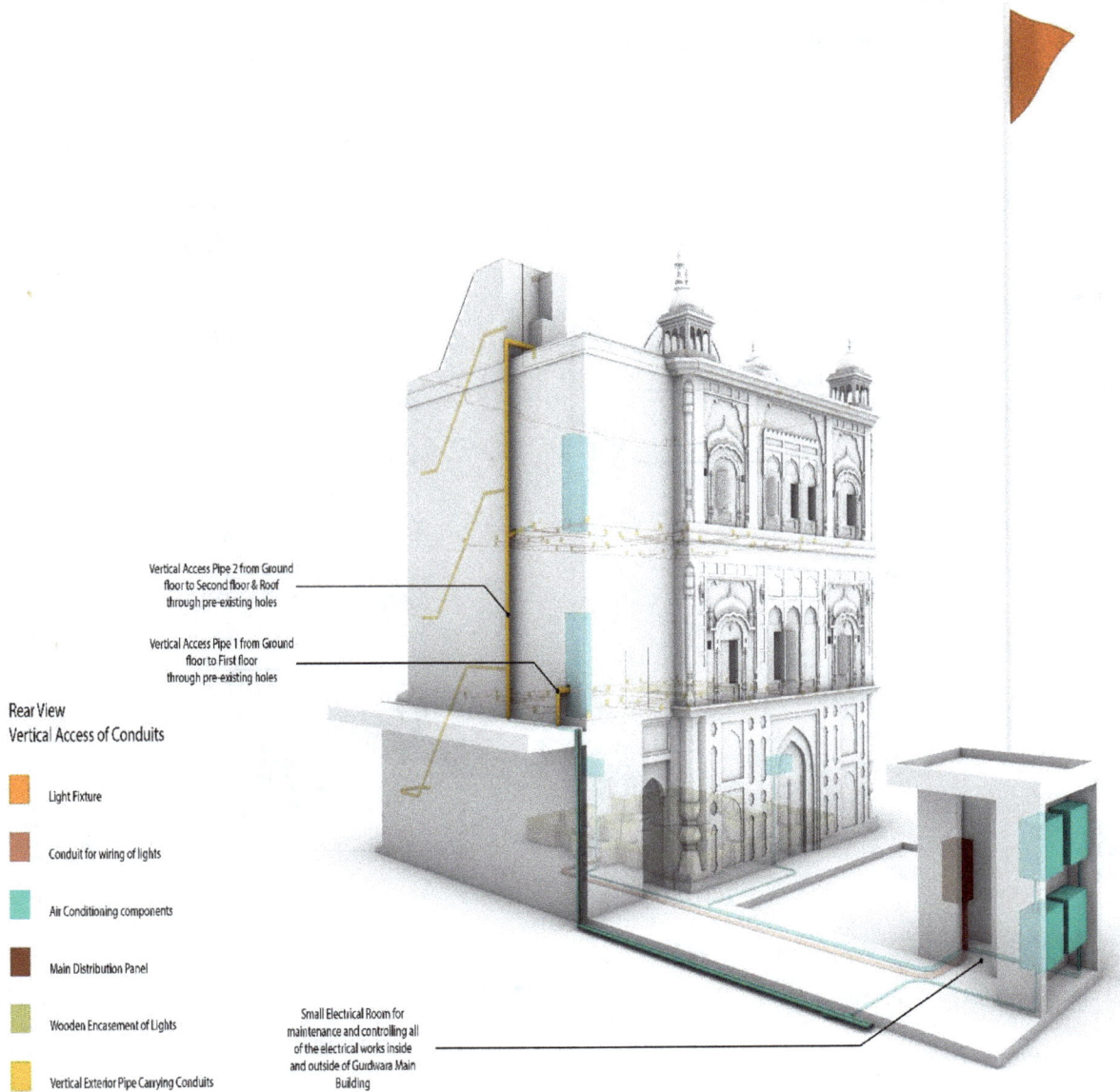

Vertical Access Pipe 2 from Ground floor to Second floor & Roof through pre-existing holes

Vertical Access Pipe 1 from Ground floor to First floor through pre-existing holes

Rear View
Vertical Access of Conduits

- Light Fixture
- Conduit for wiring of lights
- Air Conditioning components
- Main Distribution Panel
- Wooden Encasement of Lights
- Vertical Exterior Pipe Carrying Conduits

Small Electrical Room for maintenance and controlling all of the electrical works inside and outside of Gurdwara Main Building

The small electric room is used to maintain and control the electrical power and work inside and outside the main existing building of the Gurdwara Choha Sahib Ji.

179

The roof of the Gurdwara Sahib has a beautiful outside view, and illuminating it at night will get an excellent look. The roof has four Gumties (small dome), one Palki (mid-sized rectangle dome), and the Gurmat (central main dome) of the building.

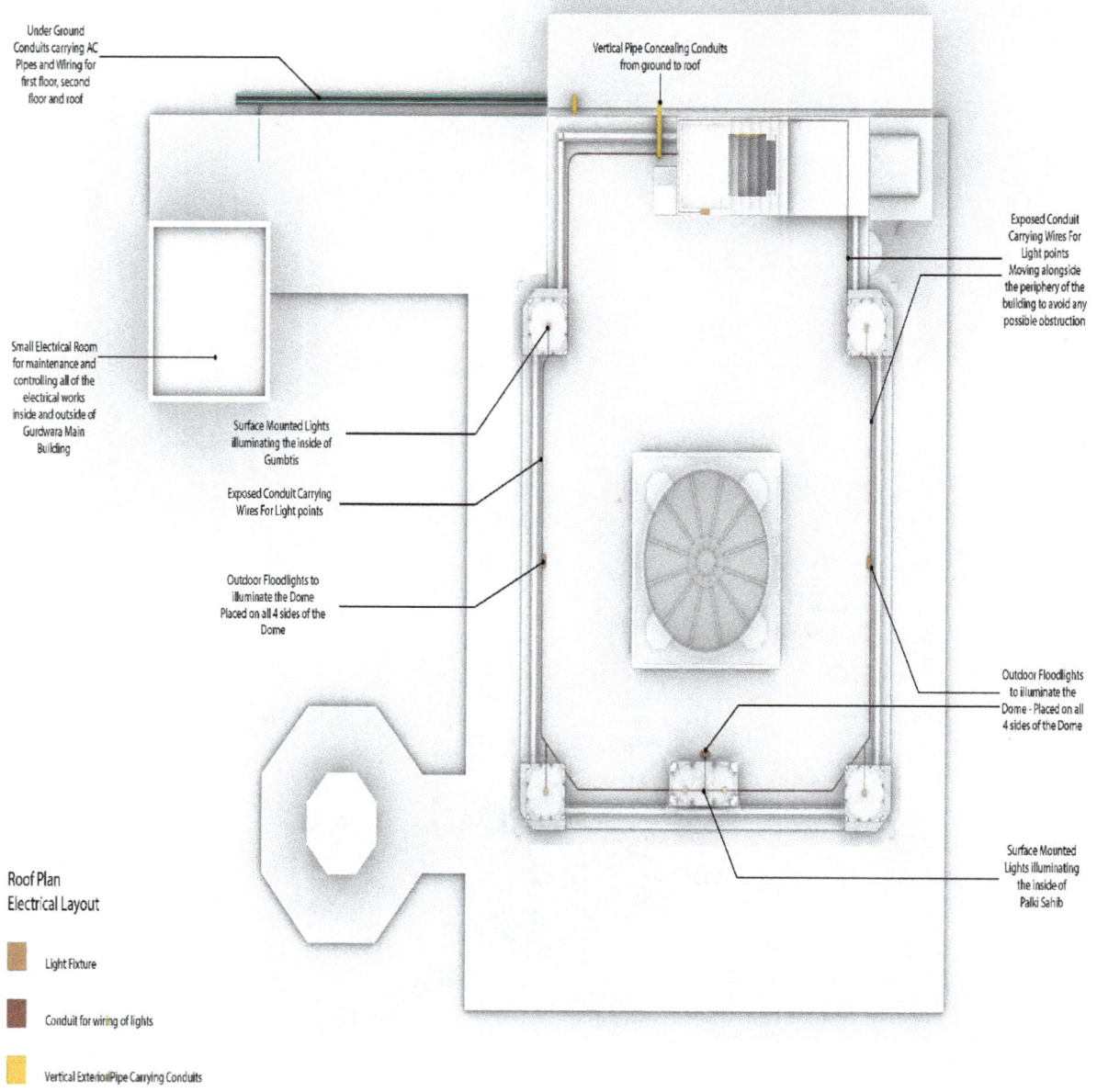

Under Ground Conduits carrying AC Pipes and Wiring for first floor, second floor and roof

Vertical Pipe Concealing Conduits from ground to roof

Exposed Conduit Carrying Wires For Light points Moving alongside the periphery of the building to avoid any possible obstruction

Small Electrical Room for maintenance and controlling all of the electrical works inside and outside of Gurdwara Main Building

Surface Mounted Lights illuminating the inside of Gumbtis

Exposed Conduit Carrying Wires For Light points

Outdoor Floodlights to illuminate the Dome Placed on all 4 sides of the Dome

Outdoor Floodlights to illuminate the Dome - Placed on all 4 sides of the Dome

Surface Mounted Lights illuminating the inside of Palki Sahib

Roof Plan
Electrical Layout

Light Fixture

Conduit for wiring of lights

Vertical Exterior Pipe Carrying Conduits

All Gumties and Main Gumat will get illuminated with electric power. Surface-mounted light is a perfect source for illumining them. Outdoor floodlights to illuminate the dome will be placed on all four sides of the central dome.

The four Gumties will be illuminated through the four different outdoor lights. The Palki will have two lights inside it because of its rectangular nature and size. The electric wire will be run through the concealed conduit on the roof floor.

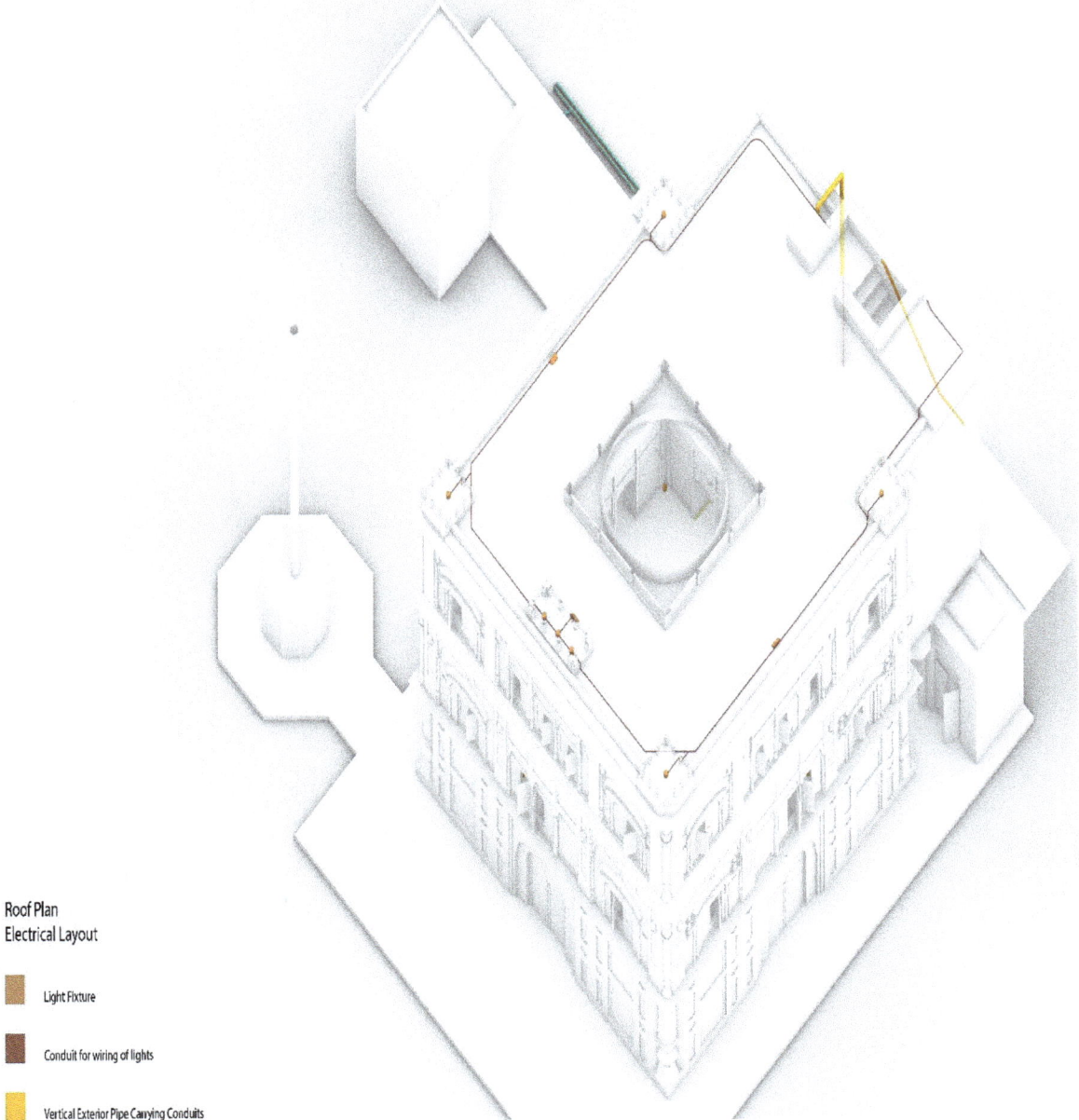

Roof Plan
Electrical Layout

Light Fixture

Conduit for wiring of lights

Vertical Exterior Pipe Carrying Conduits

The stair to the roof will be illuminated through its handrail. It will also have the floodlight and the stairs' end toward the roof.

The four floodlights were specially installed to glorify the main Gumat at night and in the dark, through the marked spots in the picture from four sides in the middles.

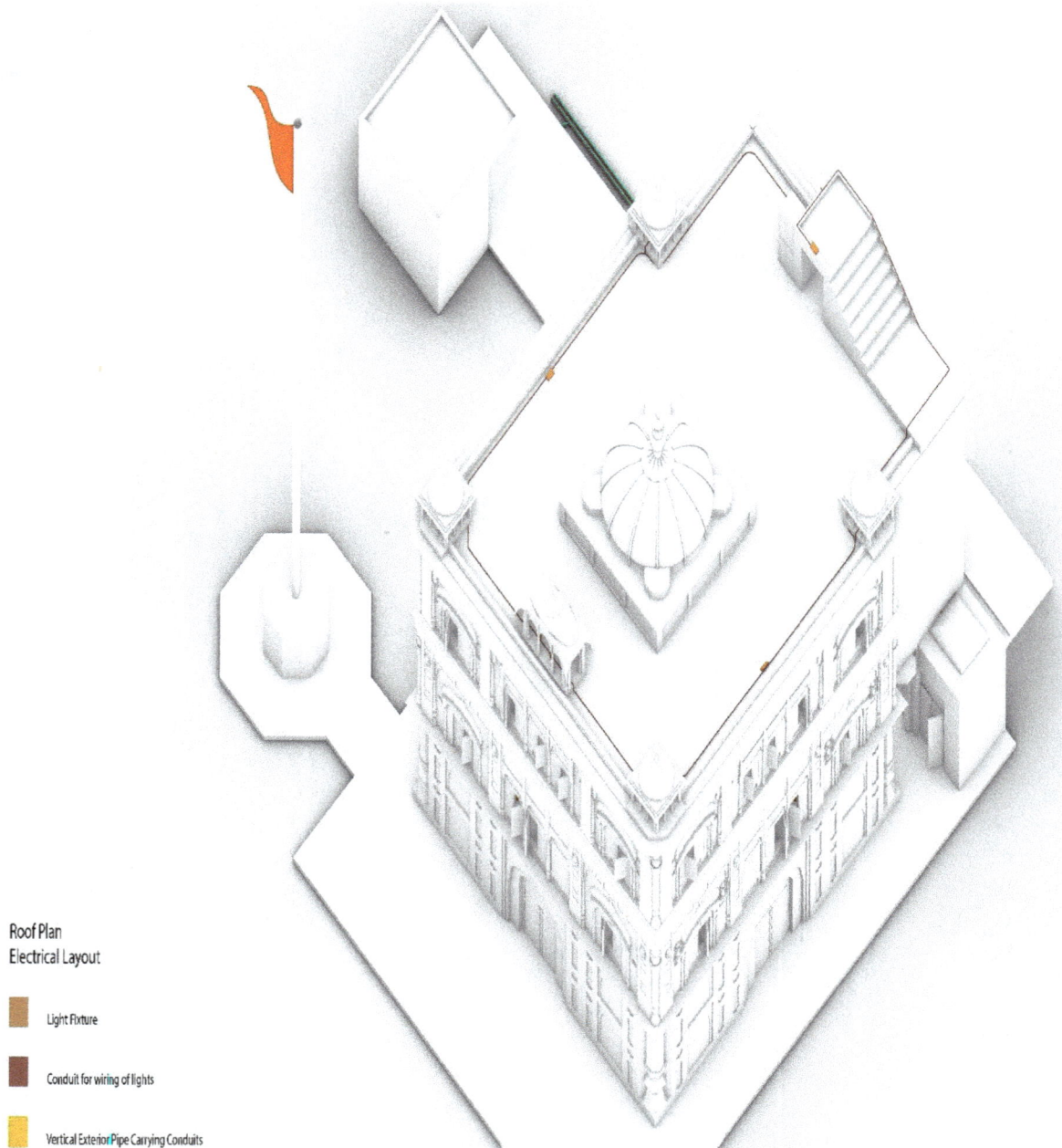

Roof Plan
Electrical Layout

Light Fixture

Conduit for wiring of lights

Vertical Exterior Pipe Carrying Conduits

The outdoor lights are also designed in a way that Nishan Sahib will get visible at night from far away roads. It will guide the needier to get help 24 hours when required in food, room, protection, or other possible ways.

Roof illuminating exposed conduit and lighting view placements in the Gumties and the middle of the sidewall and their effect on the Nishan Sahib, Gumties, and main Gumat can be seen clearly in the picture. The Nishan Sahib is 51 feet high, and the lighting from the roof will glorify it at night.

Roof View
Exposed Conduit/ Light Fixture Placement

Light Fixture

Conduit for wiring of lights

Vertical Exterior Pipe Carrying Conduits

The Electric design will glorify the Gurdwara Choha Sahib Ji at night and be visible from miles away. Gurdwaras Choha Sahib will provide the facilities to the needier and pilgrims like Langer (free kitchen to everyone), Sra (free-living quarters), medical aid, etc.

Restoration Contract of Gurdwara Choha Sahib JI

Restoration contract of Gurdwara Choha Sahib Ji, Rohtas, Jhelum

Satpreet Singh wrote the Gurdwara Choha Sahib Ji restoration contract to control the unnecessary and unwanted expenses and confusion. The architect hired for the Gurdwara Choha Sahib Ji worked with the direct instruction of Satpreet Singh to draft the bill of quantities. But as everyone knows, the countries on the Asian side have many issues and complications. The same thing happens before finalizing the restoration contract of Gurdwara Choha Sahib Ji.

Ranjit Nagara USA asked the architect and restorer to draft the bill of quantities (BOQ) and provide it to Ranjit Nagara USA before the start of the project in August 2020. But Architect team was unable to deliver before April 2021 means approximately half of the work was already completed. It was believed that the architect was intentionally delaying the BOQ and other paperwork to delay the project for a long-time of work to benefit themself. However, with the strong demand from Ranjit Nagara USA. The architect and her team send the BOQ to Satpreet Singh, the director of Ranjit Nagara, at the end of April 2021. Many things were unclear, and many were hidden in the BOQ. Satpreet Singh tried to clarify those issues with the architect and restorer. They were not answering, wasting time, and delaying the project. Even Ranjit Nagara USA was aware of the architect's hidden and clever moves in the BOQ. Ranjit Nagara USA prepared a contract given in the following pages by adding some detail and asking to sign. As per the restorer, he was not aware of the clever moves of the architects and later in December 2021 provided a statement to Ranjit Nagara that the architect told him to keep it hidden from the Ranjit Nagara USA. Ranjit Nagara USA prepared a contract to bond and control the cleverness, whether an architect or restorer.

Because of the past claver incidents of architects, In May 2021, Ranjit Nagara instructed and explained to the architect and restorer that the restorer who will restore the building would directly communicate with Ranjit Nagara USA instead of through the architect in the future. Later, those architects were removed from the project in November 2021 because of their clever move to hide things and perform detrimental unauthorized work performed at the Gurdwara Choha Sahib Ji. Each page of the restoration was either signed or initialized by the restorer. The complete contract was on the letterhead of Ranjit Nagara USA with the following information.

RANJIT NAGARA

1463 Moffat Blvd, Ste 9, Manteca, CA 95336
PH: (888) 762-4262, Fax: (209) 502-6805
Email: info@ranjitnagara.org
www.ranjitnagara.org

GURDWARA CHOHA SAHIB JI BUILDING RESTORATION CONTRACT

This Agreement, is made and entered this ____27th____ day of ____May____, 2021, by and between the RANJIT NAGARA, a California based USA Non-Profit organization ("RANJIT NAGARA") and ISHTIAQ ISHAQ DBA HERITAGE CONSTRUCTIONS ("Contractor").

WHEREAS, the Gurdwara Choha (Chowa or Choa) Sahib Ji located in Jhelum near Rohtas Fort on one side and river Ghan on the other side (hereinafter, "Gurdwara Choha Sahib Ji"); and

WHEREAS, Contractor is in the business of restoration of historical Construction and Renovation; and

WHEREAS, Contractor has indicated a willingness to undertake restoration and renovate within the Gurdwara Choha Sahib Ji; and

WHEREAS, the RANJIT NAGARA has appropriated funds equal to the payments due Contractor under this Agreement; and

WHEREAS, the RANJIT NAGARA wishes to authorize Contractor to undertake restoration and renovation within the Gurdwara Choha Sahib Ji, under the terms set forth herein.

NOW, THEREFORE, IN LIGHT OF THE FOREGOING RECITALS, THE PARTIES AGREE AS FOLLOWS:

I. Scope of Work - Contract Documents.

Attached hereto and designated Exhibit A, entitled in BOQ and dated April 10th, 2021, and Exhibit B and Exhibit C and Exhibit D and Exhibit E is a description of the scope and nature of the work contemplated under this Agreement. Exhibit A, Exhibit B, Exhibit C, Exhibit D will be the primary source of Contractor's undertakings with respect to restoration and construction services under this Agreement.

The parties understand that, given their mutual desire to complete restoration and construction within the Gurdwara Choha Sahib Ji at a cost defined herein, the scope of work under this Agreement will not be materially changed except as provided in Section II below with respect to Change Orders.

Contractor shall furnish all labor, services, materials, tools, and equipment for the restoration , renovation and construction and completion of the work described in Exhibit A, Exhibit B, Exhibit C, Exhibit D and in any Change, Orders approved as provided in Section II below.

II. Change Orders

A. Any material changes to the scope of work contemplated under Section I above shall be accomplished only as provided in this Section II.

m ishtiaq
m ishtiaq (Jun 2, 2021 23:24 GMT+5)

B. Should either party determine that a material change to the scope of work contemplated. under Section I of this Agreement is necessary or advisable, the particular change shall be set forth in a writing entitled "Change Order, [date]", and shall bear the signatures of authorized person of Contractor and RANJIT NAGARA (Head Office) of each party. Upon execution by both parties of any such Change Order, the scope of work contemplated under this Agreement shall be deemed modified and incorporated by this reference into this Agreement as if set forth fully herein. RANJIT NAGARA will retain all original Change Orders approved pursuant to this Section II, and Contractor shall be provided a copy for its files.

C. RANJIT NAGARA shall grant, deny or request a reasonable extension of time within twenty-four hours of a request for a Change Order by the Contractor. In the event a proposed change order adds to the compensable work to be performed by the Contractor, the Change Order so given shall contain written assurance by the RANJIT NAGARA that lawful appropriations to cover the costs of the additional work have been made and the appropriations are available prior to performance of the additional work.

III. Project Commencement, Progress and Completion

A. Contractor's restoration, renovation and construction services already started on November 01st, 2020. Such restoration and construction services shall be substantially completed no later than August 01st 2021 (plus/minus four (4) month, subject to weather-related delays and agreed extensions of time as authorized by the RANJIT NAGARA. Contractor will undertake the work in a thorough and workmanlike manner in every respect and in compliance with all applicable RANJIT NAGARA AND SIKH construction codes and any applicable requirements to which the Gurdwara Choha Sahib Ji is subject. In case of any conflict between the Contractor's specifications and the applicable RANJIT NAGARA (SIKH) construction codes and/or applicable requirements, the latter shall control.

B. Given the need for governmental operations within the Gurdwara Choha Sahib Ji, timely completion of the restoration and construction services contemplated herein is essential. Time is of the essence in all respects regarding the undertakings of Contractor under this Agreement. Therefore, Contractor shall carry out restoration and construction services within the Gurdwara Choha Sahib Ji with all due diligence. Contractor agrees to furnish efficient business administration and superintendence, and to use its best efforts to furnish at all times an adequate supply of workers and materials to assure the expeditious and economical completion of the restoration and construction work contemplated herein.

C. Contractor shall be responsible for providing suitable site barricading and traffic control facilities for ensuring the safety of the public during the performance of the work and for maintaining access through and adjacent to the area in which the work is to be performed.

D. Until the final acceptance of the work by the RANJIT NAGARA in writing, Contractor shall have the charge and care thereof, and shall take every necessary precaution against injury or damage to any part thereof by the effects of the elements or from any other cause. Contractor, at its own expense, shall rebuild, repair, restore, and correct all injuries or damages to any portion of the work occasioned by any causes before its completion and acceptance. In case of suspension of work from any cause whatsoever, Contractor shall be responsible for all building materials and shall properly store same, if necessary, and shall provide suitable drainage, barricades, and warning signs where necessary. Contractor shall correct

189

or replace, at its own expense and as required by RANJIT NAGARA, any building material or portions thereof which may be destroyed, lost, damaged, or in any way made useless for the purpose and use intended by the contract documents, plans, and specifications prior to final acceptance of the work. Contractor shall be relieved of the responsibilities provided in this section upon final acceptance of the work by RANJIT NAGARA, except no such relief shall apply to damages or injuries caused by or related to actions of Contractor or its subcontractors.

E. Contractor shall at all times comply with applicable workplace and occupational safety requirements under state and federal law, including but not limited to those regulations within the authority of the United States Department of Labor Occupational Safety and Health Administration and/or Pakistan labor department occupational safety and health administration.

F. The project will be considered complete when all work has been finished, the final inspection made, and the work accepted by RANJIT NAGARA in writing, and all claims for payment of labor, materials, or services of any kind used in connection with the work thereof have been paid or settled by Contractor or its surety. Contractor will then be released from further obligation except as set forth in the surety bond, and except as required in this Agreement and the contract documents regarding the Contractor's guaranty of work.

IV. Relationship of Contractor to RANJIT NAGARA

A. Contractor acknowledges that it, its employees and sub-contractors, if any, are in the relationship of independent contractor, and not as employees of the RANJIT NAGARA. Nonetheless, Contractor accepts the relationship of trust and confidence established between it and the RANJIT NAGARA by this Agreement. Contractor covenants with the RANJIT NAGARA to furnish its best skill and judgment and to assure its restoration and construction services are undertaken and completed as contemplated herein.

B. The RANJIT NAGARA's Project head for all purposes under this Agreement is SATPREET SINGH, and all communications from Contractor to RANJIT NAGARA arising out of this Agreement shall be directed to SATPREET SINGH's attention, except as he may specifically designate in writing.

V. Representations of the Parties.

A. Contractor's Representations.

1. The Contractor has familiarized itself with the nature and the extent of the contract documents, work, the locality, all physical characteristics of the area, including without limitation, improvements, soil conditions, drainage, topography, and all other features of the terrain, and with the local conditions and federal, state, and local laws, ordinances, rules, and regulations that in any manner may affect cost, progress, or performance of the work, or apply in any manner whatsoever to the work.

2. Contractor has given the RANJIT NAHARA written notice of all apparent conflicts, errors, discrepancies, or inconsistencies it has discovered in the contract documents, and such documents are acceptable to the Contractor as incorporated herein.

m ishtiaq

B. RANJIT NAGARA's Representations.

1. The RANJIT NAGARA is a USA based nonprofit Corporation, governed by the laws and Constitution of the State of California, USA and United States of America.

2. The RANJIT NAGARA has given Contractor written notice of all apparent conflicts, errors, discrepancies or inconsistencies it has discovered in the contract documents, and such documents are acceptable to the RANJIT NAGARA as incorporated herein.

VI. Payment to Contractor.

A. Contractor agrees to accept the lump-sum (26,339,567 Pakistan Rupees) set forth in the attached Exhibit E (Bid Proposal dated April 10th , 2021) as full payment (in Five Installments)for the performance of the restoration and construction services contemplated under this Agreement, which sum shall be decreased or increased only by the amount representing the associated cost of any and all Change Orders approved as provided in Section II above.

B. Notwithstanding the terms of sub-section VI (A) above, the RANJIT NAGARA shall be responsible for

the payment of all inspection fees, plan review fees, engineering consultant fees and architectural fees.

C. No funds payable under this Agreement shall become due and payable until the Contractor shall provide the RANJIT NAGARA with satisfactory assurances that Contractor has fully settled or paid for all materials and equipment used in or upon the work and labor done in connection therewith, including written evidence that all persons who have done work or furnished material for work done on the Gurdwara Choha Sahib Ji. RANJIT NAGARA may pay any or all such claims or bills, wholly or in part, and deduct the amount or amounts so paid from any funds due Contractor.

D. No later than the fifteenth day of each quarter (3 month), Contractor shall submit to the RANJIT NAGARA for review and approval an application for payment fully completed and signed by Contractor describing the work completed through the last day of the prior quarter and accompanied by such supporting documentation as may be requested by the RANJIT NAGARA. Materials on hand but not

complete in place may be included for payment at the discretion of the RANJIT NAGARA. Each subsequent application for payment shall include a certification of Contractor that all previous progress payments received on account of the work have been applied to discharge in full all of Contractor's obligations reflected in prior applications for payment. The RANJIT NAGARA shall within fifteen days of receipt of Contractor's completed application for payment, pay an amount equal to ninety percent (90%) of the requested payment, with the remaining ten percent (10%) held as

retainage.

E. Upon final completion of all restoration and construction services contemplated herein, the RANJIT NAGARA shall within ten (10) days pay to Contractor the retainage accumulated under subsection VI (D) of this Agreement in addition to any other sums properly due Contractor upon final completion.

VII. Ownership of Plans, Specifications, and Documents.

m ishtiaq

All of the plans and the contract documents are and shall remain the property of the RANJIT NAGARA.

Contractor shall be provided plans, specifications, permits, and other documents and materials

required to perform the work. The plans and specifications are not to be used on other work, and

upon final payment or termination of Contractor's services all plan sets shall be returned to RANJIT NAGARA.

VIII. Indemnification.

To the fullest extent permitted by law, the Contractor agrees to indemnify and hold harmless the RANJIT NAGARA, and its officers and its employees, from and against all liability, claims, and demands, on account of any injury, loss, or damage, which arise out of or are connected with the Work, if such injury, loss, or damage, or any portion thereof, is caused by, or claimed to be caused by, the act, omission, or other fault of the Contractor or any subcontractor of the Contractor, or any officer, employee, or agent of the Contractor or any subcontractor, or any other person for whom

Contractor is responsible. The Contractor shall investigate, handle, respond to, and provide defense for and defend against any such liability, claims, and demands, and to bear all other costs and expenses related thereto, including court costs and attorneys' fees. The Contractor's indemnification obligation shall not be construed to extend to any injury, loss, or damage which is caused by the act, omission, or other fault of the RANJIT NAGARA.

IX. Insurance and Bonds.

A. Contractor shall not commence work under this Agreement until it has presented Certificates of Insurance as required by sub-section IX (C) below, confirming it has obtained all insurance and bonds required by the Section IX, and with the minimum insurance coverage as

follows:

(1) Workers' Compensation insurance to cover obligations imposed by the Workers' Compensation Act of Pakistan and any other applicable laws for any employee engaged in the performance of Work under this contract, and Employers' Liability insurance with minimum limits of set forth in Punjab, Pakistan labor law for each accident, disease - policy limit OR Contractor will provide the signed undertaking about the insurance of the workers on site.

(2) Comprehensive General Liability insurance with minimum combined single limits of as per Punjab, Pakistan or Pakistan contractor liability law for each occurrence and aggregate. The policy shall be applicable to all premises and operations. The policy shall include coverage for bodily injury, broad form property damage (including completed operations), personal injury (including coverage for contractual and employee acts), blanket contractual, independent contractors, products, and completed operations.

The policy shall contain a severability of interests provision. OR Contractor will provide the signed undertaking about the General liability of Insurance.

(3) Comprehensive Automobile Liability insurance with minimum combined single limits for bodily injury and property damage of not less than as per Punjab Pakistan and/or Pakistan Automobile Liability insurance each accident with respect to each of Contractor's owned, hired and/or non-owned vehicles assigned to or used in performance of the services. The policy shall contain a severability of interests provision. OR Contractor will provide the signed undertaking about the Auto liability Insurance.

(4) Builder's Risk insurance with minimum limits of not less than the insurable value of the work to be performed under this contract at completion and equipment insured under installation floater insurance. The policy shall be written in completed value form and shall protect the Contractor and the RANJIT NAGARA against risks of damage to buildings, structures, and materials and equipment not otherwise covered under Installation Floater insurance, from the perils of fire and lightning, the perils included in the standard coverage endorsement, and the perils of vandalism and malicious mischief. The policy shall provide for losses to be payable to the Contractor and the RANJIT NAGARA as their interests may appear. The policy shall contain a provision that in the event of payment for any loss under the coverage provided, the insurance company shall have no rights of recovery against the Contractor or the RANJIT NAGARA. OR Contractor will provide the signed undertaking about the Builder's Risk Insurance and site equipment insurance.

(5) Installation Floater with minimum limits of not less than the insurable value of the work to be performed under this contract at completion, less the value of the materials and equipment insured under Builder's Risk insurance. The value shall include the aggregate value of any RANJIT NAGARA-furnished equipment and materials to be erected or installed by the Contractor not otherwise insured under Builder's Risk insurance. The policy shall protect the Contractor and the RANJIT NAGARA from all insurable risks of physical loss or damage to materials and equipment not otherwise covered under Builder's Risk insurance, while in warehouses or storage areas, during installation, during testing, and after the work under this contract is completed. The policy shall be of the "all risks" type, with coverage designed for the circumstances which may occur in the particular work to be performed under this contract. The policy shall provide for losses to be payable to the Contractor and the RANJIT NAGARA as their interests may appear. The policy shall contain a provision that in the event of payment for any loss under the coverage provided, the insurance company shall have no rights of recovery against the Contractor or the RANJIT NAGARA. OR Contractor will provide the signed undertaking.

B. The policies required above, except for the Workers' Compensation insurance and Employers' Liability insurance, shall be endorsed to include the RANJIT NAGARA as additional insured's. Every policy required by above shall be primary insurance, and any insurance carried by the RANJIT NAGARA, its officers, or its employees, shall not cover contractor, contractor's subcontractor, or Contractor's employee, Contractor's equipment. The additional insured endorsement for the Comprehensive General Liability insurance required above shall not contain any exclusion for bodily injury or property damage arising from completed operations. The Contractor shall be solely responsible for any deductible losses under each of the policies required above. OR Contractor will provide the signed undertaking.

C. Certificates of Insurance shall be completed by the Contractor's insurance agent as evidence that policies providing the required coverage, conditions, and minimum limits are in full force and effect, and shall be subject to review on demand by the RANJIT NAGARA. Each certificate shall identify the Project and shall provide that the coverage afforded under the policies shall not be cancelled, terminated, or materially changed until at least 30 days prior written notice has been given to the RANJIT NAGARA. The RANJIT NAGARA reserves the right to request and receive a certified copy of any policy and any endorsement thereto. OR Contractor will provide the signed undertaking.

D Failure on the part of the Contractor to procure or maintain policies as provided herein shall constitute a material breach of contract upon which the RANJIT NAGARA may immediately terminate the contract, or at its discretion may procure or renew any such policy or any extended reporting period thereto and may pay any and all premiums in connection therewith, and all monies so paid by the RANJIT NAGARA shall be repaid by Contractor to the RANJIT NAGARA upon demand, or the RANJIT NAGARA may offset the cost of the premiums against any monies due to Contractor from the Owner.

E. Contractor shall furnish a performance bond, payment bond, and warranty bond in an amount at least equal to the contract price, as security for the faithful performance and payment of all Contractor's obligations under the contract documents, including but not limited to the guarantee period provided in Section X. All bonds shall be in the forms acceptable by the RANJIT NAGARA's head office.

F. In the event the surety on any contract, performance bond, payment bond, or warranty bond given by the Contractor becomes insolvent, or is placed in the hands of a receiver, or has its right to do business in Punjab, Pakistan revoked, the RANJIT NAGARA may withhold payment of funds due Contractor until the Contractor has provided a bond or other security to the satisfaction of the RANJIT NAGARA in lieu of the bond so executed by such surety.

X. Contractor's Guarantee of Work.

Contractor shall guarantee all work under this Agreement as being free of defects. Contractor will provide signed undertaking withing 10 business days after signing this agreement that (a) Contractor material has life more than hundred (100) years from the date of final acceptance by RANJIT NAGARA, if properly maintained, (b) Contractor will not use any inferior material, defective material, poor quality material, (b) Contractor will not use poor skilled or unskilled labor for restoration, (c) Contractor will be held responsible for workmanship and fix the required defects because of workmanship for a period of 12 month free of cost to RANJIT NAGARA or Gurdwara Choha Sahib Ji, (d) Contractor will not be held or liable for anything above, if any other contract (not related to the contractor in this agreement or without

194

his chance to fix the defect) performed the restoration work in the same area where this contractor worked. Any roofing membrane and related systems will same guarantee and warranties mentioned above. If any unsatisfactory condition or damage develops within the time of Contractor's guarantee period due to defective or inferior materials or workmanship, or not constructed in accordance with the Agreement, then the Contractor shall upon notice by RANJIT NAGARA, immediately place such guaranteed work in a condition satisfactory to RANJIT NAGARA. The RANJIT NAGARA shall have all available remedies to enforce such guarantee. However, RANJIT NAGARA shall not have any work performed independently to fulfill contractor's guarantee and require Contractor to pay RANJIT NAGARA such sums as were expended by the RANJIT NAGARA for such work, unless the RANJIT NAGARA has first given notice to the Contractor of the deficiency and given the Contractor a reasonable opportunity to cure the same.

XI. Costs and Attorneys' Fees. In the event of litigation enforcing or interpreting the terms of the within Agreement, and only in the event the RANJIT NAGARA is the prevailing party, the RANJIT NAGARA shall be entitled an award of reasonable attorney fees and all costs of suit, including expert witness fees, court reporter fees and similar litigation expenses.

XII. No Assignment.

This Agreement shall not be assigned by the Contractor without the prior written approval of the RANJIT NAGARA. However, Contractor shall have the right to employ such assistance as may be required for the performance of the project, including the use of subcontractors, which employment shall not be deemed an assignment of the Contractor's rights and duties hereunder.

XIII. Governing Law, Place of Trial.

The parties agree to the jurisdiction and venue of the courts of Punjab (Pakistan) and/or Pakistan and/or International, and or United States of America, and/ or California (USA), in connection with any dispute arising out of or in any matter connected with this Agreement. The parties further agree that the interpretation and enforcement of the within Agreement shall be in accordance with United State of America and/or CA (USA) and/or International and/or Pakistan, and/or Punjab (Pakistan).

XIV. Required Pakistan resident Certification.

Under United Satates of America and/or Pakistan and/or International law., Contractor by its signature hereto certifies and represents that at this time:

(i) Contractor does not knowingly employ or contract with an illegal alien, criminal background worker who willperform work under this Contract; and

(ii) Contractor will participate in the verification of labor law program authorized under Pakistan labor law.

(iii) If Contractor obtains actual knowledge that a subcontractor performing work under this Contract

knowingly employs or contracts with an illegal alien, or has criminal background then Contractor shall:

m ishtiaq
m ishtiaq (Jun 2, 2021 23:24 GMT+5)

195

(i) Notify such subcontractor and the RANJIT NAGARA within three days that Contractor has actual knowledge that the subcontractor is employing or contracting with an illegal alien and/or criminal background worker: and

(ii) Terminate the subcontract with the subcontractor if within three days of receiving the notice required pursuant to this section the subcontractor does not cease employing or contracting with the illegal alien and/or criminal background; except that Contractor shall not terminate the contract with the subcontractor if during such three days the subcontractor provides information to establish that the subcontractor has not knowingly employed or contracted with an illegal alien or criminal background worker. Contractor shall comply with any reasonable request by the government agencies and RANJIT NAGARA.

If Contractor violates any provision of this Contract pertaining to the duties imposed by

United States of America and/or California (USA) and/or Pakistan and/or Punjab (Pakistan), the RANJIT NAGARA may terminate this Contract. If this Contract is so terminated, Contractor shall be liable for actual and consequential damages to the RANJIT NAGARA arising out of Contractor's violation.

Contractor acknowledges the enforcement of all provisions of RANJIT NAGARA, and further

acknowledges that employment of illegal aliens and/or Criminal background worker in violation thereof may result in loss of Contractor's "business license" as defined therein, together with such other enforcement measures as authorized by law.

XV. RANJIT NAGARA Labor Clause.

Contractor agrees, pursuant to RANJIT NAGARA by laws., that Contractor shall employ RANJIT NAGARA

labor (as defined below in this paragraph) to perform the Work to the extent of not less than eighty percent of each type or class of labor in the several classifications of skilled and common labor employed under this Agreement. "RANJIT NAGARA" as used in this Agreement means any person who is a resident of the PAKISTAN, at the time of employment, without discrimination as to race, color, creed, sex, sexual orientation, marital status, national origin, ancestry, age, or religion except when sex or age is a bona fide occupational qualification.

m ishtiaq
m ishtiaq (Jun 2, 2021 23:24 GMT+5)

ISHTIAQ ISHAQ
DBA HERITAGE CONSTRUCTIONS
CONTRACTOR

satpreet singh
satpreet singh (Jun 2, 2021 13:33 PDT)

SATPREET SINGH, Director
RANJIT NAGATA

Exhibit A

CONTENTS:

- Gurdwara (GR) - Ground Floor
- GR - First Floor
- GR - Second Floor
- Attachment (ATT) - First Floor, Second Floor
- Attachment Room (ATT - AR)
- Roof (RF)
- Floors (FL)
- Ceilings (CG)
- Appendix Arches, Colum ns, Chattris
- Palki and Gumties

197

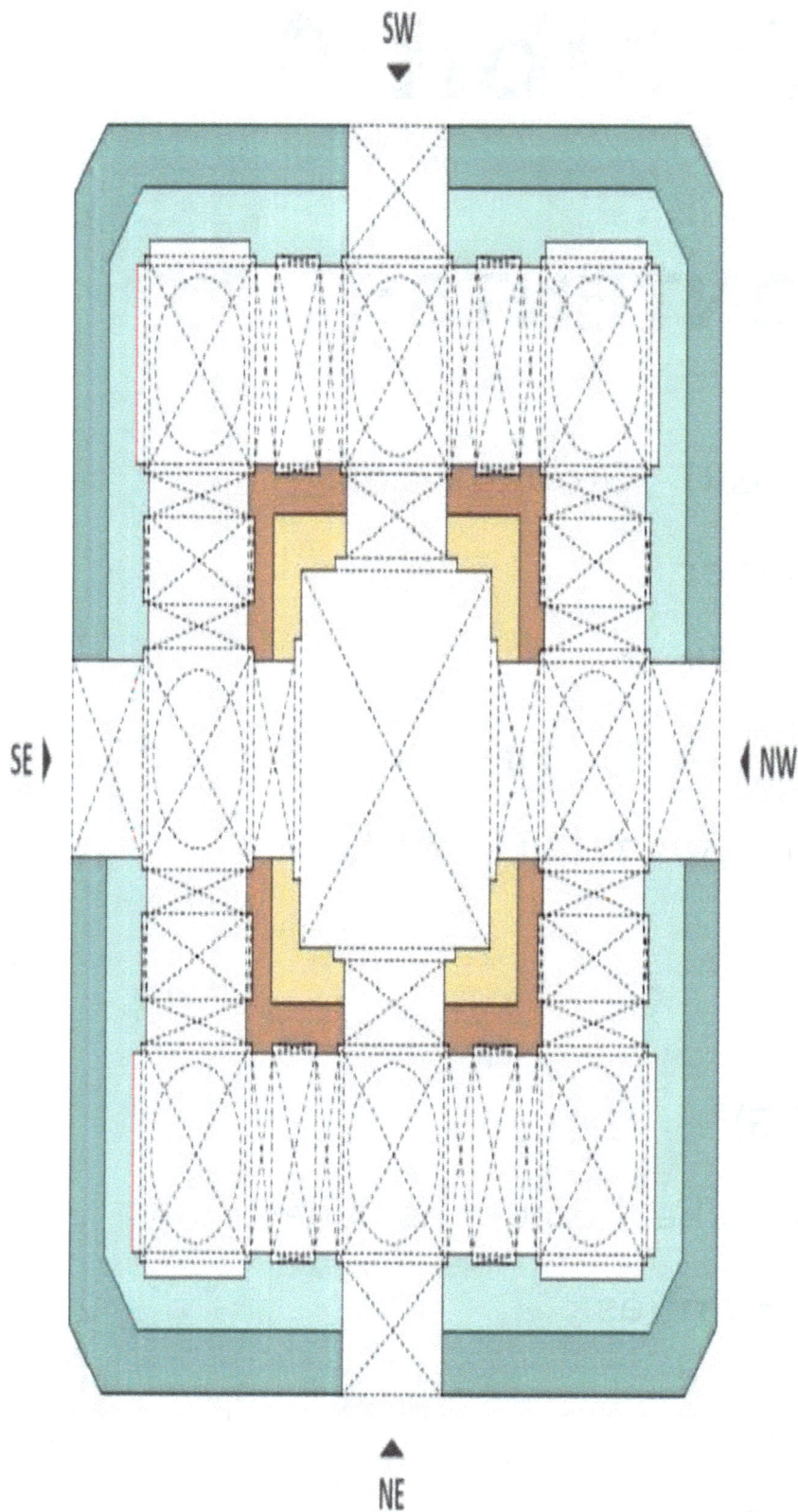

SW

SE ▶

◀ NW

NE

Gurdwara Choha Sahib
Ground Floor Plan - G.F

LAYER 4

LAYER 3

LAYER 2

LAYER 1

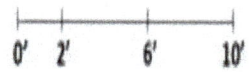

0' 2' 6' 10'

198

Level	Layer	Stage	Work to be executed	Dimensions	Sft	SW	NW	NE	SE	Total	Total Sft	Rate	Total Cost
G.F	L1	Stage 1	Removal of extraneous layers of plaster, cement work and limewash using water/mildly alkaline solution, nylon brush as well as chisel and hammer (where required) to expose red brick and preserve, in the first stage, kankar lime pointing underneath. This includes localized treatment of exposed brick/removed cement work to accentuate features that might have weathered over time, over :										
		S1.GR.GFL1	Columns (square footage measured as product of vertical length of members till spring of Attached arch, or end of capital, or associated horizontal surface that rests on it and width)										
		S1.GR.GFL1	Square column, at façade edges - Column Type B	2'-3"x 11'-2"	25.13	1	2	1	0	4	100.50	200	20100.00
		S1.GR.GFL1	Arches (Recessed) - Area for payment measured as one side as rectangle including voussoirs and brackets										
		S1.GR.GFL1	Recessed Pointed Arch, Type E2	'-4"-1/2" x 4'-1C	16.31	4	4	4	0	12	195.75	250	48937.50
		S1.GR.GFL1	Recessed Pointed Arch, Type E4	4"-1/4" x 4'-5"-3	37.42	1	1	1	0	3	112.26	250	28064.78
		S1.GR.GFL1	Arches (Structural) - Area for payment measured as one side as rectangle including voussoirs and brackets										
		S1.GR.GFL1	Arch Type E	5'-4"-1/2" x 3'-7	19.26	1	1	1	0	3	57.78	250	14445.31
		S1.GR.GFL1	Special brick elements, Type A (Stars + Stem)	8" x 9'-6"	6.33	6	6	6	0	18	114.00	250	28500.00
		S1.GR.GFL1	Cornice - 7"-1/2" High	31'-3"	31.25	1	1	1	0	3	93.75	250	23437.50
		S1.GR.GFL1	Plane Surfaces (Measured as a rectangular portion of the total wall surface, excluding arches, columns, recessed brick elements)									733.00	200	146600.00
G.F	L1	S1.GR.GFL1	Total Cost of Stage 1										310085.0911
G.F	L1	Stage 2:	Localized reconstruction/repair as stucco work in kankar lime plaster, using materials similar to specifications of original materials. Drawings/References for original state of detail/element to be approved by the Architect. Measurement in BOQ set at approximately 25% of area of element under question. Final costing to be the result of measurement on site after execution of work. Area of work to be measured as a rectangle (width x height). Categories of elements:										
		S2.GR.GFL1	Columns								25.13	2500	62812.50

M.i
m.i

199

Level	Layer	Stage	Work to be executed	Dimensions	Sft	SW	NW	NE	SE	Total	Total Sft	Rate	Total Cost
		S2.GR.GFL1	Arches (Recessed)								77.00	1000	77002.28
		S2.GR.GFL1	Arches (Structural)								14.45	1000	14445.31
		S2.GR.GFL1	Special brick elements, Type A (Stars + Stem)								28.50	1000	28500.00
		S2.GR.GFL1	Cornice								23.44	800	18750.00
G.F	L1	S2.GR.GFL1	Total Cost of Stage 2										201510.0911
G.F	L1	Stage 3	Localized reconstruction/repair in brick and kankar lime mortar, using materials similar to specifications of original materials. References for original state of detail/element to be approved by architect. Measurement in BOQ set at approximately 25% of area of element under question. Final costing to be the result of measurement on site after execution of work. Area of work to be measured as a rectangle (width x height). Categories of elements:										
		S3.GR.GFL1	Columns								25.13	2500	62825.00
		S3.GR.GFL1	Arches (Recessed)								77.00	800	61600.00
		S3.GR.GFL1	Arches (Structural)								14.45	800	11560.00
		S3.GR.GFL1	Cornice								28.50	500	14250.00
		S3.GR.GFL1	Special brick elements, Type A (Stars + Stem)								14.65	800	11720.00
		S3.GR.GFL1	Plane surfaces								183.25	500	91625.00
G.F	L1	S3.GR.GFL1	Total Cost of Stage 3										253580
G.F	L1	Stage 4	Plastering of exposed surface using kankar lime plaster matching original specifications. Over:										
		S4.GR.GFL1	Columns										
		S4.GR.GFL1	Square column, at façade edges - Column Type B3	2'-3"x 11'-2"	25.13	1	2	1	0	4	100.50	400	40200.00
		S4.GR.GFL1	Arches (Recessed)										
		S4.GR.GFL1	Recessed Pointed Arch, Type E2	'-4"-1/2" x 4'-10	16.31	4	4	4	0	12	195.75	600	117450.00
		S4.GR.GFL1	Recessed Pointed Arch, Type E4	4"-1/4" x 4'-5"-3	37.42	1	1	1	0	3	112.26	600	67355.47
		S4.GR.GFL1	Arches (Structural)										
		S4.GR.GFL1	Arch Type E	5'-4"-1/2" x 3'-7	19.26	1	1	1	0	3	57.78	600	34668.75
		S4.GR.GFL1	Special brick elements, Type A (Stars + Stem)	8" x 9'-6"	6.33	6	6	6	0	18	114.00	800	91200.00
		S4.GR.GFL1	Cornice - 7"-1/2" High	31'-3"	31.25	1	1	1	0	3	93.75	800	75000.00
		S4.GR.GFL1	Plane Surfaces								733.00	400	293200.00
G.F	L1	S4.GR.GFL1	Total Cost of Stage 4										719074.2188

Level	Layer	Stage	Work to be executed	Dimensions	Sft	SW	NW	NE	SE	Total	Total Sft	Rate	Total Cost
G.F	L2	Stage 1	Removal of extraneous layers of plaster, cement work, terrazo and limewash using water/mildly alkaline solution, nylon brush as well as chisel and hammer (where required) to expose red brick and preserve, in the first stage, kankar lime pointing underneath. This includes localized treatment of exposed brick/removed cement work to accentuate features that might have weathered over time, over :										
		S1.GR.GFL2	Columns (square footage measured as product of vertical length of members till spring of Attached arch, or end of capital, or associated horizontal surface that rests on it and width)										
		S1.GR.GFL2	Column Type B2	1'-2-"x 5'-10"	6.81	4	4	4	4	16	108.89	200	21777.78
		S1.GR.GFL2	Arches (Recessed) - Area for payment measured as one side as rectangle including voussoirs and brackets										
		S1.GR.GFL2	Recessed Pointed Arch, Type E	'-4"-1/2"x3' -7"	19.26	4	4	4	4	16	308.17	250	77041.67
		S1.GR.GFL2	Pointed Arch, Type E3	2' x 3'	6.00	2	2	2	2	8	48.00	250	12000.00
		S1.GR.GFL2	Arches (Structural) - Area for payment measured as one side as rectangle including voussoirs and brackets										
		S1.GR.GFL2	Pointed Arch, Type E	'-4"-1/2"x3' -7"	19.26	4	4	4	4	16	308.17	250	77041.67
		S1.GR.GFL2	Plane Surfaces (Measured as a rectangular portion of the total wall surface, excluding arches, columns, recessed brick elements)									596.00	200	119200.00
G.F	L2	S1.GR.GFL2	Total Cost of Stage 1										307061.1111
G.F	L2	Stage 2	Localized reconstruction/repair as stucco work in kankar lime plaster, using materials similar to specifications of original materials. Drawings/References for original state of detail/element to be approved by the Architect. Measurement in BOQ set at approximately 25% of area of element under question. Final costing to be the result of measurement on site after execution of work. Area of work to be measured as a rectangle (width x height). Categories of elements:										
		S2.GR.GFL2	Columns								27.22	2500	68055.56
		S2.GR.GFL2	Arches (Recessed)								89.04	1000	89041.67

Level	Layer	Stage	Work to be executed	Dimensions	Sft	SW	NW	NE	SE	Total	Total Sft	Rate	Total Cost
		S2.GR.GFL2	Arches (Structural}								77.04	1000	77041.67
		S2.GR.GFL2	Existing Stucco Work {Details such as caligraphy on facades}								As per site		
G.F	L2	S2.GR.GFL2	Total Cost of Stage 2										234138.8889
G.F	L2	Stage 3	Localized reconstruction/repair in brick and kankar lime mortar, using materials similar to specifications of original materials. References for original state of detail/element to be approved by architect. Measurement in BOQ set at approximately 25% of area of element under question. Final costing to be the result of measurement on site after execution of work. Area of work to be measured as a rectangle (width x height). Categories of elements:										
		S3.GR.GFL2	Columns								27.22	600	16332.00
		S3.GR.GFL2	Arches (Recessed)								50.52	800	40416.00
		S3.GR.GFL2	Arches (Structural}								77.04	800	61632.00
		S3.GR.GFL2	Existing Stucco Work {Details such as caligraphy on facades}								As per site		
		S3.GR.GFL2	Plane Surfaces								149.00	500	74500.00
G.F	L2	S3.GR.GFL2	Total Cost of Stage 3										192880
G.F	L2	Stage 4	Plastering of exposed surface using kankar lime plaster matching original specifications. Over:										
		S4.GR.GFL2	Columns										
		S4.GR.GFL2	Column Type B2	1'-2-"x 5'-10"	6.81	4	4	4	4	16	108.89	500	54444.44
		S4.GR.GFL2	Arches (Recessed)										
		S4.GR.GFL2	Recessed Pointed Arch, Type E	'-4"-1/2" x 3'-7"	19.26	4	4	4	4	16	308.17	600	184900.00
		S4.GR.GFL2	Pointed Arch, Type E3	3' x 2'	6.00	2	2	2	2	8	48.00	600	28800.00
		S4.GR.GFL2	Arches (Structural)										
		S4.GR.GFL2	Pointed Arch, Type E	'-4"-1/2" x 3'-7"	19.26	4	4	4	4	16	308.17	600	184900.00
		S4.GR.GFL2	Plane Surfaces								596.00	400	238400.00
G.F	L2	S4.GR.GFL2	Total Cost of Stage 4										691444.4444

Level	Layer	Stage	Work to be executed	Dimensions	Sft	SW	NW	NE	SE	Total	Total Sft	Rate	Total Cost
G.F	L3	Stage 1	Removal of extraneous layers of plaster, cement work, terrazo and limewash using water/mildly alkaline solution, nylon brush as well as chisel and hammer (where required) to expose red brick and preserve, in the first stage, kankar lime pointing underneath. This includes localized treatment of exposed brick/removed cement work to accentuate features that might have weathered over time, over :										
		S1.GR.GFL3	Columns (square footage measured as product of vertical length of members till spring of Attached arch, or end of capital, or associated horizontal surface that rests on it and width)										
		S1.GR.GFL3	Column Type B2	1'-2-"x 5'-10"	6.81	4	4	4	4	16	108.89	200	21777.78
		S1.GR.GFL3	Arches (Recessed) - Area for payment measured as one side as rectangle including voussoirs and brackets										
		S1.GR.GFL3	Pointed Arch, Type E3	2' x 3'	6.00	4	4	4	4	16	96.00	250	24000.00
		S1.GR.GFL3	Plane Surfaces (Measured as a rectangular portion of the total wall surface, excluding arches, columns, recessed brick elements)									348.00	200	69600.00
G.F	L3	S1.GR.GFL3	Total Cost of Stage 1										115377.78
G.F	L3	Stage 2	Localized reconstruction/repair as stucco work in kankar lime plaster, using materials similar to specifications of original materials. Drawings/References for original state of detail/element to be approved by the Architect. Measurement in BOQ set at approximately 25% of area of element under question. Final costing to be the result of measurement on site after execution of work. Area of work to be measured as a rectangle (width x height). Categories of elements:										
		S2.GR.GFL3	Columns								27.22	2500	68055.56
		S2.GR.GFL3	Arches (Recessed)								24.00	1000	24000.00
G.F	L3	S2.GR.GFL3	Total Cost of Stage 2										92055.55556

M.i
m.i

203

Level	Layer	Stage	Work to be executed	Dimensions	Sft	SW	NW	NE	SE	Total	Total Sft	Rate	Total Cost
G.F	L3	Stage 3	Localized reconstruction/repair in brick and kankar lime mortar, using materials similar to specifications of original materials. References for original state of detail/element to be approved by architect. Measurement in BOQ set at approximately 25% of area of element under question. Final costing to be the result of measurement on site after execution of work. Area of work to be measured as a rectangle (width x height). Categories of elements:										
		S3.GR.GFL3	Columns								27.22	600	16332.00
		S3.GR.GFL3	Arches (Recessed)								24.00	800	19200.00
		S3.GR.GFL3	Plane Surfaces								87.00	500	43500.00
G.F	L3	S3.GR.GFL3	Total Cost of Stage 3										79032
G.F	L3	Stage 4	Plastering of exposed surface using kankar lime plaster matching original specifications. Over:										
		S4.GR.GFL3	Columns										
		S4.GR.GFL3	Column Type B2	1'-2-"x 5'-10"	6.81	4	4	4	4	16	108.89	500	54444.44
		S4.GR.GFL3	Arches (Recessed)										
		S4.GR.GFL3	Pointed Arch, Type E3	2' x 3'	6.00	4	4	4	4	16	96.00	600	57600.00
		S4.GR.GFL3	Plane Surfaces								348.00	400	139200.00
G.F	L3	S4.GR.GFL3	Total Cost of Stage 4										251244.4444
G.F	L3	Stage 5	Use of Pakka Kalli (Milk of Lime wash) finish over kankar lime plaster. Over:										
		S5.GR.GFL3	Columns										
		S5.GR.GFL3	Column Type B2	1'-2-"x 5'-10"	6.81	4	4	4	4	16	108.89	600	65333.33
		S5.GR.GFL3	Arches (Recessed)	2' x 3'	6.00	4	4	4	4	16	96.00	700	67200.00
		S5.GR.GFL3	Pointed Arch, Type E3	2' x 3'	6.00	2	2	2	2	8	48.00	700	33600.00
		S5.GR.GFL3	Plane Surfaces								348.00	500	174000.00
G.F	L3	S5.GR.GFL3	Total Cost of Stage 5										340133.3333

Level	Layer	Stage	Work to be executed	Dimensions	Sft	SW	NW	NE	SE	Total	Total Sft	Rate	Total Cost
G.F	L4	Stage 1	Removal of extraneous layers of plaster, cement work, terrazo and limewash using water/mildly alkaline solution, nylon brush as well as chisel and hammer (where required) to expose red brick and preserve, in the first stage, kankar lime pointing underneath. This includes localized treatment of exposed brick/removed cement work to accentuate features that might have weathered over time, over :										
		S1.GR.GFL4	Columns (square footage measured as product of vertical length of members till spring of Attached arch, or end of capital, or associated horizontal surface that rests on it and width)										
		S1.GR.GFL4	Column Type B3	2' x 5'-10"	11.67	1	1	1	1	4	46.67	250	11666.67
		S1.GR.GFL4	Arches (Structural) - Area for payment measured as one side as rectangle including voussoirs and brackets										
		S1.GR.GFL4	Pointed Arch, Type E	'-4"-1/2" x 3'-7"	19.26	1	1	1	1	4	77.04	250	19260.42
		S1.GR.GFL4	Cornice- 9" High (RFT)	9'-4"	9.33	1	1	1	1	4	37.33	250	9333.33
		S1.GR.GFL4	Plane Surfaces (Measured as a rectangular portion of the total wall surface, excluding arches, columns, recessed brick elements)									224.00	200	44800.00
G.F	L4	S1.GR.GFL4	Total Cost of Stage 1										85060.41667
G.F	L4	Stage 2	Localized reconstruction/repair as stucco work in kankar lime plaster, using materials similar to specifications of original materials. Drawings/References for original state of detail/element to be approved by the Architect. Measurement in BOQ set at approximately 25% of area of element under question. Final costing to be the result of measurement on site after execution of work. Area of work to be measured as a rectangle (width x height). Categories of elements:										
		S2.GR.GFL4	Columns								11.67	2500	29166.67
		S2.GR.GFL4	Arches (Structural)								19.26	1000	19260.42
		S2.GR.GFL4	Cornice								9.33	800	7466.67
G.F	L4	S2.GR.GFL4	Total Cost of Stage 2										55893.75

M.i

Level	Layer	Stage	Work to be executed	Dimensions	Sft	SW	NW	NE	SE	Total	Total Sft	Rate	Total Cost
G.F	L4	Stage 3	Localized reconstruction/repair in brick and kankar lime mortar, using materials similar to specifications of original materials. References for original state of detail/element to be approved by architect. Measurement in BOQ set at approximately 25% of area of element under question. Final costing to be the result of measurement on site after execution of work. Area of work to be measured as a rectangle (width x height). Categories of elements:										
		S3.GR.GFL4	Columns								11.67	600	7002.00
		S3.GR.GFL4	Arches (Structural)								19.26	800	15408.00
		S3.GR.GFL4	Cornice								9.33	500	4665.00
		S3.GR.GFL4	Plane Surfaces								56.00	500	28000.00
G.F	L4	S3.GR.GFL4	Total Cost of Stage 3										55075.00
G.F	L4	Stage 4	Plastering of exposed surface using kankar lime plaster matching original specifications. Over:										
		S4.GR.GFL4	Columns										
		S4.GR.GFL4	Column Type B3	2' x 5'-10"	11.67	1	1	1	1	4	46.67	500	23333.33
		S4.GR.GFL4	Arches (Structural)										
		S4.GR.GFL4	Pointed Arch, Type E	'-4"-1/2" x 3'-7"	19.26	1	1	1	1	4	77.04	600	46225.00
		S4.GR.GFL4	Cornice- 9" High (RFT)	9'-4"	7.00	1	1	1	1	4	37.33	1000	37330.00
		S4.GR.GFL4	Plane Surfaces								224.00	400	89600.00
G.F	L4	S4.GR.GFL4	Total Cost of Stage 4										196488.33
G.F	L4	Stage 5	Use of Pakka Kalli (Milk of Lime) finish over kankar lime plaster. Over:										
		S5.GR.GFL4	Columns										
		S5.GR.GFL4	Column Type B3		11.67	1	1	1	1	4	46.67	600	28000.00
		S5.GR.GFL4	Arches (Structural)										
		S5.GR.GFL4	Pointed Arch, Type E		19.26	1	1	1	1	4	77.04	700	53929.17
		S5.GR.GFL4	Cornice- 9" High (RFT)	9'-4"	9.33	1	1	1	1	4	37.33	900	33597.00
		S5.GR.GFL4	Plane Surfaces								224.00	500	112000.00
G.F	L4	S5.GR.GFL4	Total Cost of Stage 5										227526.1667

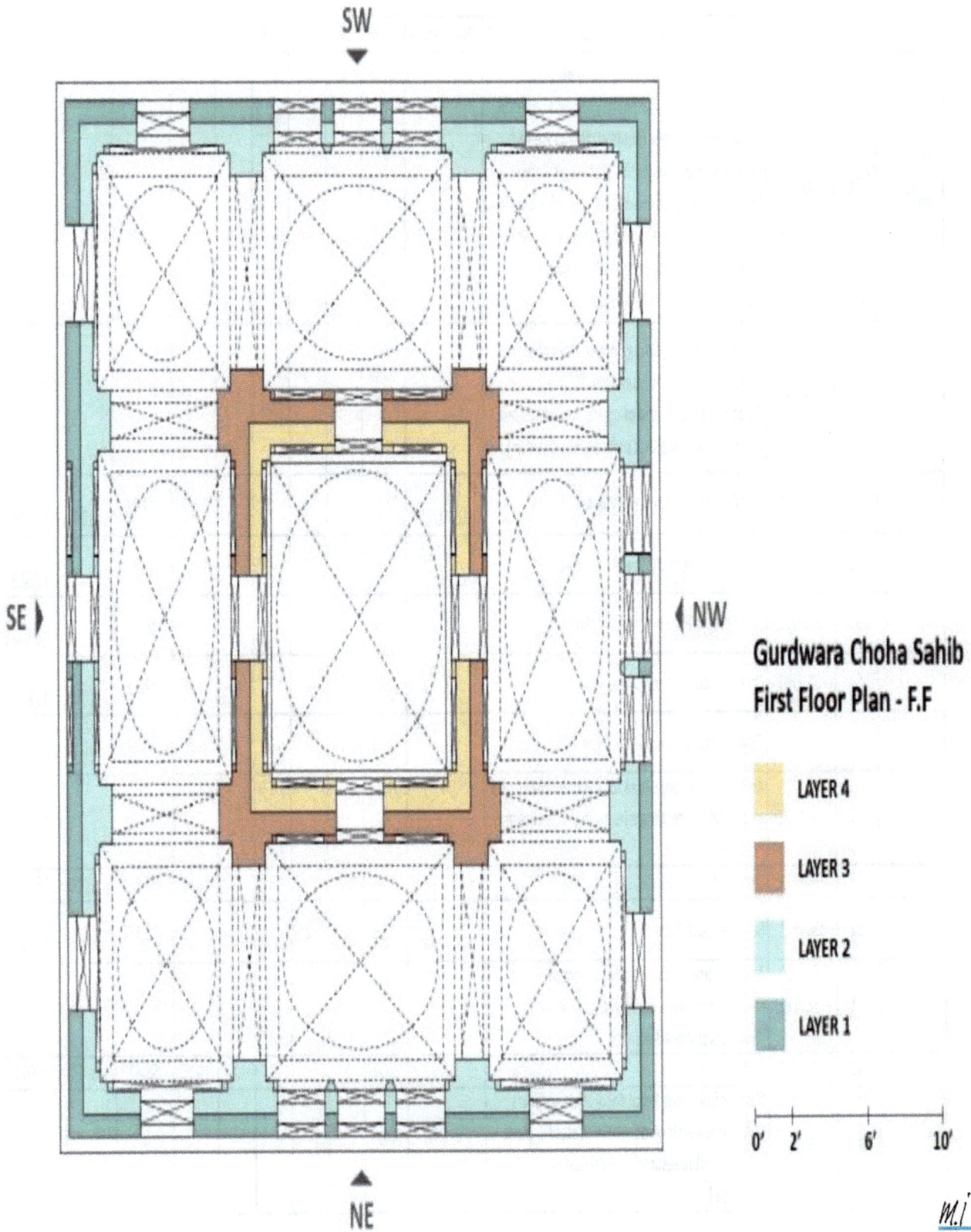

SW

SE ▶   ◀ NW

Gurdwara Choha Sahib
First Floor Plan - F.F

LAYER 4

LAYER 3

LAYER 2

LAYER 1

0'   2'   6'   10'

NE

207

m.i

Level	Layer	Stage	Work to be executed	Dimensions	Sft	SW	NW	NE	SE	Total	Total Sft	Rate	Total Cost
F.F	L1	Stage 1	Removal of extraneous layers of plaster limewash using water/mildly alkaline solution, nylon brush (where required) to expose red brick and preserve, in the first stage, kankar lime pointing underneath. This includes localized treatment of exposed brick/removed plaster work to accentuate features that might have weathered over time, over :										
	S1	GR.FFL1	Columns (square footage measured as product of vertical length of members till spring of Attached arch, or end of capital, or associated horizontal surface that rests on it and width)										
	S1	GR.FFL1	Half Octagonal columns, Type AH	4"-1/2" x 3'-10"-1/4"	1.45	8	4	8	0	20.00	28.91	1000	28906.25
	S1	GR.FFL1	Quarter Octagonal Columns, Type AQ	3"-1/2" x 5'-11"-1/2"	1.74	4	4	4	0	12.00	20.85	1000	20854.167
	S1	GR.FFL1	Half octagonal columns , Type AH2	7" x 4'-9"-1/2"	2.80	2	2	2	0	6.00	16.77	1000	16770.833
	S1	GR.FFL1	Quarter octagonal columns, Type AQ2	3"-1/2" x 4'-9"-1/2"	1.40	2	2	2	2	8.00	11.18	1000	11180.556
	S1	GR.FFL1	Quarter octagonal column, Type AQ3	10"-1/2" x9'-1"	7.95	1	2	1	0	4.00	31.79	1000	31791.667
	S1	GR.FFL1	Arches (Recessed) - Area for payment measured as one side as rectangle including voussoirs and brackets										
	S1	GR.FFL1	Recessed Arch Type C	2'-10" x 2'	5.67	3	3	3	1	10.00	56.67	1000	56666.667
	S1	GR.FFL1	Recessed Arch Type D	1'-9"-1/2" x 2'-0"-3/4"	3.70	2	2	2	0	6.00	22.17	1000	22171.875
	S1	GR.FFL1	Arches (Structural) - Area for payment measured as one side as rectangle including voussoirs and brackets										
	S1	GR.FFL1	Arch Type A	2'-10" x 2'	5.67	3	3	3	1	10.00	56.67	1000	56666.667
	S1	GR.FFL1	Chattris (including floral decoration, cupolas and internal arch work, where present). (Area for payment measured on one side as a rectangle)										

Level	Layer	Stage	Work to be executed	Dimensions	Sft	SW	NW	NE	SE	Total	Total Sft	Rate	Total Cost
	S1	GR.FFL1	Chattri Type A	5'-10" x 3'-10"	22.36	2	0	2	0	4.00	89.44	1000	89444.444
	S1	GR.FFL1	Chattri Type B (exposed not to red brick but original plaster detailing)	5'-10" x 3'-10"	22.36	0	2	0	0	2.00	44.72	1000	44722.222
	S1	GR.FFL1	Cornice - 7" High (RFT)	31'-3"	31.25	1	1	1	0	3.00	93.75	1000	93750
	S1	GR.FFL1	Niche Lights	9"-1/2" x 1'-9"-3/4"	1.43	4	4	4	2	14.00	20.09	2000	40177.083
	S1	GR.FFL1	Jali	2'-3" x 1' - 4"	3.00	3	3	3	0	9.00	27.00	2000	54000
	S1	GR.FFL1	Recessed Panels		66.00	1	1	1	0	3.00	198.00	1000	198000
	S1	GR.FFL1	Plane Surfaces (Measured as a rectangular portion of the total wall surface, excluding arches, columns, recessed brick elements)								468.75	1000	468750
F.F	L1	GR.FFL1	Total Cost of Stage 1										1233852
F.F	L1	Stage 2	Localized reconstruction/repair as stucco work in kankar lime plaster, using materials similar to specifications of original materials. Drawings/References for original state of detail/element to be approved by the Architect. Measurement in BOQ set at approximately 25% of area of element under question. Final costing to be the result of measurement on site after execution of work. Area of work to be measured as a rectangle (width x height). Categories of elements:										
	S2	GR.FFL1	Columns								27.38	2500	68439.67
	S2	GR.FFL1	Arches (Recessed)								19.71	1000	19709.635
	S2	GR.FFL1	Arches (Structural)								14.17	1000	14166.667
	S2	GR.FFL1	Chattri								33.54	2500	83854.167
	S2	GR.FFL1	Niche Lights								5.02	2500	12555.339
	S2	GR.FFL1	Jali								6.75	2500	16875
	S2	GR.FFL1	Recessed Panels								49.50	800	39600
F.F	L1	S2.GR.FFL1	Total Cost of Stage 2										255200.5

M.i

m.i

Level	Layer	Stage	Work to be executed	Dimensions	Sft	SW	NW	NE	SE	Total	Total Sft	Rate	Total Cost
F.F	L1	Stage 3	Localized reconstruction/repair in brick and kankar lime mortar, using materials similar to specifications of original materials. References for original state of detail/element to be approved by architect. Measurement in BOQ set at approximately 25% of area of element under question. Final costing to be the result of measurement on site after execution of work. Area of work to be measured as a rectangle (width x height). Categories of elements:										
		S3.GR.FFL1	Columns								98.97	2500	247425
		S3.GR.FFL1	Arches (Recessed)								19.71	1000	19710
		S3.GR.FFL1	Arches (Structural)								14.17	1000	14170
		S3.GR.FFL1	Chattri								33.54	2500	83850
		S3.GR.FFL1	Cornice								23.44	500	11720
		S3.GR.FFL1	Niche Lights								5.02	2500	12550
		S3.GR.FFL1	Jali								6.75	2500	16875
		S3.GR.FFL1	Recessed Panels								49.50	800	39600
		S3.GR.FFL1	Plane Surfaces								117.19	500	58595
F.F	L1	S3.GR.FFL1	Total Cost of Stage 3										504495
F.F	L2	Stage 1	Removal of extraneous layers of plaster limewash using water/mildly alkaline solution, nylon brush (where required) to expose red brick and preserve, in the first stage, kankar lime pointing underneath. This includes localized treatment of exposed brick/removed plaster work to accentuate features that might have weathered over time, over :										
		S1.GR.FFL2	Columns (square footage measured as product of vertical length of members till spring of Attached arch, or end of capital, or associated horizontal surface that rests on it and width)										

m.i

Level	Layer	Stage	Work to be executed	Dimensions	Sft	SW	NW	NE	SE	Total	Total Sft	Rate	Total Cost
		S1.GR.FFL2	Half octagonal columns , Type AH2 -	7" x 4'-9"-1/2"	2.80	0	2	2	2	6.00	16.77	1000	16770.833
		S1.GR.FFL2	Quarter octagonal columns, Type AQ2 -	3.5" x 4'-9"-1/2"	1.40	0	6	6	6	18.00	25.16	1000	25156.25
		S1.GR.FFL2	Half octagonal extended columns, Type AH3 -	1'-9" x 5'-3"-3/4"	9.30	0	2	2	2	6.00	55.78	1000	55781.25
		S1.GR.FFL2	Arches (Recessed) - Area for payment measured as one side as rectangle including voussoirs and brackets									1000	
		S1.GR.FFL2	Recessed Arch Type A	2'-10" x 2'	5.67	0	0	0	2	2.00	11.33	1000	11333.333
		S1.GR.FFL2	Recessed Arch Type B	6'-6" x 3'-3"-1/2"	21.40	2	2	2	2	8.00	171.17	1000	171166.67
		S1.GR.FFL2	Arches (Structural) - Area for payment measured as one side as rectangle including voussoirs and brackets									1000	
		S1.GR.FFL2	Arch Type A	2'-10" x 2'	5.67	0	5	5	3	13.00	73.67	1000	73666.667
		S1.GR.FFL2	Arch Type B	6'-6" x 3'-3"-1/2"	21.40	4	4	4	4	16.00	342.33	1000	342333.33
		S1.GR.FFL2	Recessed Panels								162.50	1000	162500
		S1.GR.FFL2	Plane Surfaces (Measured as a rectangular portion of the total wall surface, excluding arches, columns and recessed flat panel work)								403.00		1000	403000
F.F	L2	S1.GR.FFL2	Total Cost of Stage 1										1261708
F.F	L2	Stage 2	Localized reconstruction/repair as stucco work in kankar lime plaster, using materials similar to specifications of original materials. Drawings/References for original state of detail/element to be approved by the Architect. Measurement in BOQ set at approximately 25% of area of element under question. Final costing to be the result of measurement on site after execution of work. Area of work to be measured as a rectangle (width x height). Categories of elements:										
		S2.GR.FFL2	Columns								24.43	2500	61067.708
		S2.GR.FFL2	Arches (Recessed)								45.63	1000	45625

Level	Layer	Stage	Work to be executed	Dimensions	Sft	SW	NW	NE	SE	Total	Total Sft	Rate	Total Cost
		S2.GR.FFL2	Arches (Structural)								104.00	1000	104000
		S2.GR.FFL2	Recessed Panels								40.63	800	32500
F.F	L2	S2.GR.FFL2	Total Cost of Stage 2										243192.7
F.F	L2	Stage 3	Localized reconstruction/repair in brick and kankar lime mortar, using materials similar to specifications of original materials. References for original state of detail/element to be approved by architect. Measurement in BOQ set at approximately 25% of area of element under question. Final costing to be the result of measurement on site after execution of work. Area of work to be measured as a rectangle (width x height). Categories of elements:										
		S3.GR.FFL2	Columns								24.43	2500	61067.708
		S3.GR.FFL2	Arches (Recessed)								45.63	1000	45625
		S3.GR.FFL2	Arches (Structural)								104.00	1000	104000
		S3.GR.FFL2	Recessed Panels								40.63	800	32500
		S3.GR.FFL2	Plane Surfaces								100.75	500	50375
F.F	L2	S3.GR.FFL2	Total Cost of Stage 3										293567.7
F.F	L2	Stage 4	Plastering of exposed surface using kankar lime plaster matching original specifications. RECONSTRUCTION OF DETERIORATED ELEMENTS IN BRICK AND KANKAR LIME PLASTER, INCLUDED. Over:										
		S4.GR.FFL2	Columns										
		S4.GR.FFL2	Half octagonal columns , Type AH2	7" x 4'-9"-1/2"	2.80	0	2	2	2	6.00	16.77	2500	41927.083
		S4.GR.FFL2	Quarter octagonal columns, Type AQ2	3.5" x 4'-9"-1/2"	1.40	0	6	6	6	18.00	25.16	2500	62890.625
		S4.GR.FFL2	Half octagonal extended columns, Type AH 3	1'-9" x 5'-3"-3/4"	9.30	0	2	2	2	6.00	55.78	2500	139453.13
		S4.GR.FFL2	Arches (Recessed) - (Area for payment measured as one side as rectangle including voussoirs and brackets).										
		GR.S4FFL2	Recessed Arch Type A	2'-10" x 2'	5.67	0	0	0	2	2.00	11.33	800	9066.6667

Level	Layer	Stage	Work to be executed	Dimensions	Sft	SW	NW	NE	SE	Total	Total Sft	Rate	Total Cost
		S4.GR.FFL2	Recessed Arch Type B	6'-6" x 3'-3"-1/2"	21.40	2	2	2	2	8.00	171.17	800	136933.33
		S4.GR.FFL2	Arches (Structural) (Area for payment measured as one side as rectangle including voussoirs and brackets)										
		S4.GR.FFL2	Arch Type A	2'-10" x 2'	5.67	0	5	5	3	13.00	73.67	800	58933.333
		S4.GR.FFL2	Arch Type B	6'-6" x 3'-3"-1/2"	21.40	4	4	4	4	16.00	342.33	800	273866.67
		S4.GR.FFL2	Recessed Panels								162.50	500	81250
		S4.GR.FFL2	Plane Surfaces								403.00	400	161200
F.F	L2	S4.GR.FFL2	Total Cost of Stage 4										965520.8
F.F	L3	Stage 1	Removal of extraneous layers of plaster and limewash using water/mildly alkaline solution and nylon brush to expose red brick and preserve, in the first stage, kankar lime pointing underneath. This includes localized treatment of exposed brick/cleaned plaster work to accentuate features that might have weathered over time, over :										
		S1.GR.FFL3	Columns (square footage measured as product of vertical length of members till spring of Attached arch, or end of capital, or associated horizontal surface that rests on it and width)										
		S1.GR.FFL3	Quarter octagonal columns, Type AQ2	3"-1/2" x 4'-9"-1/2"	1.40	2	2	2	2	8.00	11.18	1000	11180.556
		S1.GR.FFL3	Half octagonal columns , Type AH2	7" x 4'-9"-1/2"	2.80	2	2	2	2	8.00	22.36	1000	22361.111
		S1.GR.FFL3	Half octagonal extended columns, Type AH3	1'-9" x 5'-3"-3/4"	9.30	2	2	2	2	8.00	74.38	1000	74375
		S1.GR.FFL3	Arches (Recessed) - (Area for payment measured as one side as rectangle including voussoirs and brackets).										1000	
		S1.GR.FFL3	Recessed Arch Type A	2'-10" x 2'	5.67	2	2	2	2	8.00	45.33	1000	45333.333

Level	Layer	Stage	Work to be executed	Dimensions	Sft	SW	NW	NE	SE	Total	Total Sft	Rate	Total Cost
		S1.GR.FFL3	Arches (Structural) (Area for payment measured as one side as rectangle including voussoirs and brackets)									1000	
		S1.GR.FFL3	Arch Type A	2'-10" x 2'	5.67	1	1	1	1	4.00	22.67	1000	22666.667
		S1.GR.FFL3	Recessed Panels								73.80	1000	73800
		S1.GR.FFL3	Plane Surfaces (Measured as a rectangular portion of the total wall surface, excluding arches, columns and recessed flat panel work)								329.60	1000	329600
F.F	L3	S1.GR.FFL3	Total Cost of Stage 1										579316.7
F.F	L3	Stage 2	Replastering of exposed brick using kankar lime plaster matching original specifications. RECONSTRUCTION OF DETERIORATED ELEMENTS IN BRICK AND KANKAR LIME PLASTER, INCLUDED. Over:										
		S2.GR.FFL3	Columns										
		S2.GR.FFL3	Quarter octagonal columns, Type AQ2 -	3"-1/2" x 4'-9"-1/2"	1.40	2	2	2	2	8.00	11.18	2500	27951.389
		S2.GR.FFL3	Half octagonal columns , Type AH2 -	7" x 4'-9"-1/2"	2.80	2	2	2	2	8.00	22.36	2500	55902.778
		S2.GR.FFL3	Arches (Recessed) (Area for payment measured as one side as rectangle including voussoirs and brackets)										
		S2.GR.FFL3	Recessed Arch Type A	2'-10" x 2'	5.67	2	2	2	2	8.00	45.33	800	36266.667
		S2.GR.FFL3	Arches (Structural) (Area for payment measured as one side as rectangle including voussoirs and brackets)										
		S2.GR.FFL3	Arch Type A	2'-10" x 2'	5.67	1	1	1	1	4.00	22.67	800	18133.333
		S2.GR.FFL3	Recessed Panels								73.80	500	36900
		S2.GR.FFL3	Plane Surfaces (Measured as a rectangular portion of the total wall surface, excluding arches, columns and recessed flat panel work)								329.60	400	131840
F.F	L3	S2.GR.FFL3	Total Cost of Stage 2										306994.2
F.F	L3	Stage 3	Use of Pakka Kalli (Milk of Lime) finish over kankar lime plaster. Over:										
		S3.GR.FFL3	Columns										

m.i

Level	Layer	Stage	Work to be executed	Dimensions	Sft	SW	NW	NE	SE	Total	Total Sft	Rate	Total Cost
		S3.GR.FFL3	Quarter octagonal columns, Type AQ2 -	3"-1/2" x 4'-9"-1/2"	1.40	2	2	2	2	8.00	11.18	2600	29069.444
		S3.GR.FFL3	Half octagonal columns , Type AH2 -	7" x 4'-9"-1/2"	2.80	2	2	2	2	8.00	22.36	2600	58138.889
		S3.GR.FFL3	Arches (Recessed)- (Area for payment measured as one side as rectangle including voussoirs and brackets).										
		S3.GR.FFL3	Recessed Arch Type A	2'-10" x 2'	5.67	2	2	2	2	8.00	45.33	900	40800
		S3.GR.FFL3	Arches (Structural) (Area for payment measured as one side as rectangle including voussoirs and brackets)										
		S3.GR.FFL3	Arch Type A	2'-10" x 2'	5.67	1	1	1	1	4.00	22.67	900	20400
		S3.GR.FFL3	Recessed Panels								73.80	600	44280
		S3.GR.FFL3	Plane Surfaces								329.60	500	164800
F.F	L3	S3.GR.FFL3	Total Cost of Stage 3										357488.3
F.F	L4	Stage	Work to be executed										
F.F	L4	Stage 1	Plastering of exposed brick using kankar lime plaster matching original specifications. RECONSTRUCTION OF DETERIORATED ELEMENTS IN BRICK AND KANKAR LIME PLASTER, INCLUDED. Over:										
		GR.S1FFL4	Columns (square footage measured as product of vertical length of members till spring of Attached arch, or end of capital, or associated horizontal surface that rests on it and width)										
		GR.S1FFL4	Quarter octagonal columns, Type AQ2	57"-1/2" x 3"-1/2"	1.40	2.00	2.00	2.00	2.00	8.00	11.18	2500	27951.389
		GR.S1FFL4	Half octagonal columns , Type AH2	7" x 4'-9"-1/2"	2.80	2	2	2	2	8.00	22.36	2500	55902.778
		GR.S1FFL4	Arches (Recessed)										
		GR.S1FFL4	Recessed Arch Type A	2'-10" x 2'	5.67	2	2	2	2	8.00	45.33	800	36266.667
		GR.S1FFL4	Recessed Arch Type C	2'-10" x 2'	5.67	3	3	3	3	12.00	68.00	800	54400
		GR.S1FFL4	Arches (Structural)										

M.i
m.i

Level	Layer	Stage	Work to be executed	Dimensions	Sft	SW	NW	NE	SE	Total	Total Sft	Rate	Total Cost
		GR.S1FFL4	Arch Type A	2'-10" x 2'	5.67	1	1	1	1	4.00	22.67	800	18133.333
		GR.S1FFL4	Plane Surfaces (Measured as a rectangular portion of the total wall surface, excluding arches, columns and recessed flat panel work)								329.60	400	131840
F.F	L4	GR.S1FFL4	Total Cost of Stage 1										324494.2
F.F	L4	Stage 2	Use of Pakka Kalli (Milk of Lime) finish over kankar lime plaster. Over:										
		GR.S2FFL4	Columns										
		GR.S2FFL4	Quarter octagonal columns, Type AQ2	57"-1/2" x 3" 1/2"	1.40	2.00	2.00	2.00	2.00	8.00	11.18	2600	29069.444
		GR.S2FFL4	Half octagonal columns , Type AH2	57"-1/2" x 7"	2.80	2	2	2	2	8.00	22.36	2600	58138.889
		GR.S2FFL4	Arches (Recessed) (Area for payment measured as one side as rectangle including voussoirs and brackets).										
		GR.S2FFL4	Recessed Arch Type A	2'-10" x 2'	5.67	2	2	2	2	8.00	45.33	900	40800
		GR.S2FFL4	Recessed Arch Type C	2'-10" x 2'	5.67	3	3	3	3	12.00	68.00	900	61200
		GR.S2FFL4	Arches (Structural) (Area for payment measured as one side as rectangle including voussoirs and brackets).										
		GR.S2FFL4	Arch Type A	2'-10" x 2'	5.67	1	1	1	1	4.00	22.67	900	20400
		GR.S2FFL4	Plane Surfaces (Measured as a rectangular portion of the total wall surface, excluding arches, columns and recessed flat panel work)								329.60	500	164800
F.F	L4	GR.S2FFL4	Total Cost of Stage 2										374408.3

m.i

216

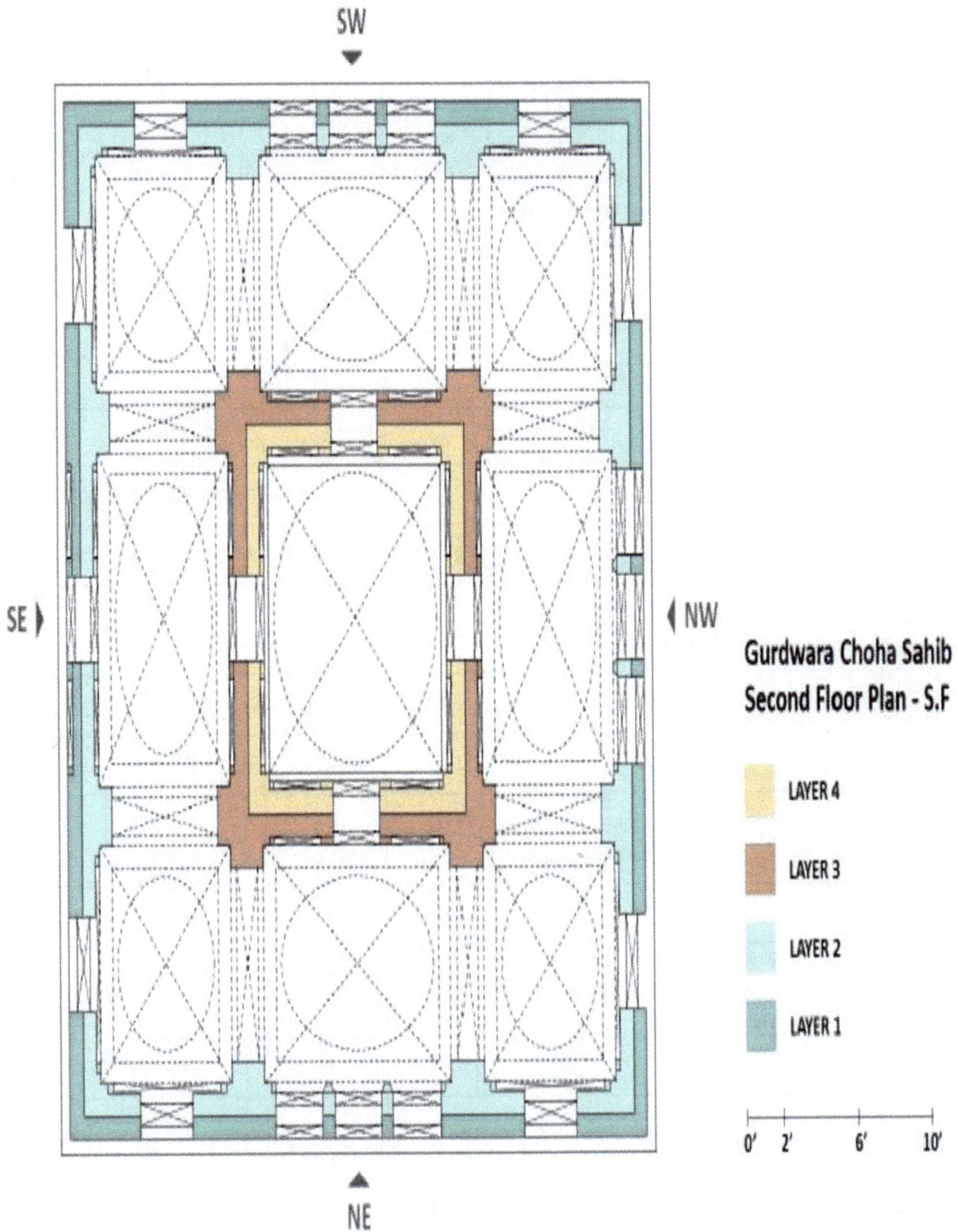

SW

SE ▶

◀ NW

NE

Gurdwara Choha Sahib
Second Floor Plan - S.F

LAYER 4

LAYER 3

LAYER 2

LAYER 1

0'   2'   6'   10'

217

Level	Layer	Stage	Work to be executed		Sft	SW	NW	NE	SE	Total	Total Sft	Rate	Total Cost
S.F	L1	Stage 1	Removal of extraneous layers of plaster limewash using water/mildly alkaline solution, nylon brush (where required) to expose red brick and preserve, in the first stage, kankar lime pointing underneath. This includes localized treatment of exposed brick/removed plaster work to accentuate features that might have weathered over time, over :										
		S1.GR.SFL1	Columns (square footage measured as product of vertical length of members till spring of Attached arch, or end of capital, or associated horizontal surface that rests on it and width)										
		S1.GR.SFL1	Half Octagonal columns, Type AH	4"-1/2" x 3'-10"-1/4"	1.45	12	12	12	0	36	52.03	1000	52031.25
		S1.GR.SFL1	Quarter Octagonal Columns, Type AQ	3"-1/2" x 5'-11"-1/2"	1.74	6	6	6	2	20	34.76	1000	34756.94444
		S1.GR.SFL1	Quarter octagonal column, Type AQ3	8'-9" x 9'-10"	7.95	1	2	1	0	4	31.79	1000	31791.66667
		S1.GR.SFL1	Arches (Recessed) - (Area for payment measured as one side as rectangle including voussoirs and brackets)									1000	
		S1.GR.SFL1	Recessed Arch Type D2 (x 2)	2'-8" x 2'-2"	5.78	2	2	2	0	6	34.67	1000	34666.66667
		S1.GR.SFL1	Recessed Arch Type D3 (x2}	1'-11" x 2'-5"	4.63	1	1	1	0	3	13.90	1000	13895.83333
		S1.GR.SFL1	Arches (Structural) (Area for payment measured as one side as rectangle including voussoirs and brackets)									1000	
		S1.GR.SFL1	Arch Type A	2'-10" x 2'-0"	5.67	3	3	3	1	10	56.67	1000	56666.66667
		S1.GR.SFL1	Chattris (including floral decoration, cupolas and internal arch work, where present). (Area for payment measured on one side as a rectangle)									1000	
		S1.GR.SFL1	Chattri Type B (exposed to original plaster detailing)	5'-10" x 3'-10"	22.36	2	2	2	0	6	134.17	1000	134166.6667
		S1.GR.SFL1	Chattri Type C (exposed to original plaster detailing)	10'-2" x 2'-2"	22.03	1	0	1	0	2	44.06	1000	44055.55556
		S1.GR.SFL1	Chattri Type D {exposed to original plaster detailing)	11'-1" x 4'-3"	47.10	0	1	0	0	1	47.10	1000	47104.16667

Level	Layer	Stage	Work to be executed		Sft	SW	NW	NE	SE	Total	Total Sft	Rate	Total Cost
		S1.GR.SFL1	Cornice - 10" High (RFT)	31'-3"	31.25	1	1	1	0	3	93.75	1000	93750
		S1.GR.SFL1	Recessed Panels								67.50	1000	67500
		S1.GR.SFL1	Niche Lights	26.63	4.34	2	2	2	0	6	26.02	2000	52031.25
		S1.GR.SFL1	Existing Detail Stucco Work (Details such as animal forms on façade)	17" x 12"	1.42	0	4	0	0	4	5.67	2000	11333.33333
		S1.GR.SFL1	Plane Surfaces (Measured as a rectangular portion of the total wall surface, excluding arches, columns and recessed flat panel work)								750.00	1000	750000
S.F	L1	S1.GR.SFL1	Total Cost of Stage 1										1423750
S.F	L1	Stage 2	Localized reconstruction/repair as stucco work in kankar lime plaster, using materials similar to specifications of original materials. Drawings/References for original state of detail/element to be approved by the Architect. Measurement in BOQ set at approximately 25% of area of element under question. Final costing to be the result of measurement on site after execution of work. Area of work to be measured as a rectangle (width x height). Categories of elements:										
		S2.GR.SFL1	Columns								29.64	2500	74112.41319
		S2.GR.SFL1	Arches (Recessed)								12.14	1000	12140.625
		S2.GR.SFL1	Arches (Structural)								14.17	1000	14166.66667
		S2.GR.SFL1	Chattri								56.33	2500	140828.9931
		S2.GR.SFL1	Cornice								23.44	800	18750
		S2.GR.SFL1	Recessed Panels								16.88	800	13500
		S2.GR.SFL1	Niche Lights								67.50	2500	168750

Level	Layer	Stage	Work to be executed		Sft	SW	NW	NE	SE	Total	Total Sft	Rate	Total Cost
		S2.GR.SFL1	Existing Stucco Work {Details such as animal forms on façade}								5.67	6000	34020
S.F	L1	S2.GR.SFL1	Total Cost of Stage 2										476268.698
S.F	L1	Stage 3	Localized reconstruction/repair in brick and kankar lime mortar, using materials similar to specifications of original materials. References for original state of detail/element to be approved by architect. Measurement in BOQ set at approximately 25% of area of element under question. Final costing to be the result of measurement on site after execution of work. Area of work to be measured as a rectangle (width x height). Categories of elements:										
		S3.GR.SFL1	Columns								29.64	2500	74112.41319
		S3.GR.SFL1	Arches (Recessed)								12.14	1000	12140.625
		S3.GR.SFL1	Arches (Structural)								14.17	1000	14166.66667
		S3.GR.SFL1	Chattri								56.33	2500	140828.9931
		S3.GR.SFL1	Cornice								23.44	500	11718.75
		S3.GR.SFL1	Recessed Panels								16.88	800	13500
		S3.GR.SFL1	Niche Lights								67.50	2500	168750
		S3.GR.SFL1	Existing Stucco Work {Details such as animal forms on façade}								5.67	6000	34020
		S3.GR.SFL1	Plane Surfaces								187.50	500	93750
S.F	L1	S3.GR.SFL1	Total Cost of Stage 3										562987.448

Level	Layer	Stage	Work to be executed	Sft	SW	NW	NE	SE	Total	Total Sft	Rate	Total Cost
S.F	L2	Stage 1	Replastering of exposed brick using kankar lime plaster matching original specifications. RECONSTRUCTION OF DETERIORATED ELEMENTS IN BRICK AND KANKAR LIME PLASTER, INCLUDED. Over:									
		S1.GR.SFL2	Columns (square footage measured as product of vertical length of members till spring of Attached arch, or end of capital, or associated horizontal surface that rests on it and width)									
		S1.GR.SFL2	Half octagonal columns , Type AH2	7" x 4'-9"-1/2"	2.80	2	2	2	2	8	22.36	2500	55902.77778
		S1.GR.SFL2	Quarter octagonal columns, Type AQ2	3"-1/2" x 4'-9"-1/2"	1.40	6	6	6	6	24	33.54	2500	83854.16667
		S1.GR.SFL2	Half octagonal extended columns, Type AH3	1'-9" x 5'-3"-3/4"	9.30	2	2	2	2	8	74.38	2500	185937.5
		S1.GR.SFL2	Arches (Recessed) (Area for payment measured as one side as rectangle including voussoirs and brackets).									
		S1.GR.SFL2	Recessed Arch Type A	2'-10" x 2'	5.67	0	0	0	2	2	11.33	800	9066.666667
		S1.GR.SFL2	Recessed Arch Type B	6'-6" x 3'-3"-1/2"	21.40	2	2	2	2	8	171.17	800	136933.3333
		S1.GR.SFL2	Arches (Structural) (Area for payment measured as one side as rectangle including voussoirs and brackets)									
		S1.GR.SFL2	Arch Type A	2'-10" x 2'	5.67	5	5	5	3	18	102.00	800	81600
		S1.GR.SFL2	Arch Type B	6'-6" x 3'-3"-1/2"	21.40	4	4	4	4	16	342.33	800	273866.6667
		S1.GR.SFL2	Plane Surfaces (Measured as a rectangular portion of the total wall surface, excluding arches, columns, recessed brick elements)								403.00	400	161200
S.F	L2	S1.GR.SFL2	Total Cost of Stage 1									988361.111
S.F	L3	Stage 1	Replastering of exposed brick using kankar lime plaster matching original specifications. RECONSTRUCTION OF DETERIORATED ELEMENTS IN BRICK AND KANKAR LIME PLASTER, INCLUDED. Over:									

Level	Layer	Stage	Work to be executed		Sft	SW	NW	NE	SE	Total	Total Sft	Rate	Total Cost
		S1.GR.SFL3	Columns (square footage measured as product of vertical length of members till spring of Attached arch, or end of capital, or associated horizontal surface that rests on it and width)										
		S1.GR.SFL3	Quarter octagonal columns, Type AQ2	3"-1/2" x 4'-9" 1/2"	1.40	2	2	2	2	8	11.18	2500	27951.38889
		S1.GR.SFL3	Half octagonal columns , Type AH2	7" x 4'-9"-1/2"	2.80	2	2	2	2	8	22.36	2500	55902.77778
		S1.GR.SFL3	Half octagonal extended columns, Type AH3	1'-9" x 5'-3"-3/4"	9.30	2	2	2	2	8	74.38	2500	185937.5
		S1.GR.SFL3	Arches (Recessed) (Area for payment measured as one side as rectangle including voussoirs and brackets).										
		S1.GR.SFL3	Recessed Arch Type A	2'-10" x 2'	5.67	2	2	2	2	8	45.33	800	36266.66667
		S1.GR.SFL3	Arches (Structural) (Area for payment measured as one side as rectangle including voussoirs and brackets)										
		S1.GR.SFL3	Arch Type A	2'-10" x 2'	5.67	1	1	1	1	4	22.67	800	18133.33333
		S1.GR.SFL3	Plane Surfaces (Measured as a rectangular portion of the total wall surface, excluding arches, columns, recessed brick elements)									330.00	400	132000
S.F	L3	S1.GR.SFL3	Total Cost of Stage 1										456191.667
S.F	L3	Stage 2	Use of Pakka Kalli (Milk of Lime) finish over kankar lime plaster. Over:										
		S2.GR.SFL3	Columns										
		S2.GR.SFL3	Quarter octagonal columns, Type AQ2	3"-1/2" x 4'-9" 1/2"	1.40	2	2	2	2	8	11.18	2600	29069.44444
		S2.GR.SFL3	Half octagonal columns , Type AH2	7" x 4'-9"-1/2"	2.80	2	2	2	2	8	22.36	2600	58138.88889
		S2.GR.SFL3	Half octagonal extended columns, Type AH3 -	1'-9" x 5'-3"-3/4"	9.30	2	2	2	2	8	74.38	2600	193375

Level	Layer	Stage	Work to be executed		Sft	SW	NW	NE	SE	Total	Total Sft	Rate	Total Cost
		S2.GR.SFL3	Arches (Recessed) (Area for payment measured as one side as rectangle including voussoirs and brackets).										
		S2.GR.SFL3	Recessed Arch Type A	2'-10" x 2'	5.67	2	2	2	2	8	45.33	900	40800
		S2.GR.SFL3	Arches (Structural) (Area for payment measured as one side as rectangle including voussoirs and brackets)										
		S2.GR.SFL3	Arch Type A	2'-10" x 2'	8.03	1	1	1	1	4	32.11	900	28900
		S2.GR.SFL3	Plane Surfaces (Measured as a rectangular portion of the total wall surface, excluding arches, columns, recessed brick elements)								330.00	500	165000
S.F	L3	S2.GR.SFL3	Total Cost of Stage 2										515283.333
S.F	L4	Stage 1	Replastering of exposed brick using kankar lime plaster matching original specifications. RECONSTRUCTION OF DETERIORATED ELEMENTS IN BRICK AND KANKAR LIME PLASTER, INCLUDED. Over:										
		S1.GR.SFL4	Columns (square footage measured as product of vertical length of members till spring of Attached arch, or end of capital, or associated horizontal surface that rests on it and width)										
		S1.GR.SFL4	Quarter octagonal columns, Type A2 - Including the following elements: Base + Stem + Capital	3"-1/2" x 4'-9" 1/2"	1.40	4	4	4	4	16	22.36	2500	55902.77778
		S1.GR.SFL4	Arches (Recessed)										
		S1.GR.SFL4	Recessed Arch Type A - (Area for payment measured as one side as rectangle including voussoirs and brackets).	2'-10" x 2'	5.67	2	2	2	2	8	45.33	800	36266.66667
		S1.GR.SFL4	Arches (Structural)										
		S1.GR.SFL4	Recessed Arch Type A	2'-10" x 2'	5.67	1	1	1	1	4	22.67	800	18133.33333
		S1.GR.SFL4	Recessed Panels	12' x 3'-3"	39.00	1	1	1	1	4	156.00	500	78000

M.i
m.i

223

Level	Layer	Stage	Work to be executed		Sft	SW	NW	NE	SE	Total	Total Sft	Rate	Total Cost
		S1.GR.SFL4	Dome										
		S1.GR.SFL4	Spherical Dome Internal Area (Dome area calculated as the product of two axial dimensions, each dimension calculated by measuring the circumference of the vertical cross section of Dome)								625.00	900	562500
		S1.GR.SFL4	Plane Surfaces (Measured as a rectangular portion of the total wall surface, excluding arches, columns and recessed panels)								330.00	400	132000
S.F	L4	S1.GR.SFL4	Total Cost of Stage 1										882802.778
S.F	L4	Stage 2	Use of Pakka Kalli (Milk of Lime wash) finish over kankar lime plaster. Over:										
		S2.GR.SFL4	Columns (square footage measured as product of vertical length of members till spring of Attached arch, or end of capital, or associated horizontal surface that rests on it and width)										
		S2.GR.SFL4	Quarter octagonal columns, Type A2	57"-1/2" x 3"-1/2"	1.40	4	4	4	4	16	22.36	2600	58138.88889
		S2.GR.SFL4	Arches (Recessed) ((Area for payment measured as one side as rectangle including voussoirs and brackets)										
		S2.GR.SFL4	Recessed Arch Type A	2'-10" x 2'	5.67	2	2	2	2	8	45.33	900	40800
		S2.GR.SFL4	Arches (Structural) (Area for payment measured as one side as rectangle including voussoirs and brackets)										
		S2.GR.SFL4	Recessed Arch Type A	2'-10" x 2'	5.67	1	1	1	1	4	22.67	900	20400
		S2.GR.SFL4	Recessed Panels	12' x 3'-3"	39.00	1	1	1	1	4	156.00	600	93600
		S2.GR.SFL4	Dome (Dome area calculated as the product of two axial dimensions, each dimension calculated by measuring the circumference of the vertical cross section of Dome)										
		S2.GR.SFL4	Spherical Dome Internal Area								625.00	1000	625000

Level	Layer	Stage	Work to be executed		Sft	SW	NW	NE	SE	Total	Total Sft	Rate	Total Cost
		S2.GR.SFL4	Plane Surfaces (Measured as a rectangular portion of the total wall surface, excluding arches, columns and recessed panels)								330.00	500	165000
S.F	L4	S2.GR.SFL4	Total Cost of Stage 2										1002938.89

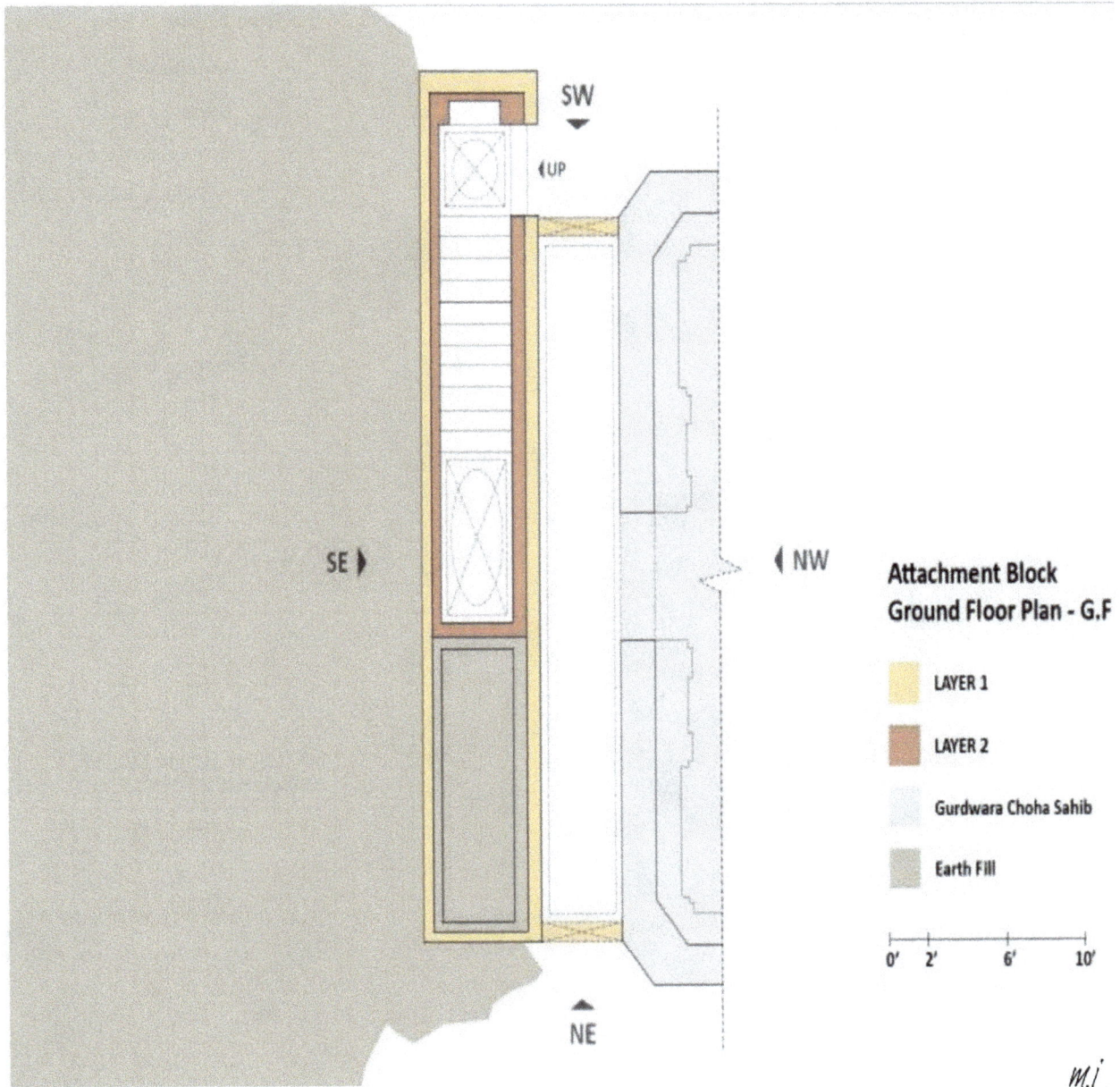

**Attachment Block
Ground Floor Plan - G.F**

LAYER 1

LAYER 2

Gurdwara Choha Sahib

Earth Fill

0'   2'   6'   10'

SW

UP

SE

NW

NE

m.i

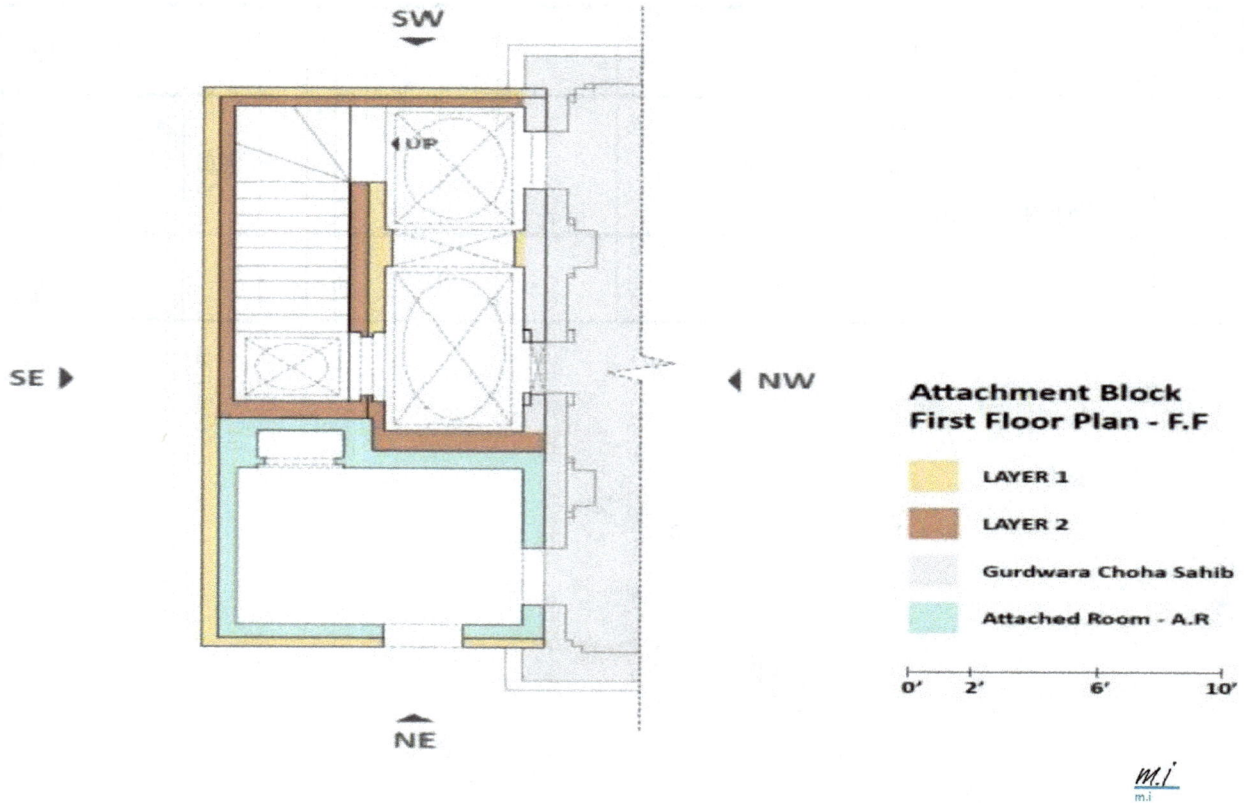

Attachment Block
First Floor Plan - F.F

- LAYER 1
- LAYER 2
- Gurdwara Choha Sahib
- Attached Room - A.R

0' 2' 6' 10'

SW
SE ▶
◀ NW
NE

m.i

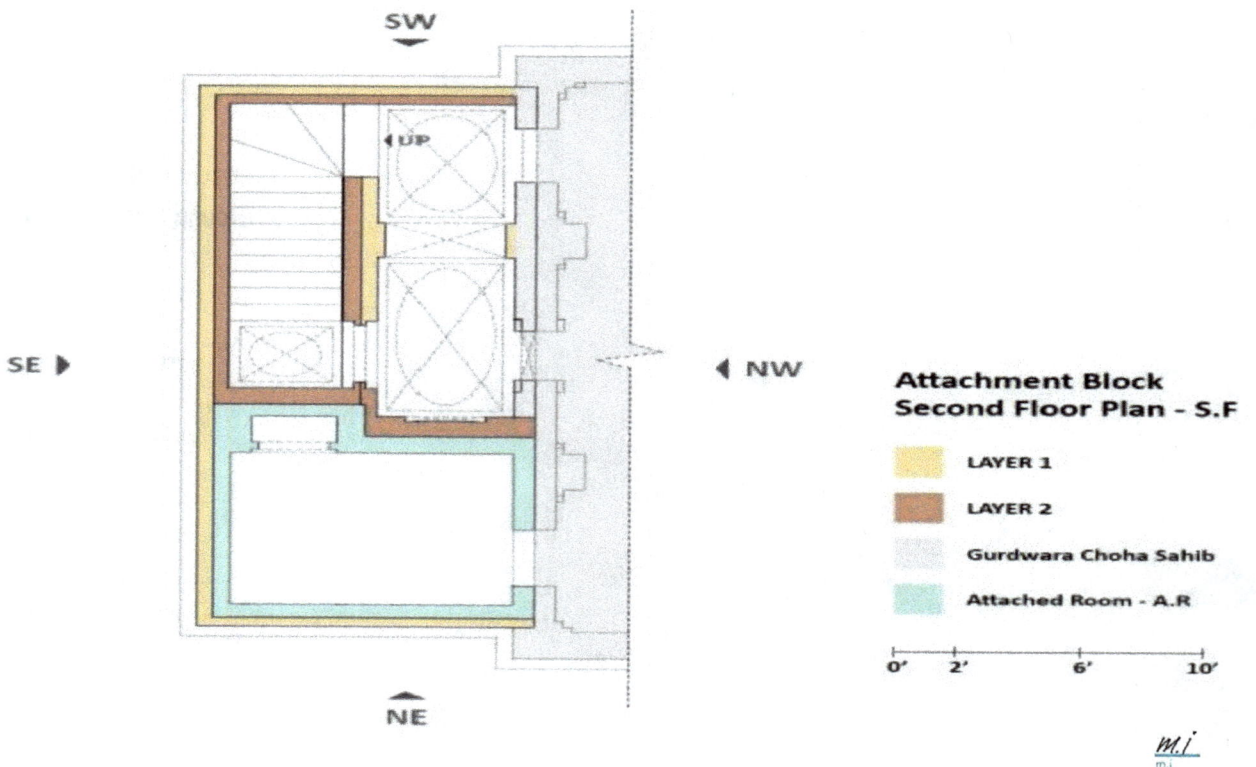

Attachment Block
Second Floor Plan - S.F

- LAYER 1
- LAYER 2
- Gurdwara Choha Sahib
- Attached Room - A.R

0' 2' 6' 10'

SW
SE ▶
◀ NW
NE

m.i

226

Level	Layer		Work to be executed	Dimension	Sft	SW	NW	NE	SE	Total No.	Total Sft	Rate	Total Cost
ATT- G.F	L1	Stage 1	Removal of extraneous layers of plaster and limewash using water/mildly alkaline solution and nylon brush to expose red brick and preserve, in the first stage, kankar lime pointing underneath. This includes localized treatment of exposed brick/cleaned plaster work to accentuate features that might have weathered over time, over :										
		S1.AT.GF.L1	Arches (Structural) (Area for arch measured on one side as rectangle including voussoirs and brackets)										
		S1.AT.GF.L1	Type E-2	4'-10"x 3'-4"-1/2"	16.3125	1	0	1	0	1	16.31	250	4077.5
		S1.AT.GF.L1	Segmental Arches - Type G	3'-8"x 1'-6"	5.5					11	60.50	250	15125
		S1.AT.GF.L1	Cornice - 7"-1/2" High (RFT)							40	40.00	250	
		S1.AT.GF.L1	Special Brick Elements (Base of missing platform)	2'-9" x 2'-6"	6.875	1	0	0	0	1	6.88	250	1718.75
		S1.AT.GF.L1	Plane Surfaces (Measured as a rectangular portion of the total wall surface, excluding arches, columns, recessed brick elements)								477.30	200	95460
ATT- G.F	L1	S1.AT.GF.L1	Total Cost of Stage 1										
ATT- G.F	L1	Stage 2	Plastering of exposed surface using kankar lime plaster matching original specifications. RECONSTRUCTION OF DETERIORATED ELEMENTS IN BRICK AND KANKAR LIME PLASTER, INCLUDED. Over:										
		S2.AT.GF.L1	Arches (Structural)										
		S2.AT.GF.L1	Type E-2	4'-10"x 3'-4"-1/2"	16.3125	1	0	1	0	1	16.31	800	13048
		S2.AT.GF.L1	Segmental Arches - Type D	3'-8"x 1'-6"	5.5					11	60.50	800	48400
		S2.AT.GF.L1	Cornice - 7"-1/2" High (RFT)							40		1000	

227

Level	Layer		Work to be executed	Dimension	Sft	SW	NW	NE	SE	Total No.	Total Sft	Rate	Total Cost
		S2.AT.GF.L1	Special Brick Elements (Base of missing platform)	2'-9" x 2'-6"	6.875	1	0	0	0	1	6.88	2000	13750
		S2.AT.GF.L1	Plane Surfaces								477.30	400	190920
ATT- G.F	L1	S2.AT.GF.L1	Total Cost of Stage 2										
ATT- GF	L2	Stage 1	Removal of extraneous layers of plaster and limewash using water/mildly alkaline solution and nylon brush to expose red brick and preserve, in the first stage, kankar lime pointing underneath. This includes localized treatment of exposed brick/cleaned plaster work to accentuate features that might have weathered over time, over :										
		S1.AT.GF.L2	Plane Area (Measured as a rectangular portion of the total wall surface, excluding arches, columns, recessed brick elements)										
		S1.AT.GF.L2	Plane Surfaces								311.42	200	62284
ATT- GF	L2	S1.AT.GF.L2	Total Cost of Stage 1										
ATT- GF	L2	Stage 2	Plastering of exposed surface using kankar lime plaster matching original specifications. RECONSTRUCTION OF DETERIORATED ELEMENTS IN BRICK AND KANKAR LIME PLASTER, INCLUDED. Over:										
		S2.AT.GF.L2	Plane Area										
		S2.AT.GF.L2	Plane Surfaces								311.42	400	124568
ATT- GF	L2	S2.AT.GF.L2	Total Cost of Stage 2										

Level	Layer		Work to be executed	Dimension	Sft	SW	NW	NE	SE	Total No.	Total Sft	Rate	Total Cost
ATT - F.F	L1	Stage 1	Removal of extraneous layers of plaster and limewash using water/mildly alkaline solution and nylon brush to expose red brick and preserve, in the first stage, kankar lime pointing underneath. This includes localized treatment of exposed brick/cleaned plaster work to accentuate features that might have weathered over time, over :										
		S1.AT.FF.L1	Plane Area (Measured as a rectangular portion of the total wall surface, excluding arches, columns, recessed brick elements)										
		S1.AT.FF.L1	Plane Surfaces								565.00	200	113000
		S1.AT.FF.L1	Arches (Structural) (Area for arch measured on one side as rectangle including voussoirs and brackets)										
		S1.AT.FF.L1	Segmental Arches - Type G	3'-8"x 1'-6"	5.50					13.00	71.50	250	17875
		S1.AT.FF.L1	Flat Arches - Type F	3'-7" x 9"	2.69	0	1	0	0	1	2.69	250	671.875
		S1.AT.FF.L1	Pointed Arch Type E-2	4'-10"x 3'-4"-1/2"	16.31	0	3	0	0	3	48.94	250	12234.375
		S1.AT.FF.L1	Columns (square footage measured as product of vertical length of members till spring of Attached arch, or end of capital, or associated horizontal surface that rests on it and width)										
		S1.AT.FF.L1	Half octagonal extended columns, Type AH3	1'-9" x 5'-3" 3/4"	9.26	1	0	1	0	2	18.52	250	4630.208333
		S1.AT.FF.L1	Cornice								40.00	250	10000
ATT - F.F	L1	S1.AT.FF.L1	Total Cost of Stage 1										

M.i
mi

229

Level	Layer		Work to be executed	Dimension	Sft	SW	NW	NE	SE	Total No.	Total Sft	Rate	Total Cost
ATT - F.F	L1	Stage 2	Plastering of exposed surface using external kankar lime plaster matching original specifications. RECONSTRUCTION OF DETERIORATED ELEMENTS IN BRICK AND KANKAR LIME PLASTER, INCLUDED. Over:										
		S2.AT.FF.L1	Plane Area										
		S2.AT.FF.L1	Plane Surfaces								565.00	400	226000
		S2.AT.FF.L1	Arches										
		S2.AT.FF.L1	Segmental Arches - Type G	3'-8"x 1'-6"	5.50					13.00	71.50	800	57200
		S2.AT.FF.L1	Flat Arches - Type F	3'-7" x 9"	2.69	0	1	0	0	1	2.69	600	1612.5
		S2.AT.FF.L1	Pointed Arch Type E-2	4'-10"x 3'-4"-1/2"	16.31	0	3	0	0	3	48.94	800	39150
		S2.AT.FF.L1	Columns										
		S2.AT.FF.L1	Half octagonal extended columns, Type AH3	1'-9" x 5'-3" 3/4"	9.26	1	0	1	0	2	18.52	2500	46302.08333
		S2.AT.FF.L1	Cornice								40.00	800	32000
ATT - F.F	L1	S2.AT.FF.L1	Total Cost of Stage 2										
ATT - FF	L2	Stage 1	Removal of extraneous layers of plaster and limewash using water/mildly alkaline solution and nylon brush to expose red brick and preserve, in the first stage, kankar lime pointing underneath. This includes localized treatment of exposed brick/cleaned plaster work to accentuate features that might have weathered over time, over :										
		S1.AT.FF.L2	Plane Area (Measured as a rectangular portion of the total wall surface, excluding arches, columns, recessed brick elements)										
		S1.AT.FF.L2	Plane Surfaces								391.88	200	78375

M.i

Level	Layer		Work to be executed	Dimension	Sft	SW	NW	NE	SE	Total No.	Total Sft	Rate	Total Cost
		S1.AT.FF.L2	Arches (Recessed) (Area for payment measured as one side as rectangle including voussoirs and brackets)										
		S1.AT.FF.L2	Recessed Arch Type A	2'-10" x 2'	5.67	0	0	1	0	1	5.67	250	1416.666667
ATT - FF	L2	S1.AT.FF.L2	Total Cost of Stage 1										
ATT - FF	L2	Stage 2	Plastering of exposed surface using external kankar lime plaster matching original specifications. RECONSTRUCTION OF DETERIORATED ELEMENTS IN BRICK AND KANKAR LIME PLASTER, INCLUDED. Over:										
		S2.AT.FF.L2	Plane Area								391.88	400	156750
		S2.AT.FF.L2	Arches (Recessed)										
		S2.AT.FF.L2	Recessed Arch Type A	2'-10" x 2'	5.67	0	0	1	0	1	5.67	800	4533.333333
ATT - FF	L2	S2.AT.FF.L2	Total Cost of Stage 2										
ATT -S.F	L1	Stage 1	Removal of extraneous layers of plaster and limewash using water/mildly alkaline solution and nylon brush to expose red brick and preserve, in the first stage, kankar lime pointing underneath. This includes localized treatment of exposed brick/cleaned plaster work to accentuate features that might have weathered over time, over :										
		S1.AT.SF.L1	Plane Area (Measured as a rectangular portion of the total wall surface, excluding arches, columns, recessed brick elements)										
		S1.AT.SF.L1	Plane Surfaces								531.38	200	106275
		S1.AT.SF.L1	Arches (Structural) (Area for arch measured on one side as rectangle including voussoirs and brackets)	Dimension									
		S1.AT.SF.L1	Segmental Arches - Type G	3'-8"x 1'-6"	5.50					12	66.00	250	16500
		S1.AT.SF.L1	Flat Arches, Type F	3'-7" x 9"	2.69	0	1	0	0	1	2.69	250	671.875

231

Level	Layer		Work to be executed	Dimension	Sft	SW	NW	NE	SE	Total No.	Total Sft	Rate	Total Cost
		S1.AT.SF.L1	Pointed Arch Type E-2	4'-10"x 3'-4"-1/2"	16.31	0	3	0	0	3	48.94	250	12234.375
		S1.AT.SF.L1	Cornice (RFT)							40.00	40.00	250	10000
ATT - S.F	L1	S1.AT.SF.L1	Total cost of Stage 1										
ATT - S.F	L1	Stage 2	Plastering of exposed surface using external kankar lime plaster matching original specifications. RECONSTRUCTION OF DETERIORATED ELEMENTS IN BRICK AND KANKAR LIME PLASTER, INCLUDED. Over:										
		S2.AT.SF.L1	Plane Area										
		S2.AT.SF.L1	Plane Surfaces								531.38	400	212550
		S2.AT.SF.L1	Arches (Structural)										
		S2.AT.SF.L1	Segmental Arches - Type G	3'-8"x 1'-6"	5.50					12	66.00	800	52800
		S2.AT.SF.L1	Flat Arches, Type F	3'-7" x 9"	2.69	0	1	0	0	1	2.69	600	1614
		S2.AT.SF.L1	Pointed Arch Type E-2	4'-10"x 3'-4"-1/2"	16.31	0	3	0	0	3	48.93	800	39144
		S2.AT.SF.L1	Cornice (RFT)								40.00	800	32000
ATT - S.F	L1	S2.AT.SF.L1	Total cost of stage 2										
ATT- SF	L2	Stage 1	Removal of extraneous layers of plaster and limewash using water/mildly alkaline solution and nylon brush to expose red brick and preserve, in the first stage, kankar lime pointing underneath. This includes localized treatment of exposed brick/cleaned plaster work to accentuate features that might have weathered over time, over :										
		S1.AT.SF.L2	Plane Area (Measured as a rectangular portion of the total wall surface, excluding arches, columns, recessed brick elements)										
		S1.AT.SF.L2	Plane Surfaces								371.25	200	74250
		S1.AT.SF.L2	Total Cost Stage 1										

Level	Layer		Work to be executed	Dimension	Sft	SW	NW	NE	SE	Total No.	Total Sft	Rate	Total Cost
		Stage 2	Plastering of exposed surface using external kankar lime plaster matching original specifications. RECONSTRUCTION OF DETERIORATED ELEMENTS IN BRICK AND KANKAR LIME PLASTER, INCLUDED. Over:										
		S2.AT.SF.L2	Plane Area										
		S2.AT.SF.L2	Plane Surfaces								371.25	400	148500
ATT- SF	L2	S2.AT.SF.L2	Total Cost Stage 2										
		S2.AT.SF.L2	Total Cost Stage 2										
ATT- SF		Stage 3	Removal of Attachment Room Flat Dome & Reconstruction with kankar lime plaster matching original. Using maxium number of bricks removed from original dome.										
		S3.AT.SF	Reconstruction of Dome	8'- x 10"	80	0	0	0	0		80.00	1450	116000

| | | | | | | | | | | | | 2077641.542 | *M.i* |

Level	Layer	Stage	Work to be executed	Dimension	Sft	SW	NW	NE	SE	Total	Total Sft	Rate	Total Cost
ATT-AR F.F		Stage 1	Removal of extraneous layers of plaster and limewash using water/mildly alkaline solution and nylon brush to expose red brick and preserve, in the first stage, kankar lime pointing underneath. This includes localized treatment of exposed brick/cleaned plaster work to accentuate features that might have weathered over time, over :										
		S1.AR.FF.L2	Plane Area (Measured as a rectangular portion of the total wall surface, excluding arches, columns, recessed brick elements)										
		S1.AR.FF.L2	Plane Surfaces								276.25	200	55250.00
		S1.AR.FF.L2	Arches (Recessed) (Area for payment measured as one side as rectangle including voussoirs and brackets)										
		S1.AR.FF.L2	Recessed Arch Type C	2'-10" x 2'	5.67	0	1	0	0	1	5.67	250	1417.50
		S1.AR.FF.L2	Arches (Structural) (Area for payment measured as one side as rectangle including voussoirs and brackets)										
		S1.AR.FF.L2	Flat Arch, Type F	3'-7" x 9"	2.69	1	0	0	0	1	2.69	250	672.50
ATT-AR F.F		S1.AR.FF.L2	Total Cost Stage 1										
ATT-AR F.F		S1.AR.FF.L2	Plastering of exposed surface using external kankar lime plaster matching original specifications. RECONSTRUCTION OF DETERIORATED ELEMENTS IN BRICK AND KANKAR LIME PLASTER, INCLUDED. Over:										
		S1.AR.FF.L2	Plane Area								276.25	400	110500.00
		S1.AR.FF.L2	Arches (Recessed)										
		S1.AR.FF.L2	Recessed Arch Type C	2'-10" x 2'	5.67		1	0	0	1	5.67	800	4536.00
		S1.AR.FF.L2	Arches (Structural)										
		S1.AR.FF.L2	Flat Arch, Type F	3'-7" x 9"	2.69	1	0	0	0	1	2.69	600	1614.00
ATT-AR F.F		S1.AR.FF.L2	Total Cost Stage 2										*M.i*

Level	Layer	Stage	Work to be executed	Dimension	Sft	SW	NW	NE	SE	Total	Total Sft	Rate	Total Cost
ATT - AR S.F		Stage 1	Removal of extraneous layers of plaster and limewash using water/mildly alkaline solution and nylon brush to expose red brick and preserve, in the first stage, kankar lime pointing underneath. This includes localized treatment of exposed brick/cleaned plaster work to accentuate features that might have weathered over time, over :										
		S1.AR.SFL2	Plane Area (Measured as a rectangular portion of the total wall surface, excluding arches, columns, recessed brick elements)										
		S1.AR.SFL2	Plane Surfaces								276.25	200	55250.00
		S1.AR.SFL2	Recessed Panel	2'-10" x 2'	5.67	1	0	0	0	1	5.67	200	1133.33
		S1.AR.SFL2	Total Cost Stage 1										
		S1.AR.SFL2	Arches (Structural) - (Area for payment measured on one side as rectangle including voussoirs and brackets)										
		S1.AR.SFL2	Structural Arch Type F	3'-7" x 9"	2.69	1	0	0	0	1	2.69	250	671.88
ATT - AR S.F		S1.AR.SFL2	Total Cost of Stage 1										
ATT - AR S.F		Stage 2	Plastering of exposed surface using kankar lime plaster matching original specifications. RECONSTRUCTION OF DETERIORATED ELEMENTS IN BRICK AND KANKAR LIME PLASTER, INCLUDED. Over:										
		S2.AR.SFL2	Plane Area								276.25	400	110500.00
		S2.AR.SFL2	Recessed Panel	2'-10" x 2'		1	0	0	0	1	5.67	500	2833.33
		S2.AR.SFL2	Arches (Structural) - (Area for payment measured on one side as rectangle including voussoirs and brackets)										
		S2.AR.SFL2	Structural Arch Type F	3'-7" x 9"		1	0	0	0	1	2.69	800	2150.00
ATT - AR S.F		S2.AR.SFL2	Total Cost Stage 2										

346528.54 *M.I*

234

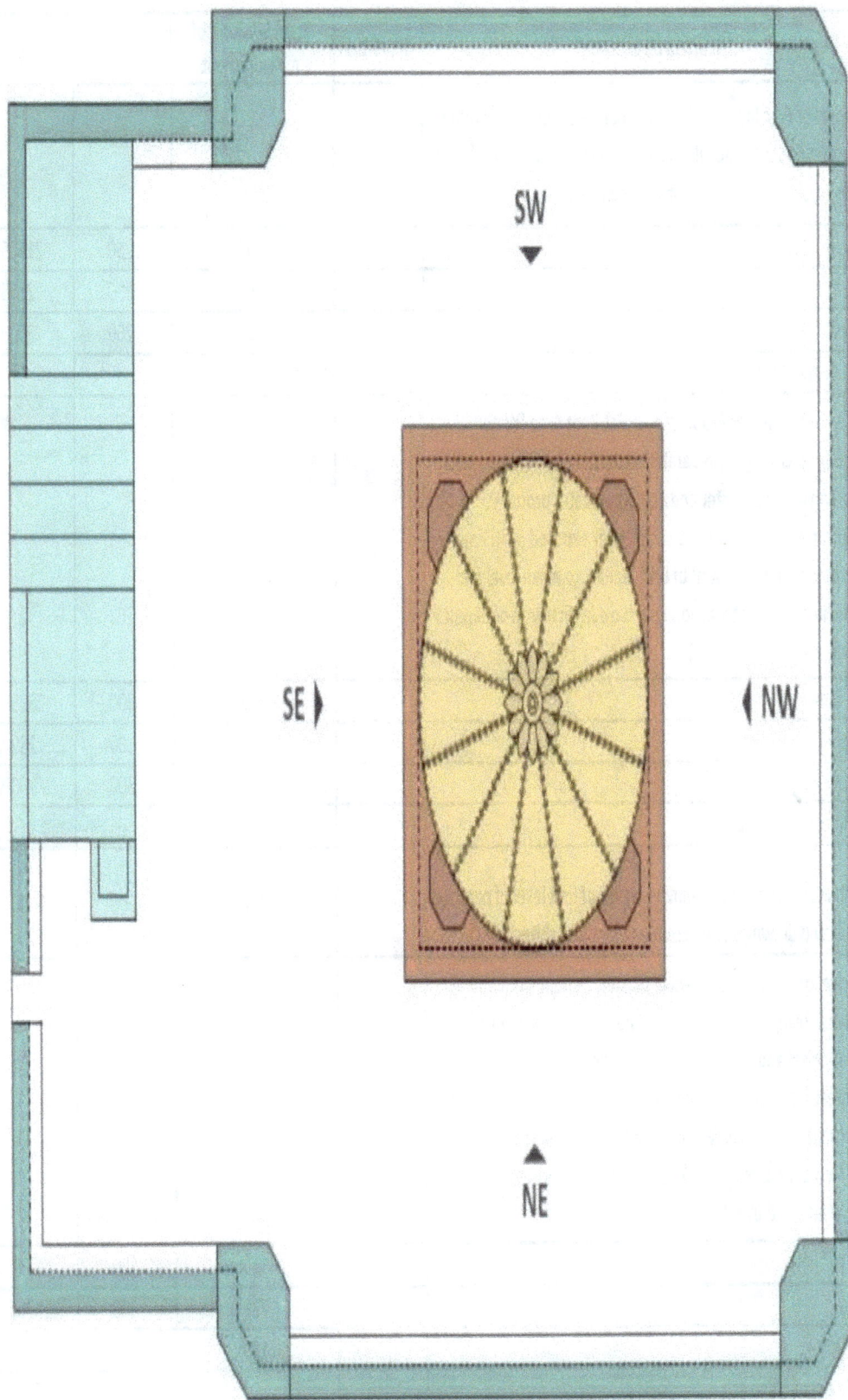

SW

SE ▶

◀ NW

NE

Gurdwara Choha Sahib
Roof Floor Plan - R.F

DOME

PEDESTAL

MUMTY

PARAPET

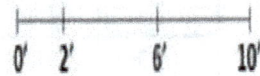

0' 2'   6'   10'

Level	Layer	Stage	Work to be executed	Dimension	Total SFT/Unit of measurement	Rate	Total Cost
	Roof	Stage 1	Removal of First layer of Plain Lime Concerete over flat portions of roof, including removal of cement concrete, wherever found, exposing second layer of plain lime concrete.				
		S1.RF	Plane Roof Area		865	250	216250
		S1.RF	Mumty		95	250	23750
		S1.RF	Parapet (rft)		120	250	30000
	Roof	Stage 1	Total Cost of Stage 1				
	Roof	Stage 2	Application of Water Proofing over flat Roof Area (Water proofing consisting of preparation of roofing for water proofing using kankar lime plaster and any other water proofing membrane, 2 coats of cold bitumen over exposed plain lime concrete, minimal amount of brick ballast to make level and bituminous felt. Water proofing to lap over first step of parapet as well as dome pedestal.)				
		S2.RF	Roof Area		865	300	259500
		S2.RF	Mumty		95	300	28500
		S2.RF	Parapet (RFT)		120	300	36000
	Roof	RF.S2	Total Cost of Stage 2				
	Roof	Stage 3	Construction of drainage channel on top of first level of parapet. Details and drawings to be approved by the architect (RFT)		120	500	60000
	Roof	Stage 4	Removal of extraneous layers of plaster, cement work and limewash using water/mildly alkaline solution, nylon brush as well as chisel and hammer (where required) to expose red brick and preserve, in the first stage, kankar lime pointing and plaster underneath. This includes localized treatment of exposed brick/removed cement work to accentuate features that might have weathered over time, over :				
		S4.RF	Pedestal (sft)		150	300	45000
		S4.RF	Dome		729	300	218700
		S4.RF	Parapet		120	300	36000
	Roof	S4.RF	Total Cost of Stage 4				

M.I
m.i

Level	Layer	Stage	Work to be executed	Dimension	Total SFT/Unit of measurement	Rate	Total Cost
	Roof	Stage 5	Localized reconstruction/repair as stucco work in kankar lime plaster, using materials similar to specifications of original materials. Drawings/References for original state of detail/element to be approved by the Architect. Measurement in BOQ set at approximately 25% of area of element under question. Final costing to be the result of measurement on site after execution of work. Area of work to be measured as a rectangle (width x height). Categories of elements:				
		S5.RF	Pedestal (incuding recessed flat panels)		37.5	1500	56250
		S5.RF	Dome (Including decorative elements at base of dome)		182.25	2500	455625
		S5.RF	Total Cost of Stage 5				
	Roof	Stage 6	Localized reconstruction/repair in brick and kankar lime mortar, using materials similar to specifications of original materials. References for original state of detail/element to be approved by architect. Measurement in BOQ set at approximately 25% of area of element under question. Final costing to be the result of measurement on site after execution of work. Area of work to be measured as a rectangle (width x height). Categories of elements:				
		S6.RF	Pedestal (incuding recessed flat panels)		37.5	800	30000
		S6.RF	Dome		182.25	1000	182250
		S6.RF	Parapet		30	800	24000
	Roof	S6.RF	Total Cost of Stage 6				
	Roof	Stage 7	Reapplication of plain lime concrete as floor finish with appropriate slope for drainage.				
		S7.RF	Flat portions of Roof		1730	500	865000
	Roof	Stage 8	Application of external lime plaster over Mumty		260	500	130000
	Roof	Stage 9	Application of water proofing over Dome				
		S9.RF	Dome area (area calculated as the product of two axial dimensions, each dimension calculated by measuring the circumference of the vertical cross section of Dome)		729	300	218700
							2915525

237

Level	Layer	Stage	Work to be executed	Sft	Rate	Total Cost
	Floors	Stage 1	Removal of layers of cement and concrete found over original Plain Lime concrete floor.			
		S1.FL	Ground Floor	687.00	200	137400
	Floors	S1.FL	Total Cost of Stage 1			
	Floors	Stage 2	Repair of original plain lime concrete floor, including brick tharras, using materials matching specifications of original. Estimated in current BOQ at approximately 25% of total floor square footage			
		S2.FL	Area with original plain lime concrete floor, including attachment and sukhasan	1100	400	440000
		S2.FL	Area with brick tharras, first and second floor	252	400	100800
		S2.FL	Total Cost of Stage 2			
	Floors	Stage 3	Laying of Plain Lime Concrete floor using materials matching specifications of original.			
		S3.FL	Ground Floor	687	500	343500
	Floors	S3.FL	Total Cost of Stage 3			
						1021700

Level	Layer	Stage	Work to be executed	Sft	Rate	Total Cost	
G.F,F.F,S.F	Ceilings	Stage 1	Removal of extraneous layers of plaster, cement work and limewash using water/mildly alkaline solution, nylon brush as well as chisel and hammer (where required) to expose ceiling surface. Over:				
		S1.CG	Ground Floor				
		S1.CG	Flat domes	383	300	114900	
		S1.CG	Pointed Barrels between Arches	197	300	59100	
		S1.CG	First Floor (Including Attachment)				
		S1.CG	Flat Domes	901	300	270300	
		S1.CG	Second Floor (Including Attachment)				
		S1.CG	Flat Domes	901	300	270300	
	Ceilings	S1.CG	Total Cost of Stage 1				714600
	Ceilings	Stage 2	Plastering of ceilings with kankar lime plaster matching specifications of original. Localized repair of ceilings included. Over:				
		S2.CG	Ground Floor				
		S2.CG	Flat domes	383	500	191500	
		S2.CG	Pointed Barrels between Arches	197	500	98500	
		S2.CG	First Floor Floor (Including Attachment)				
		S2.CG	Flat Domes	901	500	450500	
		S2.CG	Second Floor (Including Attachment)				
		S2.CG	Flat Domes	901	500	450500	
	Ceilings	S2.CG	Total Cost of Stage 2				1191000
	Ceilings	Stage 3	Treatment of Flat dome over Central Bay				
		S3.CG	Cleaning of existing fresco work	123	1000	123000	
	Ceilings	S3.CG	Total Cost of Stage 3				123000
						2028600	2028600

M.i
m.i

APPENDIX

Arches, Colum ns, Chattris

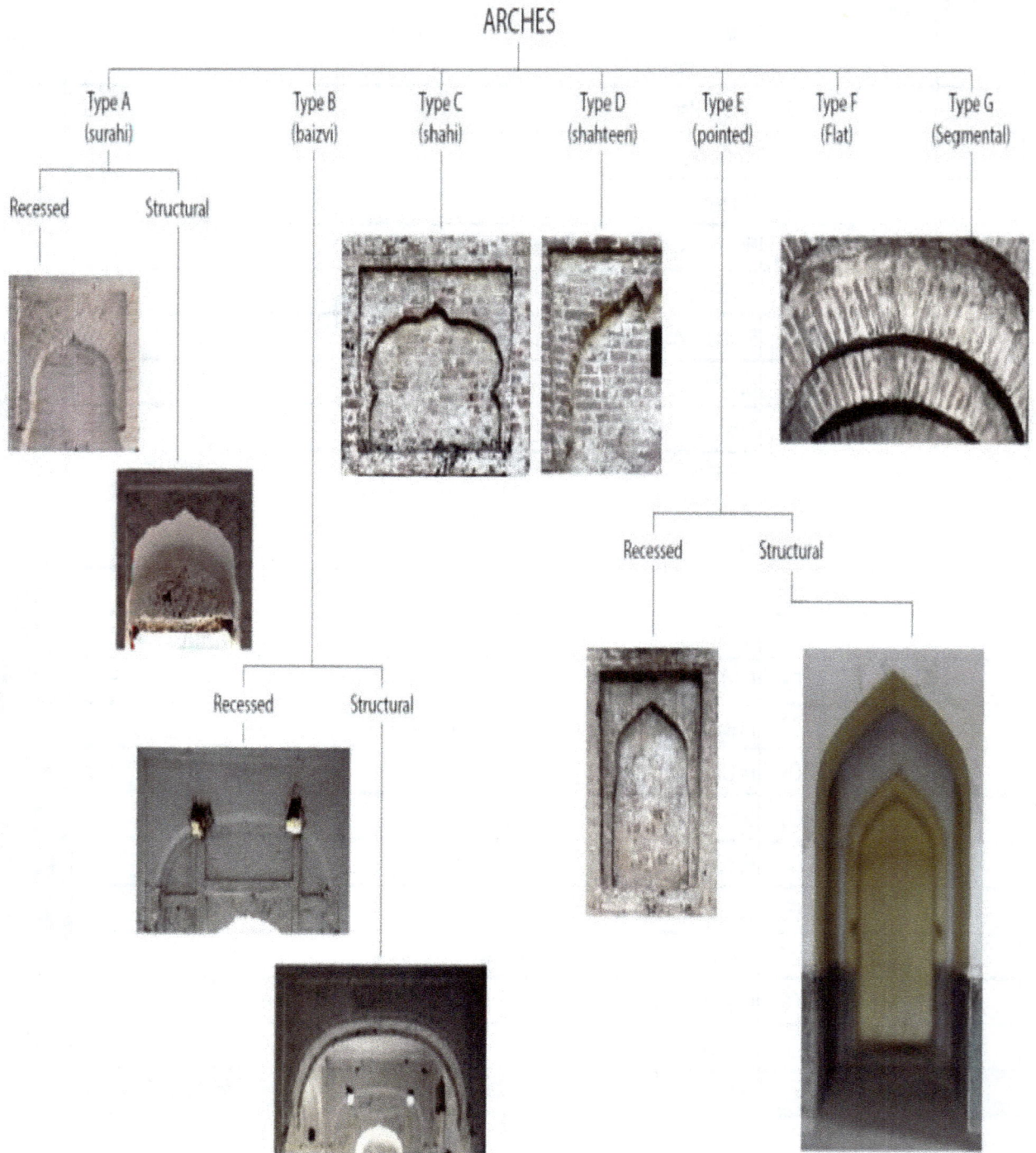

ARCHES

Type A (surahi)	Type B (baizvi)	Type C (shahi)	Type D (shahteeri)	Type E (pointed)	Type F (Flat)	Type G (Segmental)

Type A (surahi) — Recessed / Structural

Type C (shahi)

Type D (shahteeri)

Type G (Segmental)

Type B (baizvi) — Recessed / Structural

Type E (pointed) — Recessed / Structural

m.i
mi

CHATTRI

Type A

Type C

Type B

Type D

COLUMNS

```
                         COLUMNS
                            |
            ┌───────────────┴───────────────┐
         Type A                           Type B
            |                               |
      ┌─────┴─────┐                   ┌─────┼─────┐
   Quarter       Half                B1    B2    B3
   ┌──┼──┐    ┌───┼───┐
  AQ1 AQ2 AQ3 AH1 AH2 AH3
```

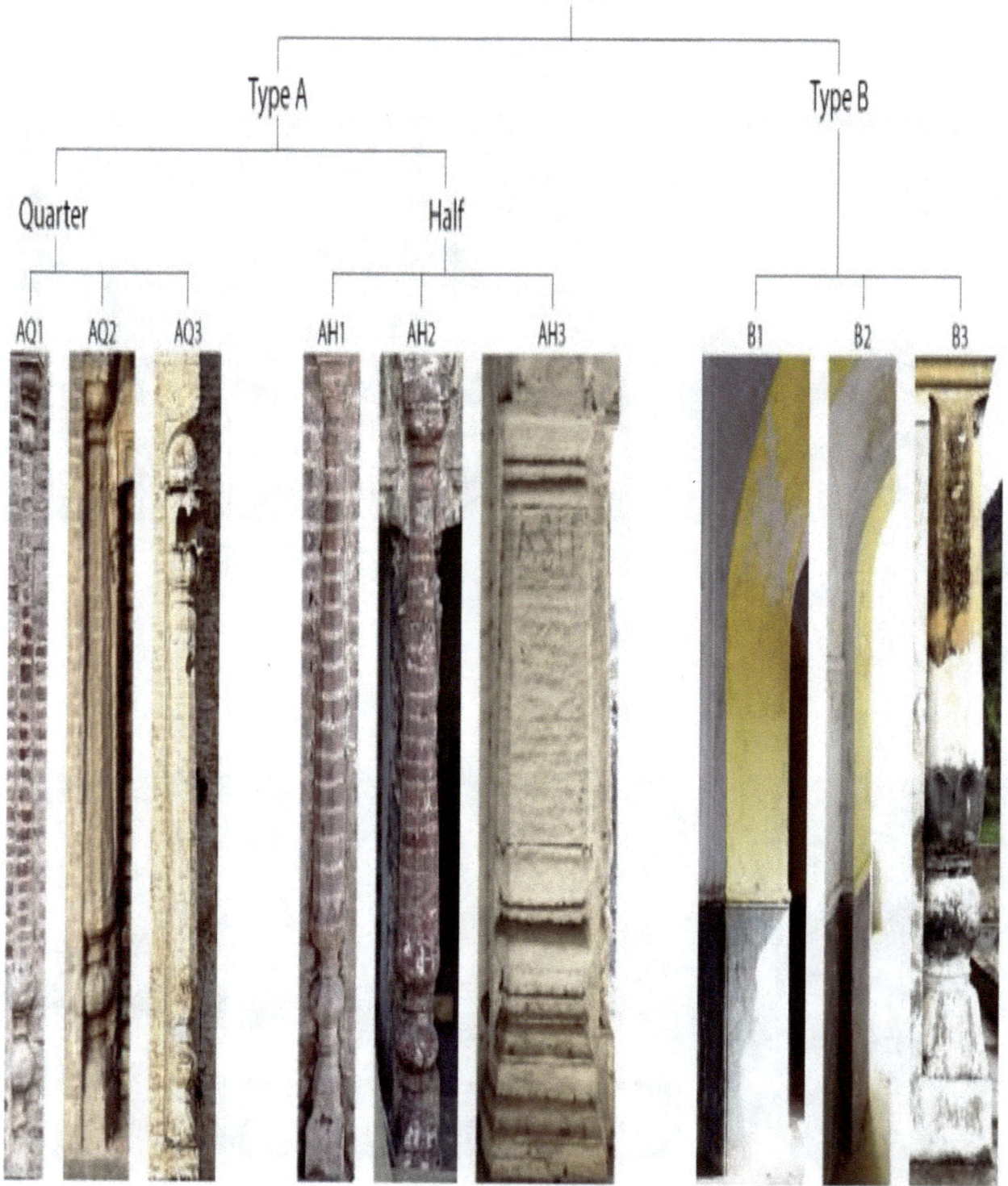

Exhibit B

Gumties

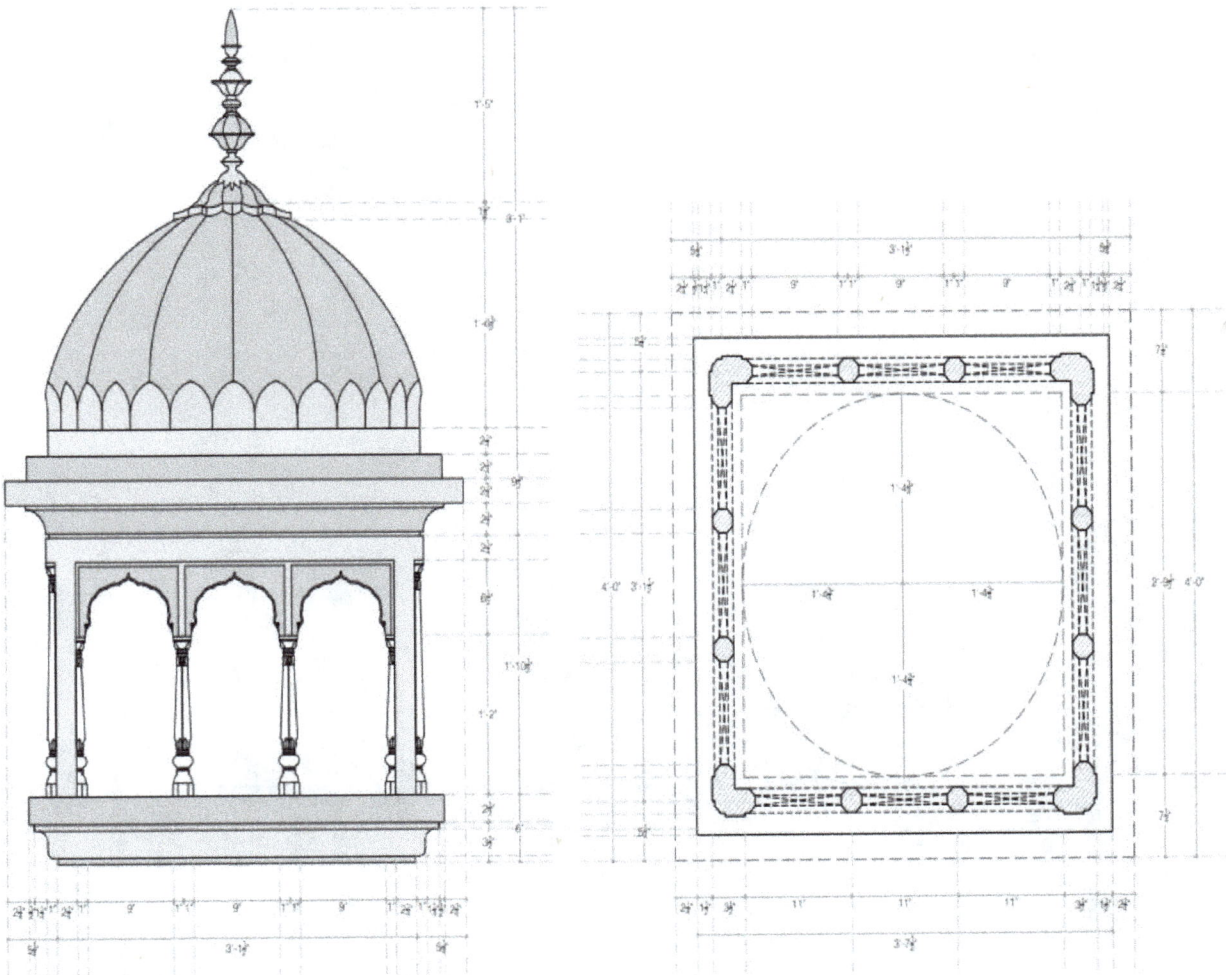

243

Exhibit C
Palki

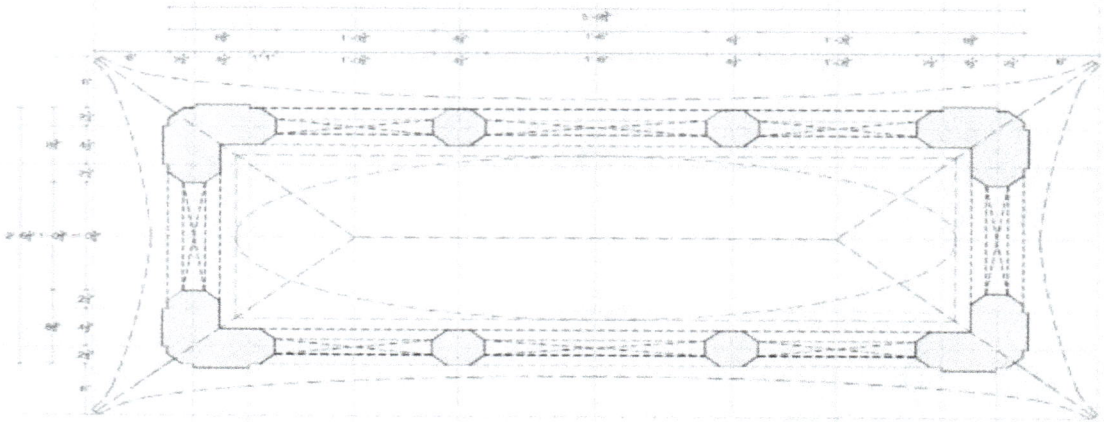

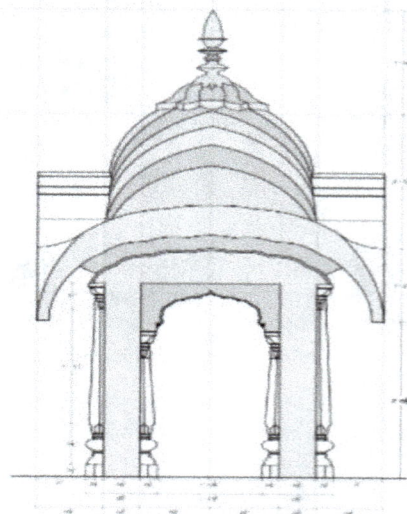

244

Exhibit D

Final Shape of Gurdwara from exterior

Exhibit E

Schedule of Payment: Total Lump-Sum Pakistan Rupees 26,339,567.00 PKR in five different installments.

Due at the end of each quarter of work completed (finished) and must be billed by contractor by the 15th day of month proceeding the quarter work completed.

Payment received by contractor as of 05/09/2021:   Pakistan Rupees 10,535,826.80 PKR (First and Second installments). Payments are always due after the reasonable work performed (otherwise subject to change).

1.	First Installment:	$5,267,913.40	Completed
2.	Second Installment:	$5,267,913.40	Completed
3.	Third Installment:	$5,267,913.40	
4.	Fourth Installment:	$5,267,913.40	
5.	Fifth Installment:	$5,267,913.40	

m ishtiaq
m ishtiaq (Jun 2, 2021 23:24 GMT+5)

The 3rd,4th, and 5th payments were paid on the following date:

Date	Amount in US dollars	Amount in Pakistan Rupees
June 21, 2021	35,165.84	5,267,913.40
August 19, 2021	33,687.05	5,267,913.40
November 08, 2021	32,663.96	5,267,913.40

The difference between the dollar amount in the three columns was caused by the currency rate difference on given dates at Bank of America in the USA.

Historical Artifacts found during the Restoration of Gurdwara Choha Sahib Ji

Historical Artifacts discovered during Restoration of Gurdwara Choha Sahib Ji

Many old artifacts are discovered during the Gurdwara Choha Sahib Ji restoration. All are documented and handover the PSGPC authorized person named Mr. Fauja Singh at the Gurdwara Choha Sahib Ji. Founding of artifacts was three types of baked clay artifacts a) Deeva, also called Small light lamp, b) Fragmented pottery, and c) letters and calligraphy. Ranjit Nagara USA asked to provide to test in laboratories for the age and other tests to find their historical significance and value. But the PSGPC authorized person took them away and refused to provide for testing. Ranjit Nagara USA cleaned all discovered artifacts by its licensed architect and restorer on-site, did the documentation, assigned them unique numbers, put them in one box. All discovered artifacts were handed over to PSGPC and ETPB authorized person in one wooden box to place them at Gurdwara Choha Sahib Ji, Rohtas.

A. **Deeva (Small tradition lamp):** Small traditional lighting clay pot with design. It is used for the lighting to remove the dark at night and stand in on steady, stable place. The total count of the Deeva's was twenty-nine. Photos are provided on the following pages: all visual size is in centimeters and discovered on the southeast side of Gurdwara Choha Sahib Ji. Each Deeva artifact in the photos from three different views:

A.01   Reference Number – GCSHAD01

A.02   Reference Number – GCSHAD02

A.03   Reference Number – GCSHAD03

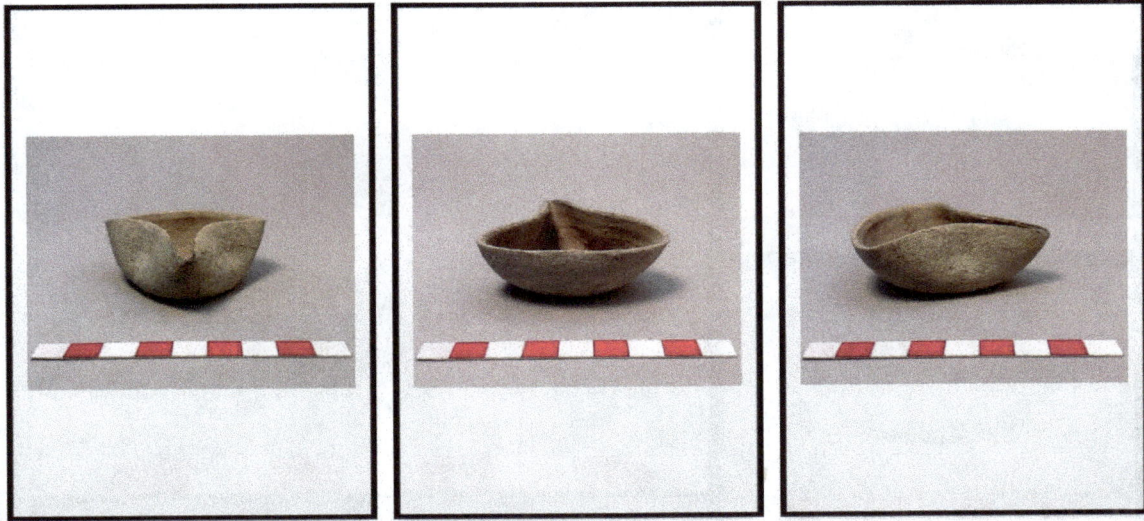

A.04   Reference Number – GCSHAD04

A.05   Reference Number – GCSHAD05

A.06   Reference Number – GCSHAD06

A.07   Reference Number – GCSHAD07

A.08   Reference Number – GCSHAD08

A.09   Reference Number – GCSHAD09

A.10   Reference Number – GCSHAD10

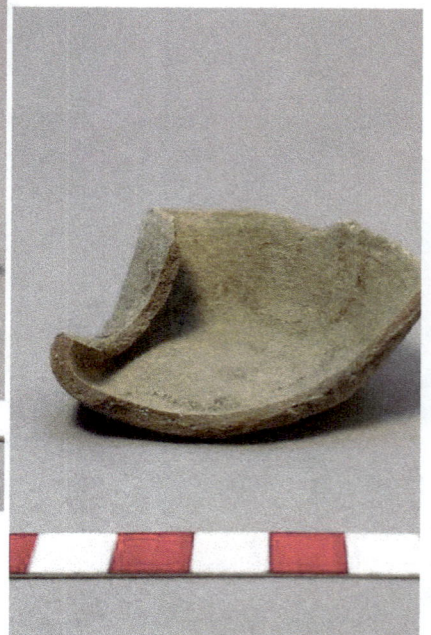

A.11   Reference Number – GCSHAD11

A.12   Reference Number – GCSHAD12

A.13   Reference Number – GCSHAD13

A.14   Reference Number – GCSHAD14

A.15　　　　　　Reference Number – GCSHAD15

A.16　　　　　　Reference Number – GCSHAD16

A.17   Reference Number – GCSHAD17

A.18   Reference Number – GCSHAD18

Reference Number – GCSHAD19

A.20   Reference Number – GCSHAD20

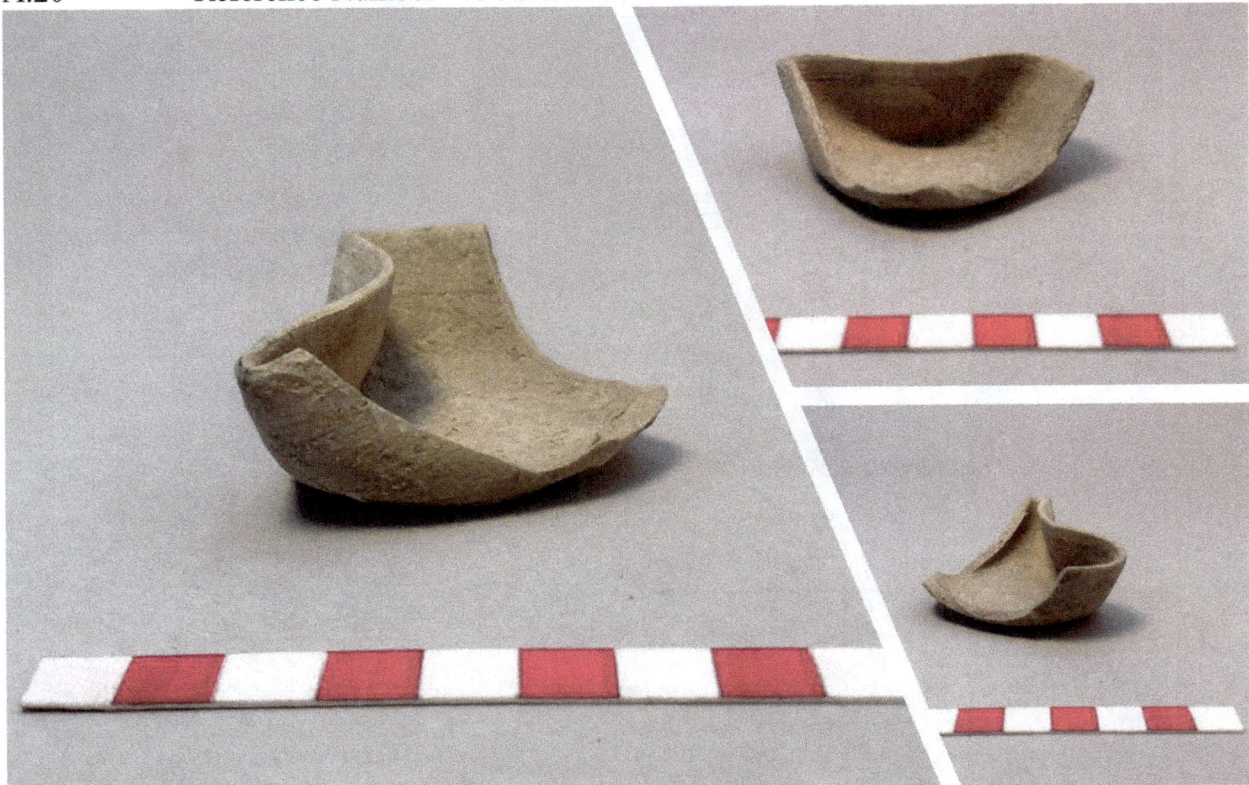

A.21   Reference Number – GCSHAD21

A.22   Reference Number – GCSHAD22

A.23   Reference Number – GCSHAD23

A.24   Reference Number – GCSHAD24

A.25   Reference Number – GCSHAD25

A.26   Reference Number – GCSHAD26

A.28   Reference Number – GCSHAD28

A.29   Reference Number – GCSHAD29

B. Pottery: Pottery can be a pot, small reservoir, or basin. It is made with baked clay with a small round base, significant middle, and a broad face. The very skilled craftsman makes the pottery pots by pottery professionals. During the restoration, the following part of the pottery was found. These pottery parts were cleaned by architects and restorers appointed for research at Gurdwara Choha Sahib Ji, Rohtas, Jhelum, Punjab, Pakistan by Ranjit Nagara USA, a non-profit organization.

B.01   Reference Number – GCSHAP01

B.02　　　　　　Reference Number – GCSHAP02

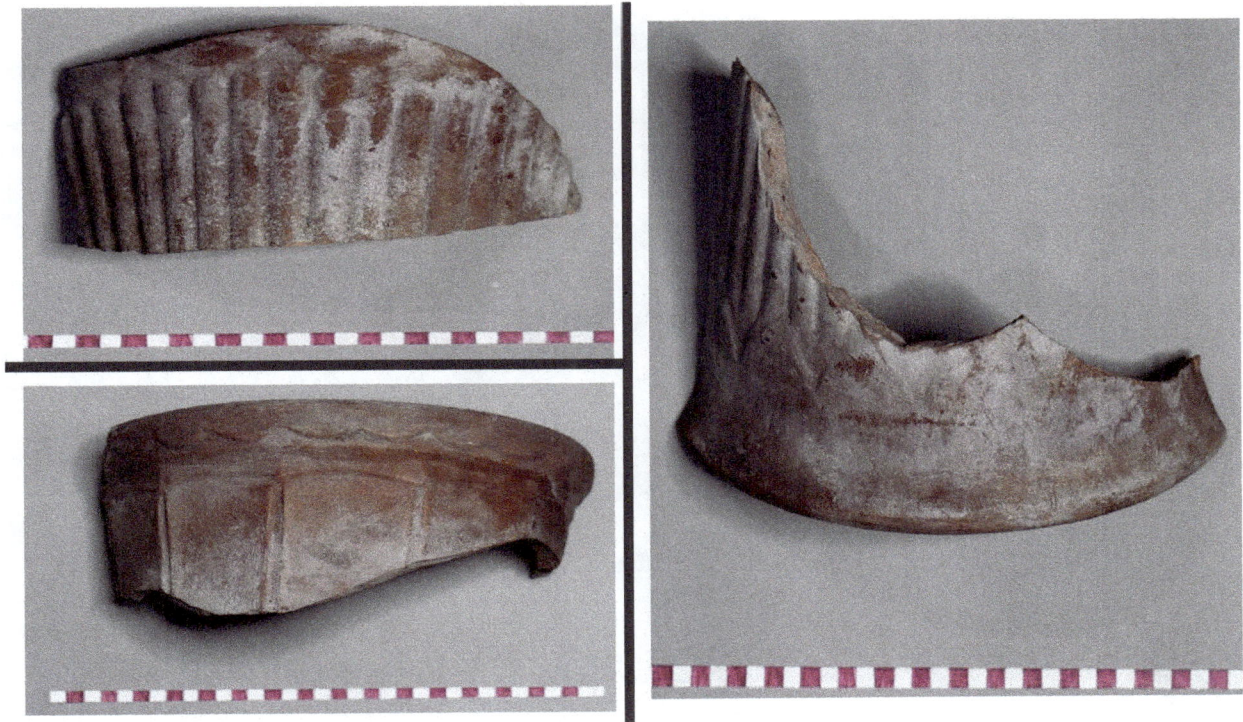

B.03　　　　　　Reference Number – GCSHAP03

B.04   Reference Number – GCSHAP04

B.05   Reference Number – GCSHAP05

B.06   Reference Number – GCSHAP06

B.07   Reference Number – GCSHA07

C.01   Reference Number – GCSHAL01

C. **Letter and Calligraphy:** Some letters and calligraphy are also found on the southeast side of the Gurdwara Choha Sahib Ji, Rohtas. These letters look in the Punjabi language ("Kan-aa"). The broken part looks like the khanda in the Khalsa Panth. Unfortunately, further digging was stopped because of pressure from the various departments and circumstances on the site. A significant area of Gurdwara Choha Sahib Ji is available for further research.

D. Iron Remains: Many Irons-made historical artifacts were found during the evacuation and digging of the southwest side of the sacred Sarovar sahib at Gurdwara Choha Sahib Ji. Initial Ranjit Nagara USA and its architects or restorer have no idea about this side. The investigation was started when Ranjit Nagara was looking for a place to build an entrance, dispensary, rooms, and other necessary facility development on Gurdwara Choha Sahib Ji land. When the historical artifacts discoveries started, Ranjit Nagara instructed the on-site architect and restorer to investigate the southwest side of Gurdwara Sahib Sarovar. The result was remarkable when the following site was discovered.

Ranjit Nagara USA gives the name to the digging site between Sarovar and Room as an archeological site and all the remains found on this site. Maharaja Ranjit Singh developed this site in 1834.

D.01   Reference Number – GCSHAD01

D.02   Reference Number – GCSHAD02

D.03   Reference Number – GCSHAD03

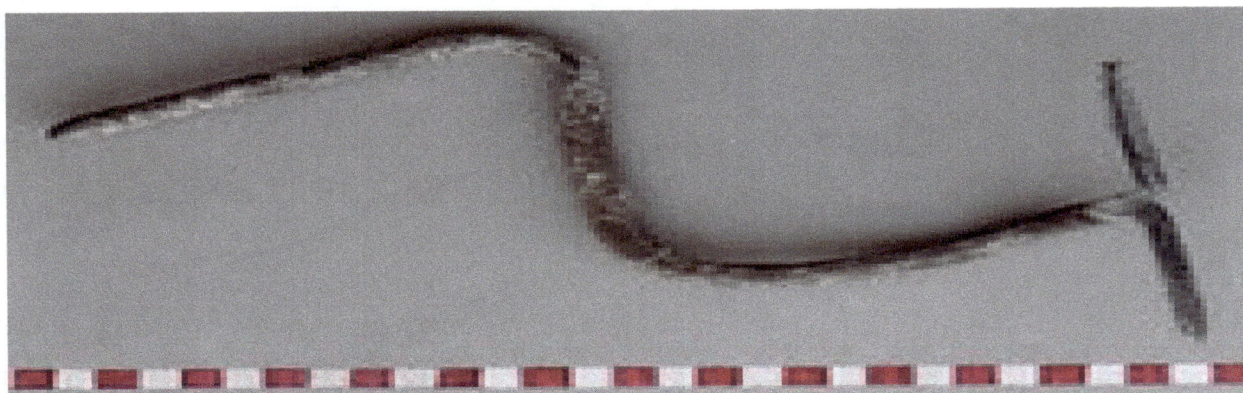

D.04   Reference Number – GCSHAD04

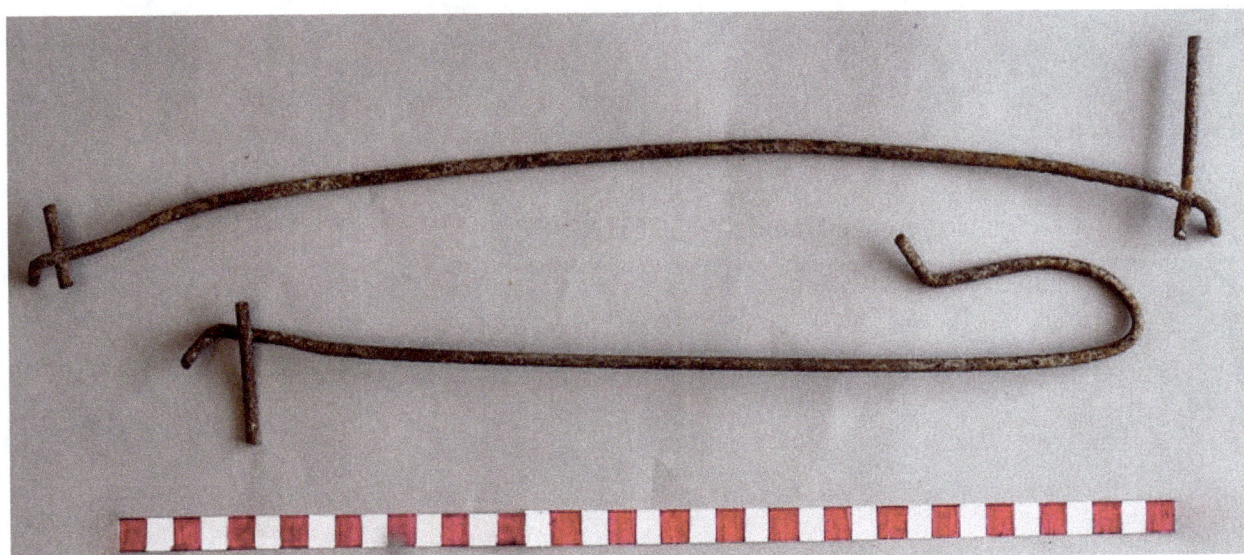

D.05   Reference Number – GCSHAD05

D.06   Reference Number – GCSHAD06

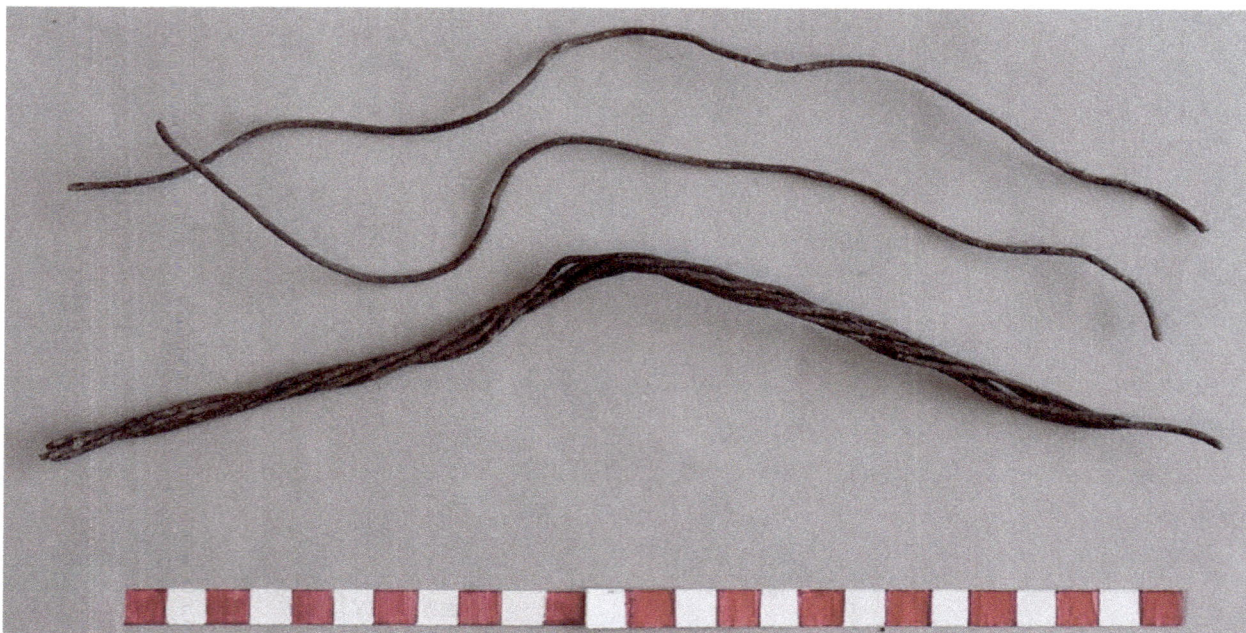

D.07   Reference Number – GCSHAD07

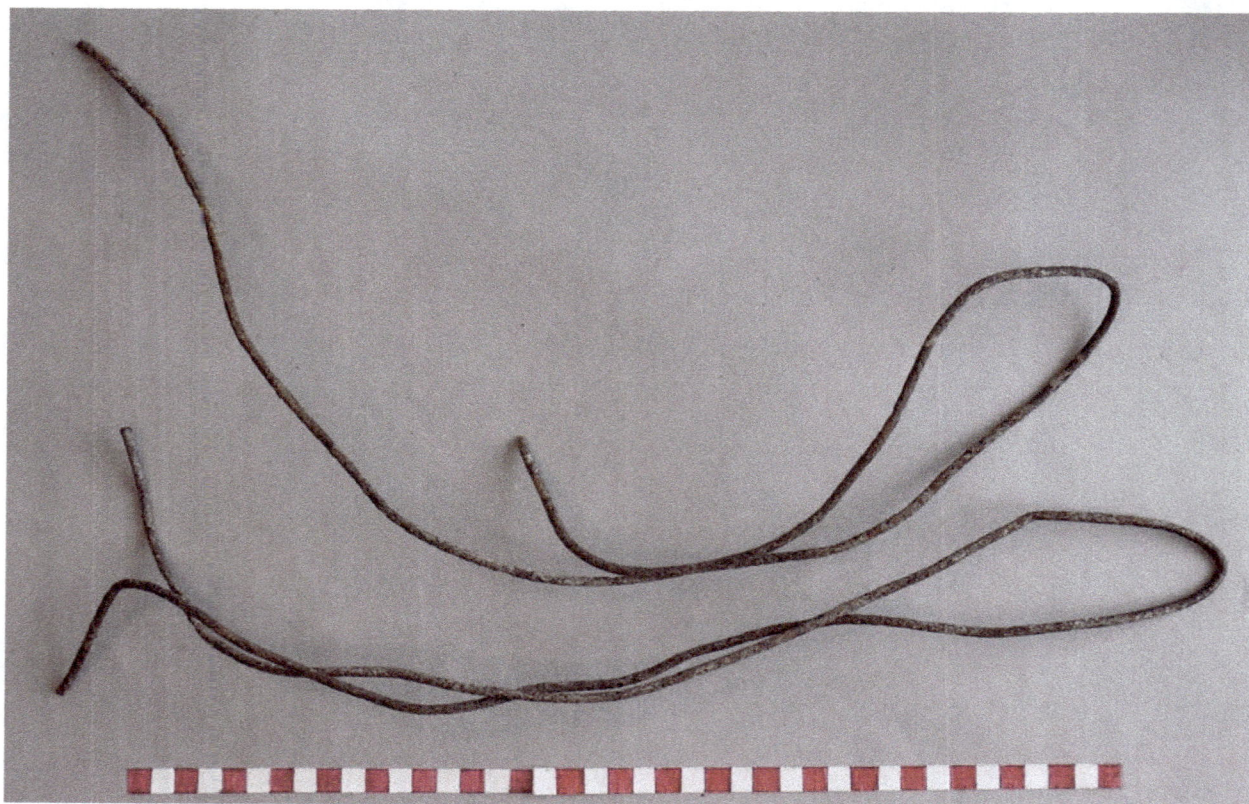

D.08   Reference Number – GCSHAD08

D.09   Reference Number – GCSHAD09   D.10 Reference Number – GCSHAD10

D.12   Reference Number – GCSHAD12

D.13   Reference Number – GCSHAD13

D.14   Reference Number – GCSHAD14   D.15   Reference Number – GCSHAD15

D.16   Reference Number – GCSHAD16

D.17   Reference Number – GCSHAD17

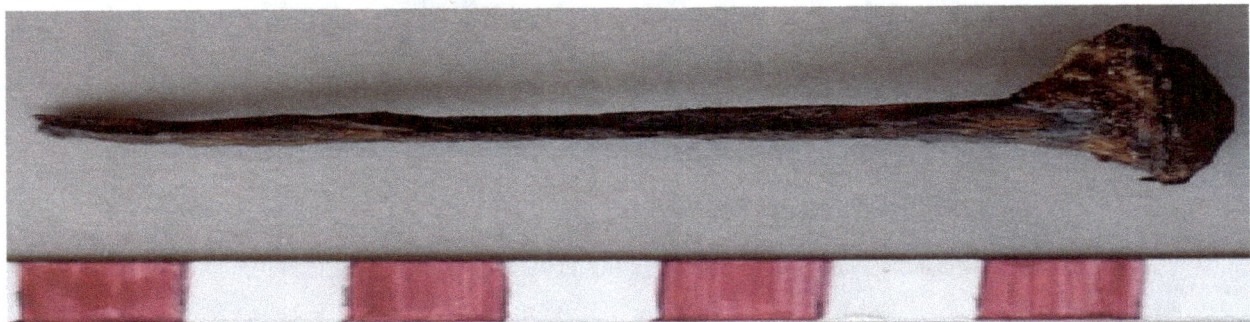

D.18   Reference Number – GCSHAD18

D.19   Reference Number – GCSHAD19   D.20   Reference Number – GCSHAD20

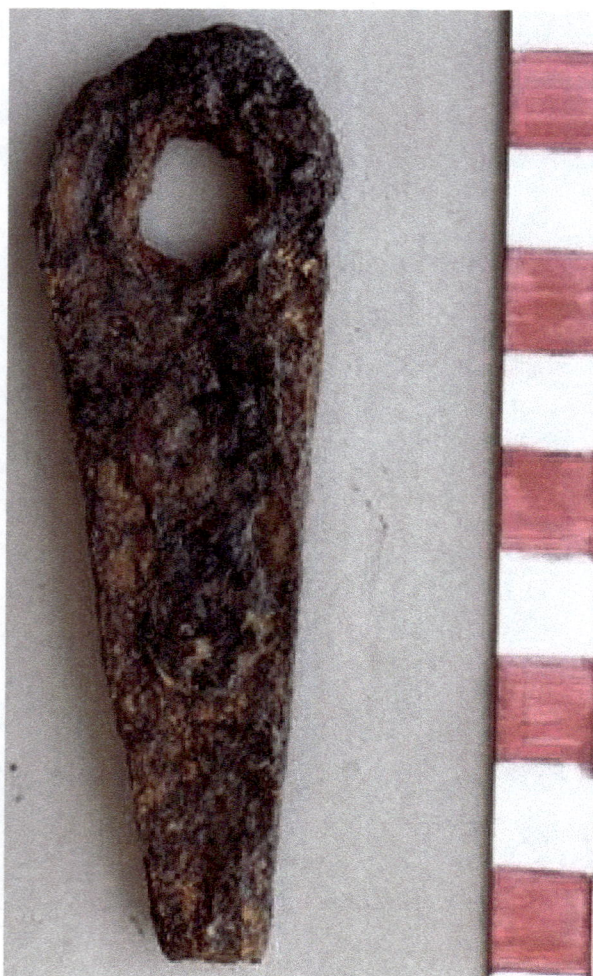

D.21   Reference Number – GCSHAD21

D.22   Reference Number – GCSHAD22

D.23   Reference Number – GCSHAD23

Contributory Religious organizations in Restoration of Gurdwara Choha Sahib Ji

Sikh Religious organizations related to restoration of Gurdwara Choha Sahib Ji, Rohtas, Jhelum, Punjab

The three leading Sikh religious organizations are contributed to the restoration of Gurdwara Choha Sahib Ji.

1. Shiromani Gurdwara Prabandhak Committee.
2. Pakistan Sikh Gurdwara Prabandhak Committee.
3. Ranjit Nagara, USA

Shiromani Gurdwara Prabandhak Committee (SGPC)

The Shiromani Gurdwara Prabandhak Committee (SGPC) was first formed in 1920 to reform the Gurdwaras movement and management. Sardar Sunder Singh Majithia played a vital role in the Gurdwara reforms and became the first president of SGPC in 1920. SGPC is the only Sikh organization to run and manage the Gurdwaras. The Sikh Gurdwara act was passed in 1925 to provide legal status to SGPC, and Baba Kharak Singh became the president in 1925. The act was passed to give the complete custody and management of the Gurdwaras to the Khalsa Panth. The head office of SGPC is in Amritsar, Punjab. SGPC is responsible for looking for the proper use of the Sikh code and conduct.

SGPC Head office, Teja Singh Samundri Hall

Currently, SGPC is running many schools, colleges, and universities to transfer knowledge and skills for a better world. SGPC is responsible for preserving the Khalsa Panth history, artifacts, archeological sites, books. It manages the financial, management, and oversight of the religious aspects of the Gurdwaras. The Gurdwara act of 1925 was amended two times in 1953 and 2016.

The SGPC organizes many Gurdwaras, Schools, Colleges, and universities and has more than 11,000 employees. The count of volunteers that work at SGPC is uncountable. The SGPC budget is enormous and can cover the Gurdwara outside their jurisdiction.

Pakistan Sikh Gurdwara Prabandhak Committee (PSGPC)

The Pakistan Sikh Gurdwara Prabandhak Committee (PSGPC) is a Sikh religious organization in Pakistan. PSGPC has no legal status by itself at this time and works under the direct supervision of the Evacuee Trust Property Board (ETPB). PSGPC and ETPB both together

are managing the Gurdwaras in Pakistan only. The PSGPC head office is in Gurdwara Dera Sahib Lahore, Punjab. Very few Gurdwara are operating in Pakistan as of April 2022, and most of the Gurdwara Sahib in Pakistan needs restoration, renovation, and reconstruction. As per Ranjit Nagara USA, more than 476 Gurdwaras are in actual critical condition and need immediate attention. The PSGPC budget is minimal, and it is requested that the Khalsa Panth preserve the Sikh Historical places before they disappear from their original locations.

Ranjit Nagara

Ranjit Nagara is formed with a mission to preserve, build, and maintain the historical Sikh gurdwaras worldwide as they're of utmost religious importance to the Sikh community. Gurdwaras are associated with the lives of the Sikh Gurus and serve as educational institutes to educate needy children, house the Sikh scriptures, and organize charitable work in the broader community on behalf of religious Sikh devotees.

Ranjit Nagara is a non-profitable, charitable, and advocacy organization of humane inhabitants, contributors, and volunteers having a shared vision of a world where everyone can exercise their rights to an adequate standard of living, they're treated with regard and dignity, where there is no poverty, agitation, or persecution, and where everyone can have access to opportunities and choices essential to a contented life. Ranjit Nagara believes that eliminating extreme poverty is possible and acts on that belief every day by empowering the deprived communities worldwide.

Ranjit Nagara aims to alter, alleviate, educate and protect the lives of underprivileged individuals and minority communities impacted by catastrophes, hunger, illiteracy, or civil/human-rights violation by fostering enduring programs regardless of complexion faith, or caste. Our utmost mission is to preserve all Sikhism historical sites worldwide, build quarters for pilgrims and religious devotees, build free occupational centers in Sikh GURDWARA, provide help to the needy, offer scholarships to deprived students and help them connect with the community. Ranjit Nagara believes that the growth of wise and progressive communities can be made possible by socially conscious individuals who commit to developing and directing human potential.

283

Restoration of Gurdwara Choha Sahib Ji Individual Contributors

Main Contributor in Restoration of Gurdwara Choha Sahib Ji

The contributors are the one who participates in the restoration work and the progress with heart and wants to accomplish the goal and objective as a team member. They can be contracted service providers, volunteers, governmental officials, and/or residents. Ranjit Nagara is a USA non-profit organization established in December 2019 and united all leading concerned authorities and people to do the Sewa (restoration) of the Gurdwara Choha Sahib Ji. It was not an easy task, but dedication and hard work provided success. The Gurdwara Choha Sahib Ji has been restored as an exemplary work in East and West Punjab. This section will give brief information about individual contributors towards the restoration Sewa of Gurdwara Choha Sahib Ji.

The list of prominent contributors is given below, and brief details are provided on the following few pages for these contributors.

1. Satpreet Singh
2. Rupinder Kaur
3. Tarlochan Singh
4. Ranjit Singh
5. Gurdev Singh
6. Amrik Singh Plaha
7. Raj Surinder Singh
8. Gurmit Singh
9. Dr. Mimpal Singh
10. Imran Gondal
11. Tariq Wazir
12. Shahid Sabbir
13. Raja Waqar

The restoration of Gurdwara Choha Sahib Ji is a great initiation in restoration history. Many buildings in the East and West Punjab were demolished in the name of old buildings. The restoration of 1834 AD Gurdwara Choha Sahib Ji set an example for all those who said there was no way to save the old building and destroy the history of Khalsa Panth in East and West Punjab.

Dr. Satpreet Singh

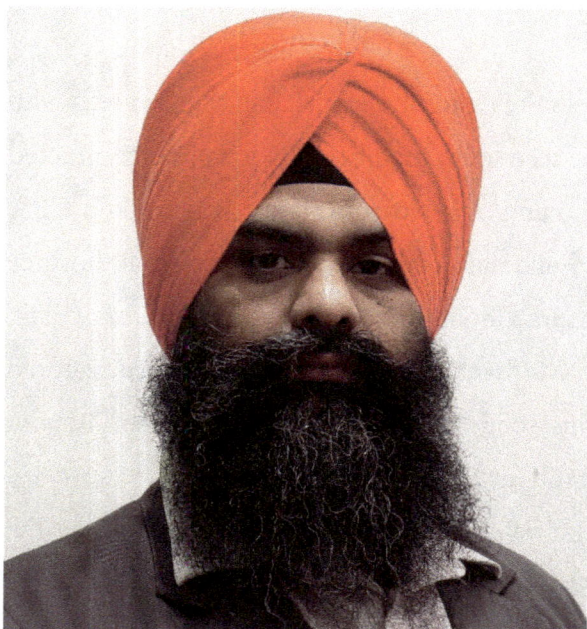

Dr. Satpreet Singh, the director and chief executive officer of the Ranjit Nagara, a USA non-profit organization, led the Gurdwara Choha Sahib Ji, Rohtas, Jhelum, Punjab. Satpreet Singh is highly educated with many professional designations in the business world. He did his Master's in computer application from Guru Nanak Dev University, Amritsar, Punjab. Satpreet Singh traveled to the United States of America as a research scholar in an offshore communication technology conference as an expert speaker. He is pursuing his Doctor of Philosophy (Ph.D.) in business administration specializing in organizational leadership in the United States of America. He is well settled in the United States as a successful business owner and a business entrepreneur. During the visit of west Punjab in December 2019, Satpreet Singh visited the Gurdwara Choha Sahib Ji with two pilgrim colleagues, Hardial Singh and Gurdial Singh. It was very sorrowful in his heart to see the current condition of Gurdwara Choha Sahib Ji and the Gurdwara Janam Asthan Mata Sahib Kaur Ji in the Rohtas. He formed a non-profit organization in the United States named Ranjit Nagara, getting all approvals from the Internal Revenue Service, California Department of Justice, Franchise tax board, and all other related departments to work outside the United States to save historical buildings worldwide. Today Ranjit Nagara USA can work in any country worldwide without any restriction toward humanity and restoring the historic building. He is also a founder and working as a chief executive officer of Sikh Reference Library USA. He continuously maintained contact with the ETPB and PSGPC from January 13, 2020, to August 01, 2020, and finally got the approval letter from ETPB to start the restoration work Gurdwara Choha Sahib Ji. He led all the panel's committees and departments and continuously guided all the teams in restoring Gurdwara Choha Sahib Ji. Satpreet Singh directly supervised the selection of teams, labor, the payment procedure, documentation. The architects, restorers, labor, and all government and the private department were in direct contact with until completing the restoration work of Gurdwara Choha Sahib Ji. He spent approximately four-five hours daily since the beginning of the restoration of Gurdwara Choha Sahib Ji till the completion of the restoration. He guided the architects and restorers at all stages, dealing with all questions and answers from the public and departments, organizing the fundraising events, and all restoration activities. He is educating the public about the meaning and importance of saving historic buildings. He is currently focusing on the coming generation to be aware of their history and heritage values. The Gurdwara Janam Asthan Mata Sahib Kaur land is also expanded in 2021 from ten by ten square feet (100 Square feet) room to 19,057 square feet with the blessing of Khalsa Panth under the supervision of Satpreet Singh. Now 19,057 square feet of land has ten feet high wall boundary with a door. He visited Gurdwara Choha Sahib Ji and Gurdwara Janam Asthan Mata Sahib Kaur Ji for the second time to check the restoration work progress in November 2021.

Rupinder Kaur

Rupinder Kaur is working as General manager at Ardass Inc. she is talented in documentation and communication with departments. She is the primary contact with the various governmental departments on behalf of Ranjit Nagara. She is the representative of Ranjit Nagara toward Internal Revenue Services, California Department of Justice, Franchise Tax Board, etc. She moved from west Punjab to the United States of America in 2000 to join her parent. She completed her higher study at San Joaquin Delta College Stockton, California. The proper filing, answers, and all documentation at Ranjit Nagara are prepared and submitted to the board by her. She is very enthusiastic and energetic in the Khalsa Panth Sewa. She conducted many interviews and provided her valuable suggestion at various stages toward restoring Gurdwara Choha Sahib Ji. She is a fully devoted volunteer and continued working as a right hand to Satpreet Singh from the beginning and constantly provided her services to Ranjit Nagara and Sikh Reference Library USA. Her services are praiseworthy toward Ranjit Nagara.

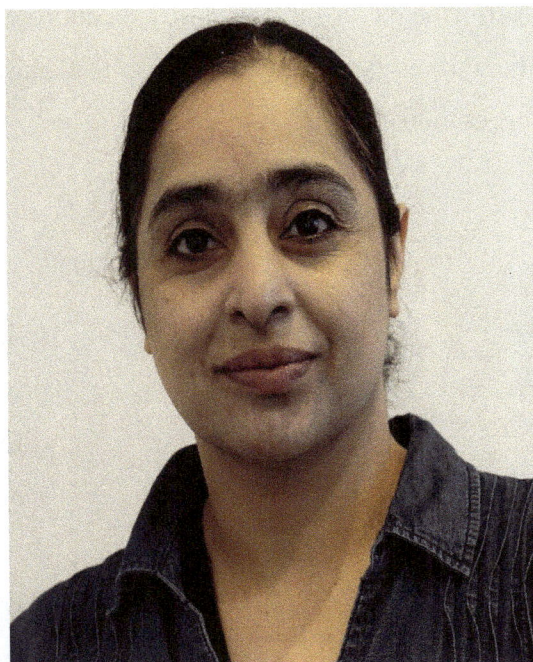

Tarlochan Singh

Tarlochan Singh is a resident of Manteca, California, and currently serves as a secretary and director of Ranjit Nagara USA. He has his very prominent place in the whole Khalsa Panth because of his contribution to the Khalsa Panth by his father Shaheed Bhai Amrik Singh and Grandfather Sant Kartar Singh Ji. He completed his Master's in computer application from Punjab Technical University Jalandhar in west Punjab. Ranjit Nagara is very honored to have him on the Board of Directors. He is currently working in a government job in California as an Informational technology specialist. His and his family's contribution to Khalsa Panth is very commendable, and the Sikhs will never forget their service.

Ranjit Singh

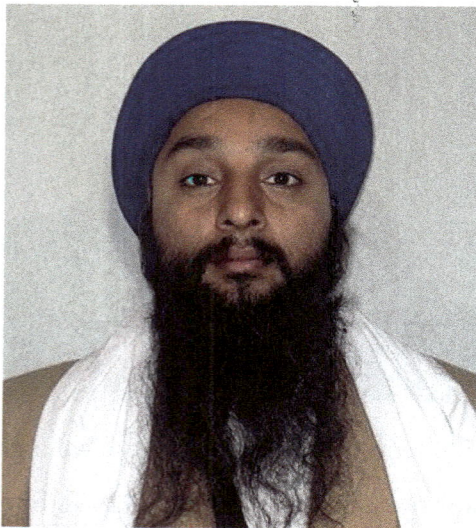

Ranjit Singh is a businessman in the transportation industry in the United States of America. Currently, he provides his services to Ranjit Nagara as treasurer and director. He is a good speaker on various religious platforms and entirely devoted to Sikhism. he always stands and works closely with the restoration project of Gurdwara Choha Sahib Ji. He also visited the Gurdwara Choha Sahib Ji during the restoration in November 2021. He is also active in teaching Sikh martial art (Gatka). Gatka is his passion and teaches many students at religious gatherings in various Gurdwara Sahiban in the United States of America.

Gurdev Singh

Gurdev Singh is a resident of Amritsar, Punjab. He completed his Master's degree in Mathematics and MTech degree in Information technology from Guru Nanak Dev University, Amritsar. He played a vitally important role in selecting Ranjit Nagara's name to Satpreet Singh during the prior filing procedure. He is very close to Satpreet Singh and participates in many historical discussions. He is currently self-employed and running various research journals. His study in multiple fields makes him an expert advisor to history at multiple stages. He is entirely devoted to Sikhism and Khalsa Panth. His services toward Ranjit Nagara are appreciable.

Amrik Plaha

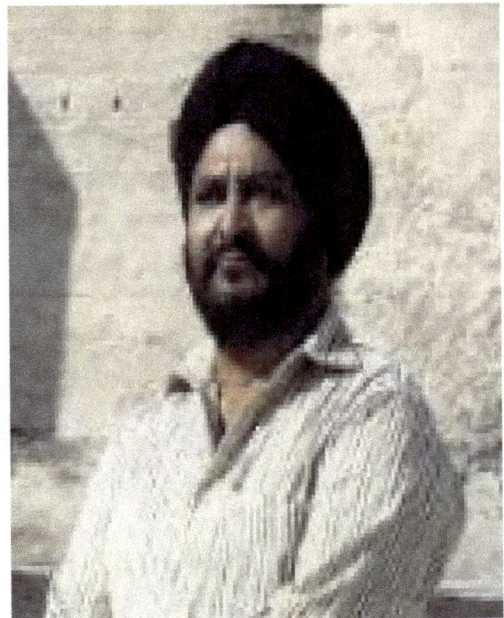

Amrik Plaha is a restorer of historical monuments at the Government of Fujairah UAE. When Satpreet Singh contacted him to provide his restoration service to Ranjit Nagara to restore Gurdwara Choha Sahib Ji, he immediately accepted and provided his expert advice and guidance to the on-ground architects and restorers. He promised Ranjit Nagara that he always becomes available voluntarily for the sewa of restoration. He has 41 years of experience and restored the 14th and 15th-century historical sites and forts. His expertise as a restorer became the gem for the Ranjit Nagara to restore Gurdwara Choha Sahib Ji. He is currently working as the restorer government of Fujairah UAE and providing his expert services voluntarily to Ranjit Nagara as head of the restoration department of Ranjit Nagara USA. He is the gem of the restoration world.

Raj Surinder Singh

Raj Surinder Singh is a very motivated poet and lyric. He had written many Dhadi Varra, Songs, Poems. Many dhadi Jathas and singers sang his poetry. He provided his volunteer service to Ranjit Nagara USA and wrote two historical poems named "Sewa Naal Ne Karam Kamaye Jande" and "Mata Sahib Kaur Ji." Currently, he is self-employed in the transportation industry and living in Stockton, California.

Gurmit Singh

Gurmit Singh lives in Fresno, California, and works as a life insurance agent with New York Max life Insurance. He is working as the head of the advisory committee of Ranjit Nagara. His proficient interpersonal and communication skills. He is very dedicated to the Sewa of restoration toward Gurdwara Choha Sahib Ji. He is continuously attached to the Ranjit Nagara and helped raise funds for the Sewa of Gurdwara Choha Sahib Ji. He participates in all local religious ceremonies at various Gurdwara Sahiban in California.

Dr. Mimpal Singh

Dr. Mimpal Singh is the first Sikh Doctor in Pakistan. He is also an assistant professor in the pediatric wing of Pakistan's Specialized healthcare & medical education department. He is a member of the Pakistan Sikh Gurdwara Prabandhak Committee. The restoration work at Gurdwara Choha Sahib Ji started with his help, and he provided his full support of exemplary restoration work at Gurdwara Choha Sahib Ji.

Imran Gondal: Mr. Imran Gondal is a secretary of shrines in Pakistan's Evacuee trust property board. All the Sikh Gurdwaras are in direct control of

Mr. Imran Gondal is a primary contact for any type of work on Gurdwara Sahiban in Pakistan. Satpreet Singh talked to him in January 2020 and continues in touch with him until the completion of restoration till February 28, 2022.

Tariq Wazir: Mr. Tariq wazir was an additional secretary of Evacuee Trust property board before current additional secretary Mr. Rana Shahid. Mr. Tariq Wazir was very helpful when on January 13, 2021, Ranjit Nagara noticed stopping the restoration work and was forced to stop for some reason locally in west Punjab. He directly interferes and helps Ranjit Nagara to continue restoration work on Gurdwara Choha Sahib Ji. The restoration was started again after two days, on January 15, 2021.

Shahid Shabbir

Shahid Shabbir is an west Punjab Youtuber, blogger, and social media activist. He has been working as a social media activist for a long time. He is passionate about historical building awareness. Satpreet Singh contacted him to work for Ranjit Nagara and provide his audio and video services toward the knowledge of the exemplary restoration work of Gurdwara Choha Sahib Ji. He worked directly with Satpreet Singh for his services and made a commendable effort for Ranjit Nagara. Ranjit Nagara is very thankful to him for his services. He provided a continuous video update of Gurdwara Choha Sahib Ji for Ranjit Nagara.

Raja Waqar

Raja Waqar is a local Jhelum journalist working in 24 news channels. He is in the media industry for a long time. He played a vital role in purchasing homes for the Janam Asthan Mata Sahib Kaur Ji under the direct supervision of Satpreet Sing from Ranjit Nagara. He conducted various governmental official interviews for the Ranjit Nagara at multiple stages. The 10 feet wall and the measurements of the 19,057 square feet purchased land were also completed by him, and documentation was provided to Ranjit Nagara via postal mail.